CAMBRIDGE READINGS IN
THE LITERATURE OF MUSIC

General Editors: John Stevens and Peter le Huray

Music in early Christian literature

CAMBRIDGE READINGS
THE LITERATURE OF MUSIC

Cambridge Readings in the Literature of Music is a series of source
materials (original documents in English translation) for students of the
history of music. Many of the quotations in the volumes will be substantial,
and introductory material will place the passages in context. The period
covered will be from antiquity to the present day, with particular emphasis
on the nineteenth and twentieth centuries. The series is part of *Cambridge
Studies in Music*.

Already published:
Peter le Huray and James Day, *Music and Aesthetics in the Eighteenth and
    Early-Nineteenth Centuries*
Andrew Barker, *Greek Musical Writings*: 1 *The Musician and his Art*
Bojan Bujić, *Music in European Thought 1851–1912*

Music in early Christian literature

Edited by
James McKinnon
Professor of Music
State University of New York at Buffalo

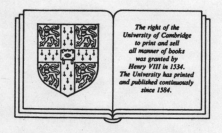

The right of the
University of Cambridge
to print and sell
all manner of books
was granted by
Henry VIII in 1534.
The University has printed
and published continuously
since 1584.

Cambridge University Press

Cambridge
New York   Port Chester
Melbourne   Sydney

Published by the Press Syndicate of the University of Cambridge
The Pitt Building, Trumpington Street, Cambridge CB2 1RP
32 East 57th Street, New York, NY 10022, USA
10 Stamford Road, Oakleigh, Melbourne 3166, Australia

First published 1987
Reprinted 1988
First paperback edition 1989

Printed in Great Britain at
the University Press, Cambridge

British Library cataloguing in publication data

Music in early Christian literature. –
(Cambridge readings in the literature of
music)
1. Music – Religious aspects – Christianity
– Sources 2. Music – History and
criticism – To 400 – Sources
I. McKinnon, James
261.5'7   BR115.M8

Library of Congress cataloguing in publication data

Music in early Christian literature.
(Cambridge readings in the literature of music)
Bibliography.
Includes index.
1. Church music – To 500 – Sources. 2. Music and
literature. 3. Music – To 500 – Philosophy and
aesthetics. I. McKinnon, James. II. Series.
ML3865.M88   1987   780'.901   86–21545

ISBN 0 521 30497 0 hard covers
ISBN 0 521 37624 6 paperback

Contents

Preface

The typical early Christian reference to music is an incidental remark made by a church father in some lengthy work on an entirely different subject. This circumstance of non-musical context has posed difficulties of interpretation for the music historian, while just as serious is the problem of inaccessibility resulting from the way in which these remarks are scattered over so vast a body of literature. One hopes that the present volume makes at least a modest contribution in the area of interpretation, but it is designed primarily to alleviate the latter problem of inaccessibility. Towards this end it presents several hundred brief passages, arranged by author in chronological order, from the New Testament to approximately 450 AD.

It aims to be inclusive rather than representative in its selection of material and to be a research tool for the serious student of music history rather than merely a pedagogical resource in the manner of the typical anthology of source readings. Thus, in an important area like liturgical psalmody, virtually every passage known to the author that makes a unique contribution to the subject, however slight, is included. The same is true of references to music as one of the liberal arts. Indeed there are so few of these that it is practical to reproduce, or at least to cite, virtually every known passage. On the other hand, in the broad area of musical metaphor, where the material is often more of theological or literary interest than musical, it seems best to turn from a policy of inclusiveness to one of representative-ness. Still the selection is generous, including the earlier appearances in the literature of the more prominent musical images and enough subsequent material to provide a brief survey of the genre.

In sum it is hoped that the individual engaged in the research and writing of music history can use the volume with confidence that the essential literary evidence for the music of the period is available in its pages. It is true that most of the material appears already in secondary sources. Indeed the method of collection employed was to work through these, tracing each citation to its original. It is true also that certain of the secondary sources such as Johannes Quasten's *Musik und Gesang* (1930) have made enormous contributions to our knowledge of the period. Yet it is fair to say that in general our discipline remains faced with material not yet brought sufficiently under control. Some of our most estimable music historians when constrained to venture into the period can still be observed to use mis-leading translations, give inaccurate citations, quote pseudo-authors as genuine, and more seriously present evidence selectively without an over-view of the literature. Hence the need for a uniform presentation of this material within one conveniently available volume.

This being said, it should be emphasized how qualified any claims made here for definitiveness must be. The basic qualification is that a musical reference must possess some degree of historical importance or intrinsic interest in order to be reproduced or cited. It is possible that I have mistakenly rejected certain items as lacking in significance and equally possible that others have escaped my notice: this is inevitable in dealing with so vast a range of possibilities. In due course, a sufficient accumulation of such omissions might warrant the publication of a supplement in some appropriate journal. Meanwhile I proceed with the hope that the collection meets the general needs of the music historian.

The arrangement of materials follows that used in the standard manuals of Patrology. Each chapter covers a specific chronological and regional span, with its authors appearing in chronological order. The chapters are intro-duced by a paragraph or two of basic background material, and the indi-vidual authors by a skeletal biography based on standard reference works like Frank L. Cross's *Oxford Dictionary of the Christian Church* and Johannes Quasten's *Patrology*. These are generally not cited, whereas others used in the composition of the introductions and biographies – for example a recent biography or a particularly valuable monograph on some region or period – are. The individual passages of a particular author are arranged according to their appearance in his works, and the works in turn are arranged accord-ing to an order which seems suited to display the musical material to best advantage. Generally this order is announced at the close of an author's biography.

Every passage is introduced with a minimal head note that begins with a three-fold citation: (1) the place within the author's oeuvre (2) the place within Migne's *Patrologia*, and (3) the place within a modern critical edition when available. Latin titles are given in the original Latin, while Greek and Syriac titles are given variously, usually in Latin or English, as they appear in Quasten (1950–60) and Altaner-Graef (1960). In the rare instances where Migne's *Patrologia* presents a substantially inferior text to that of more recent critical editions (for example the genuine Ignatian letters) reference to it is omitted. The translations are of course based on the critical editions. The head note concludes with brief remarks on the content of the passage to follow. It is intended to focus attention on the central point of the quotation or highlight some interesting detail. In the case of difficult or controversial passages, references to relevant secondary literature may be supplied and some comment offered that reveals the author's viewpoint. Yet the interpretation of controversial passages is ultimately the task of the reader, in keeping with the primary function of this volume to make materials accessible rather than to interpret them.

Readers searching for material on a specific topic, such as antiphonal psalmody or music at pagan weddings, should follow these through from the index, and from cross-references in the head notes. (Such cross-references are indicated by giving the name of the cited author in capitals.) The volume has also been prepared with continuous reading in mind, and certain portions of it may reward such use, for example those devoted to fascinating personages like John Chrysostem and Augustine or to an important movement like desert monasticism.

Most of the material consists in brief passages of a few sentences or less. Some passages of original text do however run to several pages. Where the argument is rambling and repetitious, the significant material has been extracted, and presented in units, each of which makes a separate point, is readily quotable and easily indexed. In such cases details of the editorial omissions are supplied in the head note and reference to a translation of the entire passage is given when one is available.

The translations have all been newly prepared for the volume. At an earlier stage of the project it was thought best to include previously published translations. These are available for some three-quarters of the material in a number of monumental series: most notably the nineteenth-century British *Ante-Nicene Fathers* (*ANF*) and *Nicene and Post-Nicene Fathers* (*NPNF*), and the more recent American *Fathers of the Church* (*FC*) and *Ancient Christian Writers* (*ACW*). All of these are satisfactory as far as rendering the general sense of the text is concerned. Indeed certain items within *ACW* in particular appear to be models of modern academic translation, while *ANF* and *NPNF*, for all their Victorian flavor, are frequently admirable in their rotund idiomatic fluency. Yet in addition to the obvious discrepancies of style among translations made over a period of one hundred and fifty years, there is a more substantial difficulty in using them. While satisfactory in rendering the general sense, they tend to be inadequate with regard to technical detail; liturgical and musical terms are frequently rendered loosely, anachronistically and even inaccurately.

The ideal pursued in the present translations is that of literalness – not of course to the extent that the demands of idiomatic English were ignored, but in every instance where there was a choice between a graceful English expression which almost fitted the meaning and a somewhat more awkward one which still more closely fitted it, the former was sacrificed to the latter. Above all any hint of anachronism was strenuously avoided. This seems necessary in a volume which purports to furnish scholars with material they can use confidently in the writing of history. Accordingly, musical terms are rendered consistently by their English cognates. This is true, for example, of all the common Greek and Roman instruments like aulos, lyre, tibia, syrinx, etc., the one exception being the Greek *salpinx* and Latin *tuba* which are rendered 'trumpet'. When there are divergent transliterations to choose from, the Latin is preferred over the Greek – thus cithara and tympanum rather than kithara and tympanon. When a less common term is encountered or when the principle of transliteration by cognate must be overridden, this is indicated by placing the original language term in parentheses after its translation. The same principles apply to liturgical terminology so that *uigiliae* for example is rendered vigils not matins, and *lucernarium* lamp-lighting not vespers. The latter term is also included in parentheses because it is not precisely literal. The verbs *cantare* and *canere*, and their Greek equivalents are always translated 'to sing', but the verb *dicere*, in phrases like *dicere psalmum*, can be given as to 'say', 'recite', or 'sing', as the context suggests. Again in instances of substantial doubt the original language term appears in parentheses.

Liturgical and practical musical terminology provide few difficulties, but the area of music theory is something of an exception. Theoretical terminology is problematic enough when used by music theoreticians, but it can become hopelessly vague and ambiguous when used by non-professionals. There is an attempt here to maintain the above-described scheme of translation by cognate and the use of the original language terms in parentheses when a cognate is inappropriate, but it breaks down occasionally, particularly in passages with a proliferation of loosely used Greek synonyms for the idea of harmony.

For biblical excerpts that appear in patristic passages I have tried to use the familiar *Revised Standard Version*. This works well enough for the New Testament but not for the Old, particularly the Psalter. The *Revised Standard Version* derives ultimately from the Hebrew, whereas the church fathers generally used the Septuagint or Latin translations of it, a tradition better reflected in the *Douay-Rheims Version*. This was used for Old Testament quotations when the match was close, but there are many instances where either the particular translation employed by a church father or his tendency to quote from memory provides a passage that corresponds to no modern version and hence must be translated independently. The numbering of the psalms employed here, incidentally, is that of the patristic sources themselves, again derived from the Septuagint, not that of the Hebrew and Protestant tradition. To provide the latter in parentheses as is frequently done seems unnecessary.

I owe a very special debt to Dr Keith Dickson of Wheaton College, Massachusetts, who edited virtually all of the Greek and Latin translations. He made countless suggestions to render them more accurate and precise and to improve the English prose. I find it hard to imagine how I could have proceeded without him. Fr Sidney Griffith of the Catholic University of America generously provided a similar service for the Syriac translations from Ephraem and, more than that, rescued me from my badly dated view of that great author. Ms Cynthia Kahn of the same institution verified all the page references to the Latin and Greek works. I also owe much to Mrs Rosemary Dooley, formerly of the Cambridge University Press, who first suggested that I prepare this volume; to the series editors Dr Peter le Huray and Prof. John Stevens, who have behaved with kindness to me over a period that long pre-dates the present project; and to the current editor Mrs Penny Souster, who ably presided over the final stages of preparation. Most of all I am grateful to my wife Sally, who has consistently supported and encouraged me in this effort, and tolerated my neglect of much else. To her it is dedicated.

Buffalo, New York, February 1986

Introduction

In working with early Christian references to music one comes gradually to distinguish four principal categories of material. The most obvious perhaps is that chorus of denunciation directed against pagan musical customs, concentrating with special fervor on musical instruments. A second, seemingly contradictory, category is made up of passages that signal acceptance of music as one of the liberal or encyclical arts. The third consists in musical images or figures of speech. And finally there is the category of most interest to music historians, passages that shed some light on early liturgical chant.

Clearly this is a practical categorization rather than one with absolute logical validity. The categories differ in kind: one of them – musical imagery – is a mode of expression while the other three have to do with particular subjects. Occasionally there is overlap among them: the same passage might for example contrast the lascivious music of a pagan banquet with sober monastic pslamody. And then one encounters from time to time a passage that falls outside the system, for instance, an unbiased historical reference to some facet of music in classical Greece. It is nonetheless true that the categorization has considerable value as a first step in sorting out an initially confusing mass of material, and that a surprisingly large majority of patristic references to music is well served by it.

The first category cited, the polemic against pagan music and music instruments, has attracted considerable attention among contemporary scholars. This is due one assumes to the extravagant manner in which it is expressed. John Chrysostom, for example, refers to musical instruments along with dancing and obscene songs as the 'devil's garbage', and on another occasion declares that, 'Where the aulos is, there, by no means, is Christ'; while Arnobius of Sicca enquires sarcastically, 'Was it for this that God sent souls, that in men they become male prostitutes, and in women harlots, sambuca-players and harpists?' Such vehemence prompts the modern reader to wonder about its motivation. An attempt to identify it will be made presently, but first a few remarks on the historical background of the phenomenon.

Patristic musical puritanism did not come about in a cultural vacuum; there were precedents for it in both Greco-Roman and Jewish society. It is well known that Plato already wished to exclude from his ideal state the 'many-stringed' and 'many-keyed' professional instruments along with the 'slack' modes like the Lydian and Ionian (*Republic* 399). A number of Roman philosophers and historians expressed views even closer to those of the church fathers; Livy, for example, included the employment of women harpists at banquets among the undesirable luxuries introduced to Rome from Asia (39, 6, 7). The prophet Isaiah said of the new urban rich in Israel that, 'they have lyre and harp, timbrel and flute and wine at their feasts; but they do not regard the deeds of the Lord' (Is 5.12). Several centuries later Rabbi Johanan commented upon the passage, 'Whoever drinks to the accompaniment of the four musical instruments brings five punishments to the world' (Sotah 48a). Without doubt both pagan and Jewish moralism contributed each in its own way to the patristic position, but the latter remains in a class by itself for its vehemence and uniformity. There is hardly a major church father from the fourth century who does not inveigh against pagan musical practice in the strongest language.

This reference to the fourth century raises a point of chronology. Hermann Abert (1905, p. 93) followed by Eric Werner (1959, pp. 335 and 344) has told us, plausibly enough, that in the beginning the poorly educated Christians were greatly opposed to pagan music, but the sophisticated figures of the fourth century were more liberal on the subject. However, the reader of this anthology, arranged chronologically as it is, will observe that this is a one hundred and eighty degree reversal of the truth. The first hint of the polemic against pagan music appeared in the work of the late second-century converted rhetorician Tatian, who wrote: 'I do not wish to gape at many singers, nor do I care to look benignly upon a man who is nodding and motioning in an unnatural way.' The polemic grew in explicitness and intensity throughout the third century, particularly with Latin Africans like Tertullian and Arnobius, and became a commonplace among the major figures of the fourth like John Chrysostom, Ambrose and Augustine. Pseudo-Basil provides us with a typical example:

You place a lyre ornamented with gold and ivory upon a high pedestal as if it were a . . . devilish idol, and some miserable woman, rather than being taught to place her hands upon the spindle, is taught by you . . . to stretch them out upon the lyre. Perhaps you pay her wages or perhaps you turn her over to some female pimp, who after exhausting the licentious potential of her own body, presides over young women as the teacher of similar deeds.

Why the polemic should have been absent from the writings of earlier church fathers and so prominent in those of later ones is not easy to explain. Perhaps it was because most Christians were likely to succumb to the abuses in question only after the mass conversions of the third and fourth centuries. Or perhaps it was due to cultural factors precisely the opposite of those suggested by Abert and Werner. Werner refers to the 'intransigent puritanism' of the primitive church, while its attitude might better be characterized by what Dom Gregory Dix calls 'simplicity' and 'directness' (1945, p. 314). The later fathers on the other hand, all thoroughly educated in the classical tradition, might be said to have shared the musical puritanism of pagan intellectuals, taking it – for reasons of their own – beyond all precedent.

What these reasons might be is the question raised earlier and left unanswered. Quasten, while acknowledging the factor of moralism, sees the principal motivation of the patristic polemic as the close association of pagan musical practice with the 'pagan cult of idols' (1930, pp. 126–30). Indeed in commenting upon the passage from Pseudo-Basil quoted above he focuses on its incidental reference to a 'devilish idol' in making this point. Certainly he also presents better evidence, and no one will dispute the close association of much pagan musical practice with pagan cults. One need look no further than the omnipresent theatrical music of the day and recall the cultic origins of the theatre. Tertullian for one demonstrates his awareness of such associations when he says of the theatre that 'whatever transpires in voice, melody, instruments and writing is in the domain of Apollo, the Muses, Minerva and Mercury. You will detest, O Christian, those things whose authors you cannot but detest.'

Nevertheless the reader of this volume is likely to conclude that the motivation of moralism is at least as strong as that of antipathy toward idolatry. The polemic makes reference to a limited number of contexts: most notably the theatre, marriage celebrations and banquets. Typically singled out are items of moral concern like the lewd aspect of theatrical musicians, the coarseness of marriage songs and the dubious profession of the female musicians employed at banquets. Obviously it is not so much morality in general that is at stake here, but sexual morality in particular, a subject concerning which the church fathers display the most acute sensitivity. It is not an altogether attractive trait; anyone wishing to defend it without qualification should first read Jerome's extraordinary letter to Eustochium (XXII) on the subject of her virginity. Still it should not come entirely as a surprise, given on the one hand the real excesses of Late Antiquity, and on the other the inclination among intellectuals of the time, pagan and Christian alike, to pit the spirit against the flesh. An awareness of this latter tendency is essential to an understanding of the period and the reader wishing to be introduced to it might consult E. R. Dodds (1965, especially pp. 20–36).

Before leaving the category of polemic there is a final question to be raised: what relationship is there between the polemic against instruments and the *a cappella* performance of sacred music? Music historians have tended to assume that there is a direct connection, that is, that ecclesiastical authorities consciously strove to maintain their music free from the incursion of musical instruments. There is little evidence of this in the sources however. What one observes there are two separate phenomena: a consistent condemnation of instruments in the contexts cited above, and an ecclesiastical psalmody obviously free of instrumental involvement. It is puzzling to the modern mind that the church fathers failed to forge an ideological link between the two – leaving this apparently to the *a cappella* partisans of the nineteenth century. It is true that a few exceptional passages exist where there is a hint of such a connection – where the two are juxtaposed at least on the level of phenomenon if not of doctrine. The most striking is one in which John Chrysostom writes admiringly of a monastic community that rises before daybreak for prayer and psalmody:

They sing the prophetic hymns with great harmony and well ordered melody. Neither cithara, nor syrinx, nor any other musical instrument emits such sound as can be heard in the deep silence and solitude of those holy men as they sing.

One would have to deny the larger context to see this as an example of incipient *a cappella* doctrine. The truth remains that the polemic against musical instruments and the vocal performance of early Christian psalmody were – for whatever reason – unrelated in the minds of the church fathers.

Examples of the second category, passages dealing with music as one of the encyclical or liberal arts, are comparatively rare and at the same time uniform in their central point. The church fathers, in seeming contradiction to their stand on pagan music in real life situations, accepted the idea of music as an academic discipline. They did so as part of the overall compromise that the church worked out with classical learning. At the heart of the classical system were the so-called seven liberal arts (Wagner, 1985, pp. 1–31). The scheme had its beginnings in the teaching of Plato, Aristotle and the Pythagoreans, and achieved its definitive formulation in the *De nuptiis Philologiae et Mercurii* of the early fifth-century encyclopedist Martianus Capella. The seven arts are divided into a trivium of three language arts – grammar, rhetoric and dialectic – and a quadrivium of four mathematical arts – arithmetic, music, geometry and astronomy. The latter group reflects the view that nature is somehow composed of number, a conception epitomized in the term Augustine uses in his *De musica* – *numerositas*, which might best be translated 'numberliness'. Music within this context is well defined by Cassiodorus as 'the discipline which speaks of numbers . . . that are found in sound' (*Institutiones musicae* 4). Thus the *ars musica* is most characteristically a matter of number, in particular the fractions defining the intervals of the tonal system and the ratios underlying the rhythmical and metrical systems. It includes other considerations also such as ethos doctrine and classifications of musical instruments according to their method of tone production, but everything is dealt with in a manner so far removed from everyday music that there is no real contradiction in the fact that the church fathers accepted it while rejecting pagan musical practice.

The principal use to which they put it, along with the other disciplines, was as an aid to the elucidation of Scripture. Augustine explains this in *De doctrina christiana*, a treatise on biblical exegesis:

We must not shun music because of the superstition of the heathen, if we are able to snatch from it anything useful for the understanding of the Holy Scriptures; and we need not be involved with their theatrical frivolities, if we consider some point concerning citharas and other instruments which might be of aid in comprehending spiritual things.

If the passage seems obscure on first reading, its meaning should be clear enough in present context. One can reject the 'theatrical frivolities' of everyday music and still seek out in the received doctrine of *ars musica* whatever information contributes something to understanding the Bible. The specific point Augustine appears to have in mind when citing 'citharas and other instruments' is one encountered again and again in the patristic psalm commentaries. It is that the cithara has its sound chamber in the lower part of the instrument while harps have theirs in the vertical member of the triangle, a higher placement. The distinction is put to use when the two instruments are encountered together in passages such as that of Psalm 150.3: 'Praise him with psaltery and cithara'. The result, according to the generally employed method of allegorical or figurative exegesis, is the commonplace that the cithara whose sound 'comes from below' symbolizes the more mundane virtues, while the psaltery, a type of harp, whose sound 'comes from above' symbolizes the higher virtues like contemplation.

Such specific applications might strike the modern reader as trivial or far-fetched, but the general attitude of acceptance toward music as a liberal art is of profound importance in the history of western music. It shared, of course, the overall significance of the Christian compromise with pagan learning, but it had a significance peculiar to itself. Its immediate manifestation was in the treatises on the *ars musica* by transitional figures like Cassiodorus and Boethius, who preserved summaries of classical music theory. Their work bore little relationship to the music of the time, but their successors, the theorists of the Carolingian era, took the momentous step of applying classical theoretical conceptions to the Gregorian repertory and the beginnings of ecclesiastical polyphony. This is significant enough in itself but Walter Wiora for one (1961, especially pp. 125–30) sees it as only the start of a process unique to western music, whereby factors such as the vertical rationalization we call harmony and the horizontal rationalization we call rhythm and form resulted in architectonic creations like the products of Viennese musical classicism. However far one wishes to take such thinking, it seems fair to say that western music would not have been quite the same had the church fathers adopted a different policy toward the *ars musica*.

It was acknowledged above that musical imagery, as a mode of expression rather than a subject heading, is not analogous to the three other categories. Yet from a practical point of view it may be precisely the one most necessary to bring to the attention of the reader. For the first three centuries at least it far surpasses the other categories in frequency of appearance, and perhaps the most common sort of misinterpretation of patristic musical reference is to draw unwarranted conclusions from a passage involving musical figures of speech. It is true that there are passages where the context or a chance remark of the author reveals his attitude on some aspect of music, but these are distinctly in the minority and must be demonstrated as such in each case.

Perhaps the most popular of all musical figures invokes the harmony existing among the strings of the cithara. It is encountered first in Ignatius of Antioch, who writes to the citizens of Ephesus:

It is fitting that you concur with the intention of your bishop, as in fact you do. For your renowned presbytery, worthy of God, is attuned to the bishop as strings to a cithara. Hence it is that Jesus Christ is sung in your unity of mind and concordant love.

This is an attractive figure and there are others of comparable quality such as Origen's identification of the trumpet with the Gospel and Tertullian's imaginative play upon the complexity of the hydraulis. Such aesthetic considerations aside, patristic musical imagery can be of special interest to the theologian. It is after all the musical manifestation of a world view – shared by many church fathers with the pagan proponents of Platonism's later stages – that sees material objects as signs of spiritual reality. In this way of thinking, what strikes us as a mere figure of speech amounts to the expression of a metaphysical bond between the sign and the thing signified. Thus the idea of a musical instrument – if not the actual instrument – becomes so to speak a sacrament.

While paying respect to such beliefs, it is necessary in a volume addressed primarily to music historians to take the pragmatic tack indicated above. This is especially true when dealing with the psalm commentary, that genre where the majority of later patristic musical imagery is to be found. The psalm commentary works its way through the one hundred and fifty psalms, commenting upon each verse and indeed virtually every key word, including the many instances where musical instruments are mentioned. The mode of commentary is the so-called allegorical method. It was employed earlier by Hellenistic scholars, who used it to explain away the unedifying escapades of gods and goddesses. Thus when Athena is said to have come in to Telemachus, this means only that she, as the personification of thought, caused Telemachus to reflect upon the profligacy of the suitors (Hatch, 1889, p. 62). The reader of this introduction is by now prepared to see in such interpretation not a cynical evasion of the truth but simply another example of how thinkers of the time tended to look upon the spiritual world as the real one and the material world as an illusion. In any case the method came to be employed by the Jewish contemporary of Jesus, Philo of Alexandria, in interpreting the Old Testament, and after him by the Christian Alexandrians, Clement and Origen, who established it as standard for Christian biblical exegesis. In commenting upon the instruments of the Psalter, the exegete would ignore their historical usage in

Israel and their contemporary usage in pagan society, and compose instead instrumental metaphors. The Pseudo-Origen commentary, for example, has this to say of the instruments mentioned in Psalm 150:

The cithara is the practical soul activated by the commandments of Christ. The tympanum is the death of covetousness through goodness itself . . . The strings are the harmony of the balanced sound of virtues and instruments . . . The well-sounding cymbal is the active soul . . . the clangorous cymbal is the pure mind made live by the salvation of Christ.

Metaphors such as these – not all equally arresting in a poetic sense – were repeated again and again in the psalm commentaries of various authors and are therefore quoted sparingly in the present volume. The reader wishing to pursue the subject further has only to identify the places in the psalms themselves that cite instruments and turn then to the corresponding places in the commentaries.

In addition to the typical allegorical type there is a minority group of commentaries that better serves the music historian. The exegetes of the school of Antioch, figures like John Chrysostom and Theodoret of Cyrus, asserted the need for biblical interpretation of a more literal and historical nature. As a result they provide us with commentary that strictly speaking falls outside the category of musical imagery, but for that very reason offers an instructive perspective on Old Testament instruments. What Theodoret has to say on the instruments of Psalm 150 is quite different from Pseudo-Origen:

Of old the Levites used these instruments as they hymned God in his holy Temple, not because God enjoyed their sound but because he accepted the intention of those involved. We hear God saying to the Jews that he does not take pleasure in singing and playing: 'Take away from me the sound of your songs; to the voice of your instruments I will not listen' (Amos 5.23). He allowed these things to happen because he wished to free the Jews from the error of idols. For since they were fond of play and laughter, and all these things took place in the temple of the idols, he permitted them . . . thus avoiding the greater evil by allowing the lesser.

The argument, then, is that God, in order to entice the Jews away from the worship of idols, which was of course accompanied by instrumental music, permitted them the pleasure of using instruments in the Temple at Jerusalem, so that by allowing a lesser evil a greater evil was avoided. The argument is expanded and repeated several times in the writings of the Antiochene exegetes. Its anti-semitic tone aside (Wilken, 1983), it leaves no doubt about their opposition to instruments and serves as a corrective to the notion occasionally expressed by modern scholars, that the allegorical treatment of musical instruments in psalm commentaries somehow implies their acceptance in real life.

If the category of most interest to music historians is that of references to liturgical chant, it remains the one where the least progress has been made to date. This is so simply because of the great difficulty involved. It is comparatively easy to make substantially sound generalizations about, say, the patristic attitude toward music at pagan banquets, but here an entirely different kind of effort is required. It is necessary to reconstruct a detailed chronological sequence of events in the development of psalmody and hymnody over a period of several centuries. The evidence – plentiful for some periods, but more often scarce – is generally fragmentary in character and widely scattered in the sources. The situation is reflected in the secondary literature, which while occasionally providing an excellent work on a limited subject like Helmut Leeb's *Die Psalmodie bei Ambrosius* (1967), has made little progress toward an overview of the period since Peter Wagner's pioneering *Einführung in die gregorianischen Melodien* (1895).

It is hoped that the present volume makes a modest contribution in this respect by suggesting a fresh approach. In recent years the more commonly employed approach has been topical rather than chronological, perhaps even inductive rather than deductive. Generalizations on a few salient themes are put forth and a scattering of references provided in support. This may seem the only way to cope with an obscure period for authors hard-pressed to produce an opening chapter for their surveys of music history. Yet it should be possible to achieve an immediate improvement by the simple expedient of collecting the available literary evidence – there is of course virtually no other – and assembling it in chronological and regional order. A thorough analysis of the material thus arranged is a project of at least book-length proportions, but it might be appropriate here to suggest certain positive points that are immediately apparent, as well as to define gaps and perplexities that may remain with us indefinitely.

In general the subject is much more difficult in its earlier than its later phases. The New Testament passages are particularly elusive in character, and the second and third centuries are silent on some of the most essential questions, while the abundant evidence of the fourth and early fifth centuries offers opportunities for dramatic advances in our understanding of the period.

Of the New Testament material it can at least be said that it creates the impression of a positive attitude toward liturgical song. Moreover, one can console oneself with the thought that the difficulty in arriving at knowledge of specific musical practice might stem from the circumstance that musical practice, along with liturgical practice in general, was not yet fixed. An important question which unfortunately the evidence presented here does little to advance is that of non-biblical hymnody in the primitive church. It is maintained by many with some plausibility that this was more common at the time than the singing of the Old Testament psalms. There is some material germane to this subject presented here, but not much, and it must remain one where specialists will continue to speculate without benefit of the sort of tangible evidence that most music historians prefer.

Yet there is one brief reference in the New Testament that might prove eventually to be of great significance. Appearing identically in the gospels of Matthew and Mark, it indicates that the Last Supper was concluded with the singing of a 'hymn'. This singing by Jesus and the Apostles at a Jewish ceremonial meal, whether the Passover Seder or not, furnishes a link with Jewish musical practice on the one hand and, on the other, with the Christian practice of the immediately succeeding centuries (Smith, 1984). If the second and third century material is relatively sparse, as mentioned above, it favors us nevertheless with several striking vignettes of psalmody at common Christian meals, whether the *agape* or a less clearly defined gathering. These passages suggest that it was primarily in this context that the New Testament enthusiasm for sacred song continued to be fostered. Lending weight to this idea is the near total absence of reference to psalmody in the Eucharist. Justin omits mention of it in his detailed description of the mid-second century Eucharist at Rome, and the one apparent reference, from Tertullian's *De anima*, might very well involve non-biblical song rather than Old Testament psalms. Thus, while the lack of material from the second and third centuries makes the historian's task only marginally easier than for the Apostolic period, what we do have points to common meals rather than the Eucharist as the principal context for Christian song.

The situation changes greatly in the fourth and fifth centuries: a number of important points emerge from the abundant evidence, allowing one to discern the broad outlines of psalmodic development during the period and also to speculate more confidently about some of the problematic areas of the earlier period. To engage in such speculation is not appropriate here, but a few of the more salient fourth century phenomena should be noted.

Among them is the role played by the desert monks of Egypt and Palestine. Music historians have tended to look upon these redoubtable ascetics as exercizing a negative influence; we are familiar from many secondary sources with the monk Pambo's harsh denunciation of the frivolities of urban psalmody. Actually this anecdote is apocryphal – probably sixth century in origin (Wessely, 1952) – and there is nothing like it in the authentic sayings of Pambo or any of his fourth century colleagues. Instead we observe these monks chanting the Psalter from memory for a substantial part of the day and night. We observe also, as the monastic movement developed and spread in the second half of the fourth century, how the original Egyptian mode of virtually continuous prayer and psalmody was relaxed, and the day was broken down into set times for common meetings. These corresponded precisely to the six medieval office hours of matins, lauds, terce, sext, none and vespers with only prime and compline yet to be established. By the second half of the fourth century, monastic communities had been established in the principal eastern urban centers, and the monastic office virtually inundated the cathedral office with psalmody. The rest of this momentous chapter in the history of early liturgical music is too complex for easy summary, but let it be suggested here by way of hypothesis that it includes that wave of enthusiasm for psalmody that we observe in the literature, as it sweeps from east to west culminating in the remarkable sermon of Niceta of Remesiana. A careful analysis of the principal sources involved, such as Basil's much quoted Epistle 207 and even Augustine's famous description of Ambrose's musical innovations at Milan, might very well reveal a key role for the monastic movement.

To retreat for the moment from broad generalization to a more specific point – the manner of psalmodic performance – the reader will note numerous clear examples of responsorial psalmody ranging chronologically from Tertullian to Augustine. Responsorial psalmody is understood here in the conventional sense of the chanting of the psalm verses by a soloist with the congregation adding a single verse, or an exclamation like Alleluia, in response to each verse. The abundance of references makes it clear that this is the normal manner of psalmodic performance. And what of the other type of psalmody generally mentioned in the same breath as responsorial psalmody – the so-called antiphonal psalmody? In the early medieval sources this type appears in its commonly understood meaning of two choirs singing psalm verses in alternation. There is, however, just one example of dual choir psalmody given in this volume, from Basil's Epistle 207, and it fails to use the term antiphonal. The term does begin to appear, generally as a noun, in late fourth century monastic circumstances like those described by Egeria and Cassian, but here there is nothing suggesting a dual choir performance. In short, antiphonal psalmody in the early Christian period is one of those 'perplexities' referred to above, for which this volume can serve at best only as a starting point.

Turning finally to eucharistic psalmody in the fourth century, one observes unambiguous references to just two places in the service – the communion and the gradual. There is a small number of late fourth century references to a communion psalm – John Chrysostom, Pseudo-Cyril of Jerusalem and the *Apostolic Constitutions* – which make up in explicitness for their paucity. References to the gradual psalm, conversely, are plentiful but offer difficulties of interpretation. Before discussing them a brief comment on the omission of the alleluia would seem to be in order. Music historians continue to assume that authors like Augustine, Jerome and Hilary were referring to the alleluia in their vivid descriptions of the *jubilus*. They identify the melismatic style of the alleluia of the Mass as known from medieval sources with the most striking characteristic of the *jubilus*, its lack of text. This is a completely arbitrary identification, however, not hinted at by the patristic authors themselves. On the contrary they describe the *jubilus* as a secular genre, not an ecclesiastical chant; it is a kind of wordless song with which workers, especially farmers, accompanied their labors (Wiora, 1962). They introduce it into the psalm commentaries when the word *jubilare* – not *alleluia* – appears in a psalm, and then in the accustomed manner of allegorical exegesis they attempt to discover in its wordlessness some facet of spiritual truth. It is true that many other passages indicate that the alleluia was sung during Paschaltide, but none of these specify *the* alleluia of the pre-Eucharist; rather they seem to refer to the word's use as an exclamation or response made at various points in the liturgy. The first unambiguous references to the alleluia psalm in the pre-Eucharist appear in the fifth century Armenian Lectionary, which reflects the liturgy at Jerusalem (Renoux, 1961–2); there is no comparable evidence from the contemporary west.

Returning to the gradual psalm there is a peculiarity of most references to it which bears careful study. They do not describe it in the way we have come to understand it from the later literature, that is, as a lyric response to a reading from Scripture. Rather they refer to it as a reading in its own right. This observation suggests the following hypothesis: the gradual psalm was originally simply one of the Old Testament readings of the pre-eucharistic 'service of the Word'. Thus prior to the fourth century it would have figured occasionally, perhaps even frequently, among the readings, but in the late fourth century – that period of singular enthusiasm for psalmody – it was singled out and made a discrete musical event at every Eucharist. This hypothesis rejects the conventional wisdom that the gradual psalm goes back to the synagogue service at the time of Jesus, yet it conforms much better to the available evidence – the lack of a single unambiguous reference to the gradual psalm prior to the fourth century, the conception of it as a reading when it finally appears, and other points not yet mentioned in this introduction, such as the absence of the clerical cantor from the sources until the late fourth century, and the remarkable testimony of Augustine in his *Retractationes* that eucharistic psalmody was looked upon by some of his contemporaries as an objectionable innovation.

Most of what is suggested here on the early history of ecclesiastical chant is at variance with the conventional wisdom, that is, the commonly held views of music historians as expressed in recent surveys of music history. Yet it is neither so daring nor so original when matched with the conclusions of an entirely different body of secondary literature – the specialized studies on individual phases of early Christian music by scholars like Helmut Hucke, Juan Mateos, Helmut Leeb and most recently Peter Jeffery. Where I hope that the present volume makes a unique contribution is in demonstrating that it is now feasible to develop a new overview, one that employs the critical standards of the latter group. Gaps will remain, particularly for the earlier centuries, but by the careful arrangement of what evidence does exist we can see what we do know and what we do not, thus replacing wishful thinking with controlled speculation. For the later centuries, where we have considerable evidence, we should be able – again by studying it systematically rather than selectively – to establish much that is both new and of central importance. And finally there is a good possibility that periods of abundance will shed light on those less favored. Nearly a century has elapsed since the appearance of Wagner's *Einführung*; some measure of advance beyond his noble effort seems long overdue.

CHAPTER I

The New Testament

'The Christian Church was born in song' (Martin, 1964, p. 39). One might be inclined to agree after reading the quotations presented in this chapter, but there is a distinction to be made. It is true that considerable evidence of warmth toward the notion of praising God in song appears in the pages of the New Testament, but there is a singularly elusive quality about most of the references in question. While singing is mentioned frequently, it is extremely difficult to determine just what is being sung and in what liturgical circumstances. There has been an attempt in any case to assemble here every passage that can reasonably be construed to describe religious song. Omitted, on the other hand, are actual quotations of putatively sung texts. The most obvious of these are the three canticles from the early chapters of Luke: Mary's *Magnificat* (1.46–55), Zachariah's *Benedictus* (1.67–79), and Simeon's *Nunc dimittis* (2.29–35). There are also numerous shorter passages that many scholars claim to be fragments of early Christian hymns woven into the text. Just one of these – 1 Tim. 3.16, a less controversial example – is included by way of illustration, while the reader is referred to Martin (1963) for a particularly cogent exposition of the subject.

In addition to passages that might have a bearing on sacred song, there are several that fall outside not only this category but any of the others discussed in the Introduction – for example incidental references to music in contemporary Palestinian life. The majority of these are not given here; for exhaustive citation of them one can consult Smith (1962).

The material is arranged according to the traditional succession of New Testament books, although this does run contrary in some cases to their probable chronology; all the gospels, for example, are later than the genuine Pauline epistles. For a summary of modern scholarship on considerations of this sort, see Kümmel (1965).

1   Mt 14.6–8; see also Mk 6.22–5

> The infamous dance of Salome (she is not named here, but is in Josephus, *Ant.*, xviii, 136). It is invoked in subsequent condemnations of dance by the church fathers.

When the birthday of Herod came, the daughter of Herodias danced in their midst and pleased Herod, so that with an oath he promised to give her whatever she might ask. Prompted by her mother, she said, 'Give me here upon a platter the head of John the Baptist.'

2   Mt 21.9

> Jesus enters Jerusalem as the crowd exclaims 'Hosanna', an event com-
> memorated on Palm Sunday and in the Sanctus of the Mass.

And the crowds that went before him and those that followed were crying
out saying: 'Hosanna to the Son of David! Blessed is he who comes in the
name of the Lord! Hosanna in the highest!'

3   Mt 26.30; Mk 14.26

> This verse, identical in Matthew and Mark, concludes their descriptions of
> the Last Supper. Commentators, accepting the Synoptic Gospels' place-
> ment of the Last Supper on the first night of the Passover, identify the meal
> as the Passover Seder and accordingly the hymn sung at it as the Hallel (Ps
> 113–18). One must caution that John appears to place the Last Supper on
> the preceding day, but the passage remains a crucially important link in a
> chain of evidence that connects the singing of psalms at Jewish and
> Christian ceremonial meals.

And after singing a hymn (ὑμνήσαντες), they went out to the Mount of
Olives.

4   Lk 2.13–14

> Angels sing the initial words of the *Gloria in excelsis*, the hymn that comes to
> be sung in the eastern morning office and the western Eucharist. The
> passage concludes the scene, referred to eventually as 'The Annunciation
> to the Shepherds', which plays an important role in liturgical drama,
> medieval musical iconography (McKinnon, 1976) and the tradition of
> renaissance and baroque pastoral music.

And suddenly there was with the angel a multitude of the heavenly host,
praising God and saying: 'Glory to God in the highest, and on earth peace
among men of [his] good will'.

5   Acts 2.46–7

> In this passage, describing the ritual behavior of Christians immediately
> after the first Pentecost, the term 'praising' might be taken to imply the
> singing of psalms or hymns. See also Acts 4.25, where the community
> appears to sing Psalm 2, 'Why did the Gentiles rage?'.

And continuing daily in the Temple with one accord, and breaking bread in
their homes, they shared their food in gladness and simplicity of heart,
praising God and having favor with all the people.

6   Acts 16.25–6

> Paul and Silas sing in prison at Thyatira.

At about midnight Paul and Silas were praying and singing (προσευχόμενοι ὕμνουν) to God, and the prisoners were listening to them. Suddenly there was a great earthquake so that the foundations of the prison were shaken, and immediaitely the doors were open and the fetters of all were unfastened.

7   Rom 15.5–6

> Whether or not this passage refers directly to liturgical song, as some commentators believe it does, it expresses two musical conceptions that will become common in patristic literature: living in harmony and exclaiming in a single voice, the *una uoce dicentes* of the eucharistic prayer (Quasten, 1930, pp. 66–72).

May the God of patience and encouragement grant that you live in harmony with each other (τὸ αὐτὸ φρονεῖν ἐν ἀλλήλοις), in accord with Christ Jesus, so that together with one mouth you may glorify God and Father of our Lord Jesus Christ.

8   1 Cor 13.1

> 1 Corinthians is by far the most rich in musical references of all New Testament epistles. Werner (1960) claims that this famous passage expresses Paul's Pharisaic scorn for the instruments of the Temple at Jerusalem.

If I should speak with the tongues of men and of angels, but have not love, I have become sounding brass or a clanging cymbal (χαλκὸς ἠχῶν ἢ κύμβαλον ἀλαλάζον).

9   1 Cor 14.7–8

> This reference appears in an extended passage that cautions against placing too high a value on speaking in tongues. An essential characteristic of this gift is its lack of intelligibility, and here Paul makes a comparison with musical instruments which must produce distinct notes to be musically intelligible. There is no reason to assume that he refers to the instruments disparagingly.

Yet if inanimate things that give voice, such as aulos and cithara, provide no distinction among notes, how can one tell what is piped or plucked; and indeed, if the trumpet produces an uncertain sound, who will prepare for battle?

10   1 Cor 14.15

> Again Paul, while allowing for 'spiritual' activity, calls for intelligible activity as well.

What then? I will pray with the spirit, and I will pray with the mind also. I will sing (ψαλῶ) with the spirit, and I will sing with the mind also.

11   1 Cor 14.26–7

> Here we are granted a glimpse of early Corinthian liturgy. The context remains Paul's attempt to restrain the Corinthian tendency to rely excessively upon inspired gifts. This tendency makes it more likely that the 'psalm' mentioned here is a spontaneous creation rather than an Old Testament psalm. It is in any case true that the terms psalm and hymn as used in early Christian literature do not necessarily correspond to the modern meanings of Old Testament psalm and individually composed hymn. For recent commentary of exceptional value on Corinthian liturgy, see Meeks (1983, pp. 14–63).

What then, brethren? When you come together each one has a psalm, has a teaching, has a revelation, has a tongue, has an interpretation.

12   1 Cor 15.51–2

> Perhaps the most stirring reference to the trumpet in early Christian literature. Together with other New Testament references to the trumpet, in particular Mt 24.30–1, it inspires the rich medieval iconography of angel trumpeters (Hammerstein, 1962).

Behold, I tell you a mystery. We shall not all sleep, rather we shall all be changed – in a moment, in the twinkling of an eye, at the last trumpet. For the trumpet will sound, and the dead will rise uncorrupted and we shall be changed.

13, 14 Eph 5.18–20; Col 3.16–17

> This pair of famous passages has been subjected to widely divergent and sometimes incautious interpretations (Kraeling and Mowry, 1957). They serve as prime examples of the elusiveness of New Testament musical reference. The traditional translation 'making melody', incidentally, is retained here for want of a better alternative. The verb ψάλλειν originally meant 'to pluck a string instrument', but by New Testament times it came to mean simply 'to sing', with or without an instrument. To translate it here as 'singing', however, would create an obviously undesirable repetition.

And do not become drunk with wine, for that is debauchery, but be filled with the spirit, speaking to one another in psalms and hymns and spiritual songs, singing and making melody (ψάλλοντες) in your hearts to the Lord, giving thanks at all times for everything in the name of our Lord Jesus Christ to God the Father.

Let the word of Christ dwell in you abundantly; in all wisdom teach and advise each other with psalms, hymns and spiritual songs; sing in your hearts to God with pleasure. And whatever you do in work or deed, [do] all in the name of the Lord Jesus, giving thanks through him to God the Father.

15   1 Tim 3.16

> An example of a putative hymn fragment embedded in the New Testament text. It is looked upon as hymnic in character because of the parallelism of the concluding six Greek phrases, but it could be argued that the same device is compatible with rhetorical prose.

> And great, certainly, is the mystery of our religion:
>> Who was manifested in the flesh
>> was vindicated in the spirit
>> seen by angels
>> preached among the nations
>> believed in the world
>> taken up in glory.

16   Heb 13.15

> It can be argued that the phrase 'sacrifice of praise' is a synonym for the singing of psalms or hymns.

Through him then let us continually offer up a sacrifice of praise to God, that is, the fruit of lips confessing his name.

17   Jas 5.13

Is anyone among you in distress? Let him pray. Is anyone cheerful? Let him sing (ψαλλέτω).

18   Rev 4.8

> There is considerable musical allusion in the Book of Revelation, some of it incidental, like the opening comparison of the heavenly voice to a trumpet, and some more substantial, like the singing in the visionary liturgical scenes of chapters 4, 5, 14 and 18; the angel trumpeters that announce the seven plagues of chapters 8 through 11; and the destruction of 'Babylon the great' along with its musicians (chapter 14). Of most relevance to the subject of liturgical song perhaps is the great vision of chapters 4 through 5, which some see as a reflection of early Christian liturgy (Mowry, 1952). It seems probable, however, that it owes more to Jewish Temple liturgy or the

contemporary imperial court than the simple domestic Christian liturgy of the time. Two short excerpts from it are given here, the first of which mentions the Sanctus (Is 6.2–3).

And the four living creatures, each of them with six sings, are full of eyes round about and within; and day and night they do not rest from saying:

> Holy, holy, holy, the Lord God Almighty,
> who was, who is and who is to come.

19   Rev 5.8–9

As the vision continues the twenty-four elders now hold citharas in their hands, a circumstance of great importance for medieval musical iconography. One might also note the curious reference of the so-callled John of Cotton (*De musica* iii) to a string instrument that he calls the *fiala*.

And when he had taken the scroll, the four living creatures and the twenty-four elders fell down before the lamb, each holding a cithara and golden bowls (φιάλας) full of incense, which are the prayers of the saints. And they sing a new song saying:

> Worthy art thou to take the scroll and open its seals . . .

CHAPTER 2

The Christian literature of the first and second centuries

The literature of this period consists primarily in the work of the Apostolic Fathers and the second century Greek Apologists. The Apostolic Fathers, figures like Clement of Rome and Ignatius of Antioch, are so called because of their proximity in time to the New Testament authors. The Greek Apologists, the best known of whom is Justin Martyr, were educated converts who set out to defend their new faith from contemporary misconceptions. Unfortunately neither group contributes much to our knowledge of early Christian song, but they do provide us with a variety of musical imagery. And toward the end of the period the beginnings of the polemic against pagan musical practice can be discerned.

Also included in this chapter are the *Odes of Solomon*, a collection of post-biblical Christian psalms; and other sources from outside the patristic mainstream such as the Apocryphal New Testament and the *Sibylline Oracles*.

A The Apostolic Fathers

Clement of Rome (fl. c.96)

He was probably the third Bishop of Rome, with the shadowy figure of Linus intervening between him and Peter. His one authenticated work is the First Epistle to the Corinthians.

20   1 *Corinthians* XXXIV, 5–7; *PG* I, 276–7; *AF* I, 51–2

Some see this passage as an early reference to the Sanctus of the Eucharist, but its language is by no means conclusive in this respect.

Let us consider the entire multitude of his angels, how standing by you they minister to his will. For the Scripture says: 'Ten thousand times ten thousand stood by him and a thousand times a thousand ministered to him and cried out, "Holy, holy, holy is the Lord of Sabaoth, the whole of creation is full of his glory" (Is 6.3)'. Let us, therefore, gathered together in concord by conscience, cry out earnestly to him as if with one voice, so that we might come to share in his great and glorious promises.

Ignatius of Antioch (c.35–c.107)

Probably of Syrian birth, he was, according to Origen, the second bishop of Antioch and as such Peter's direct successor, while according to Eusebius a certain Euodius intervened between the two. He wrote letters to the various city churches at stages of his journey to Rome, where he was to be martyred. On occasion he employed musical figures of speech.

21   *Ephesians* IV, 1–2; *PG* V, 733–6; *AF* I, 81

A central passage in the history of musical imagery, introducing the comparison of Christian harmony with the strings of a cithara. Foster (1962–3) takes the view that the passage suggests instrumentally accompanied liturgical music at Ephesus. For a passage in which Ignatius invokes the image of the cithara somewhat less successfully, see *Philadelphians* 1.2.

Wherefore it is fitting that you concur with the intention of your bishop, as in fact you do. For your most renowned presbytery, worthy of God, is attuned (συνήρμοσται) to the bishop as strings to a cithara. Hence it is that Jesus Christ is sung in your unity of mind and concordant love. 2 And to a man you make up a chorus, so that joined together in harmony and having received the godly strain (χρῶμα Θεοῦ) in unison, you might sing in one voice through Jesus Christ to the Father, that he might hear you and recognize you through your good deeds as members of his son. It is beneficial, then, for you to be in blameless unity so that you might always partake of God.

22   *Romans* II, 2; *PG* V, 805; *AF* I, 95–5

The term chorus is used frequently in early Christian musical imagery. The passage refers to Ignatius' impending martyrdom in Rome – the west, where the sun sets.

Grant me nothing more than to be poured out for God, while an altar is still at hand, so that forming a chorus in charity you might sing to the Father in Christ Jesus, because God has considered the bishop of Syria worthy to be found at the setting of the sun, having been summoned from its rising.

23   Pseudo-Ignatius, *Antiochenes* XII, 1–2; *PG* V, 908; *AF* II, 220–2

The eight spurious epistles of Ignatius, among which is that addressed to the Antiochenes, date from the late fourth century, a point not observed by several scholars who cite this passage as evidence for the establishment of the clerical office of cantor already in the second century. For a recent study on the cantor which avoids such errors, see Foley (1982).

I greet the holy presbytery. I greet the sacred deacons . . . 2 I greet the sub-deacons, the readers, the cantors (ψάλτας), the porters, the laborers, the exorcists and the confessors. I greet the keepers of the sacred gateways and the deaconesses in Christ.

B The Greek Apologists

Justin Martyr (c.100–c.165)

The foremost of the Apologists, he was born at Sechem in Samaria. Before discovering Christianity he sought truth among the various pagan philosophies. He was one of the first to strive for a formal reconciliation of his faith with reason. His mature years were spent at Rome where he addressed his literary defense of Christianity to the Emperor and the Senate.

One notes, for what it is worth, a reference by Eusebius (*Ecclesiastical History* IV, xviii, 5), repeated by Jerome (*De uiris illustribus* 23), to a lost work of Justin's entitled *Psaltes*, the Greek term for clerical cantor.

24   *Apology* I, 13; *PG* VI, 345; *Otto* I, 40

> Rather than participate in bloody sacrifice, one must offer prayers and hymns of thanksgiving.

We have been instructed that only the following worship is worthy of him, not the consumption by fire of those things created by him for our nourishment but the use of them by ourselves and by those in need, while in gratitude to him we offer solemn prayers and hymns for his creation and for all things leading to good health.

25   *Apology* I, 67; *PG* VI, 429; *Otto* I, 184–6

> This important text is a detailed description of Sunday morning Eucharist that fails to mention psalmody.

And on the day named for the sun there is an assembly in one place for all who live in the towns and in the country; and the memoirs of the Apostles he Prophets are read as long as time permits. Then, finished, he who presides speaks, giving admonishment and exhortation to imitate those noble deeds. Then we all stand together and offer prayers. And when, as we said above, we are finished with the prayers, bread is brought, and wine and water, and he who presides likewise offers prayers and thanksgiving, according to his ability, and the people give their assent by exclaiming Amen. And there takes place the distribution to each and the partaking of that over which thanksgiving has been said, and it is brought to those not present by the deacon.

26   *Dialogue with Trypho* 2; *PG* VI, 477; *Otto* II, 8

> A Pythagorean recommends the mathematical arts, including music, to the young Justin. This is apparently the earliest reference to music as a liberal art in Christian literature.

Since my spirit was still bursting to hear what was proper to and special about philosophy, I approached a particularly eminent Pythagorean, a man who prided himself greatly on his wisdom. Then, as I conversed with him, indicating that I wished to attend his lectures and be his disciple, he said, 'What? Are you not acquainted with music, astronomy and geometry? Or do you expect to comprehend what leads to happiness without first learning what will draw the soul away from sense objects and render it fit for things of the mind, so that it perceives the Beautiful itself and what is Good itself?'

27   *Dialogue with Trypho* 106; *PG* VI, 724;

> Justin sees in Psalm 21.23 a prophecy of Christ's singing with the Apostles at the Last Supper.

And the rest of the psalm reveals that he hymned God while with them, which in fact is set forth in the memoirs of the Apostle. Here are the words: 'I will declare thy name to my brethren; in the midst of the church will I hymn thee'.

28   Pseudo-Justin, *Hortatory Address to the Greeks* 8; *PG* VI, 256–7; *Otto* III, 40

> The author, a contemporary of Justin, sees divine inspiration using the Prophets as instruments, an idea encountered a number of times among the Apologists: see also Athanagoras, *Supplication for the Christians*, 7; and Theophilus, *To Autolycus* II, 9.

For neither by nature nor by human understanding is it possible for men to know things so great and divine, but by the gift descending from above at that time upon those holy men, to whom there was no need of verbal artifice nor of saying anything in a contentious or quarrelsome way, but to present themselves pure to the working of the divine Spirit, so that the Divinity itself, coming down from heaven like a plectrum and using those just men as an instrument like the cithara or lyre, might reveal to us the knowledge of divine and heavenly things. Therefore, as if from one mouth and one tongue, in conformity and harmony (συμφώνως) with one another, they have taught us about God, about the creation of the world, about the fashioning of man . . .

Tatian (fl. c.160)

Born in Assyria and educated in rhetoric and philosophy, he was converted at Rome before 165, where he was a pupil of Justin Martyr. His tendency to rigorism caused him to stray from the path of orthodox Christianity, and, after his return to the east, to found an ascetic sect of the Gnostic-Encratite type. His apologetic work is characterized by a bitter attack upon paganism.

29   *Discourse to the Greeks* 1; *PG* vi, 804–5; *TU* iv, 1, 1

> Tatian's charge that the Greeks deceitfully take credit for the musical
> inventions of earlier peoples, whether barbarians or Jews, will become a
> commonplace of patristic literature and eventually of medieval music
> theory. On the latter see McKinnon (1978).

Cease, then, to call these imitations your discoveries. For Orpheus taught
you to compose and sing poetry, and also to participate in the mysteries.
The Tuscans taught you to sculpt, the chronicles of the Egyptians taught
you to write history; you acquired the art of aulos playing from Marsyas and
Olympus, while these same two rustic Phrygians contrived the harmony of
the syrinx. The Tyrrhenians invented the trumpet . . .

30   *Discourse to the Greeks* 22; *PG* vi, 857; *TU* iv, 1, 25

> In this and in the following passage appear the first hints of the patristic
> polemic against pagan musical immortality – unless one wishes to grant
> priority to *Sibylline Oracles* viii, 113–21, quoted below. See also this work, 8
> and 24.

I do not wish to gape at many singers nor do I care to look benignly upon a
man who is nodding and motioning in an unnatural way.

31   *Discourse to the Greeks* 33; *PG* vi, 873; *TU* iv, 1, 34

And this Sappho is a lewd, lovesick female who sings to her own licentiousness, whereas all our women are chaste, and the maidens at their distaffs
sing of godly things more earnestly than that girl of yours.

Athenagoras (fl. c.175)

He was active at Athens. His attitude toward Greek culture was not quite so
unfriendly as that of Tatian.

32   *Supplication for the Christians* 16; *PG* vi, 921; *TU* iv, 2, 17

> One should honour the Creator – the player, not creation – the instrument;
> a similar point is made by TERTULLIAN, *Ad nationes* ii, v, 9.

Now if the cosmos is an harmonious instrument set in rhythmic motion, I
worship him who tuned it, who strikes its notes and sings its concordant
melody, not the instrument. Nor do the judges at the contests pass over the
cithara players and crown their citharas.

Theophilus (later 2nd century)

Born near the Euphrates, he was converted to Christianity as an adult and became bishop of Antioch. His one surviving work is *To Autolycus*, in the second book of which he opposes the Greek poets and philosophers with the teaching of Genesis and the Prophets.

33   *To Autolycus* II, 30; *PG* VI, 1100; *SC* XX, 172–4

The same argument encountered in TATIAN, *Discourse to the Greeks* 1.

Lamech took unto himself two wives, whose names were Adah and Zillah. Thence came about the beginning of polygamy and also of music. For three sons were born to Lamech: Jabal, Jubal and Tubal. Jabal became a man who lives in tents and keeps cattle; Jubal is he who invented the psaltery and cithara and Tubal became a smith, a worker in brass and iron . . . But as for music, some claimed frivolously that Apollo was its inventor, while others say that Orpheus discovered it in the sweet song of birds. But their story is manifestly groundless and foolish, for these were born many years after the deluge.

C Literature other than patristic

Odes of Solomon

This collection of forty-two psalm-like compositions was discovered by J. Rendel Harris in 1909. It has been a matter of dispute whether their original language was Greek or the extant Syriac, and also whether they are Gnostic or orthodox Christian in character. A view enjoying some currency at present is that they were written in Syriac by a Palestinian or Syrian Christian toward the end of the first century (Chadwick, 1970). There are several musical passages in the Odes including images involving the cithara and references to the act of composition. In addition to the examples quoted here, see Ode VI, 1–2. VII, 19–20; XXI, 3–4 and XLI, 16–17.

34   Ode XIV, 7–8; *Charlesworth*, 65

Teach me the songs of thy truth,
    that I may yield fruits in thee;
And open the cithara of thy Holy Spirit to me,
    that with every note I may praise thee, O Lord.

35   Ode XVI, 1–2; *Charlesworth*, 69

As the task of the husbandman is the plough,
    and the task of the helmsman the steering of the ship,
    so also is my task the psalm of the Lord in his hymns;

My craft and my occupation are in his hymns
    because his love has nourished my heart,
    and even unto my lips he poured out his fruits.

36   Ode xxvi, 1–3; *Charlesworth*, 103

I poured out praise to the Lord,
    because I am his.
I will pronounce his holy song,
    because my heart is with him;
For his cithara is in my hands,
    and the songs of his rest shall not be still.

37   Ode xxxvi, 1–2; *Charlesworth*, 126

I rested on the Spirit of the Lord,
    and it lifted me to the height;
And caused me to stand upon my feet in the high place of the Lord,
    before his fulness and his glory,
    while I was praising him in the creation of his songs.

The Apocryphal New Testament

The term applies to a somewhat loosely defined category of early Christian literature which modern scholarship is still in the process of bringing under control.
These works have in common that they adopted titles similar to those of the
canonical New Testament with a view toward enjoying apostolic authority. Some of
them are quite orthodox in character, but most are tinged with heresy, particularly
Gnosticism. For a sympathetic and readable treatment of Gnosticism, see Pagels
(1979).

The Apocryphal New Testament is not particularly rich in musical allusion. Most
notable are three long hymns: one sung by St Thomas at a marriage feast (*Acts of
Thomas* 3–6); another sung by him, the so-called 'Hymn of the Pearl' (*Acts of Thomas*
108); and the well known 'Hymn of Jesus' (*Acts of John* 94–7). The first two of these
are more of theological and literary interest than musical and are not quoted here,
but a portion of the 'Hymn to Jesus' is. All three are available in modern translation
in Wilson (1963–5, vol. 2) and discussed in Kroll (1921). For more recent discussion
of the hymns from the *Acts of Thomas* see Adam (1959). In addition to the hymns there
are two brief references to psalmody in defective Coptic fragments of the *Acts of Paul*.
They are translated provisionally in Wilson (vol. 2, pp. 380 and 388) pending the
forthcoming *editio princeps*.

38   *Acts of John* 94–7; *Bonnet* 2, 1, 197–9

The *Acts of John*, a composite work like many of the pseudepigrapha, is a
romance on the exploits and travels of the Apostle John. Although some
claim a second-century Ephesian origin for it, it is of uncertain date and

provenance, with the earliest incontrovertible reference to it coming from Eusebius. The famous dance and hymn of Jesus is from a Gnostic portion of the work. Quoted here is the surrounding narrative and short portions of the hymn itself. The hymn supplied the text for Gustav Holst's 'Hymn of Jesus'.

Its existence in early Christian – albeit heretical – literature has occasioned some loose speculation on the early Christian attitude toward dance; for a more creditable discussion of that subject see Andresen (1958).

Before his arrest by the lawless Jews, who are given their laws by the lawless serpent, he gathered us all together and said: 'Before I am given over to them, let us sing a hymn to the Father, and thus go to meet what lies ahead'. So he bade us form a circle, as it were, holding each other's hands, and taking his place in the middle he said: 'Answer Amen to me'. Then he began to hymn and to say:

'Glory be to thee, Father.'

And we, forming a circle, responded 'Amen' to him.

'Glory be to thee, Word,
Glory be to thee, Grace.' 'Amen.'
'Glory be to thee, Spirit,
Glory be to thee, Holy One,
Glory be to thy Glory.' 'Amen.'
'I wish to play on the aulos;
Dance, all of you.' 'Amen.'
'I wish to mourn;
Beat your breasts, all of you.' 'Amen.'
'The one octad sings with us.' 'Amen.'
'The twelfth number dances above.' 'Amen.'
'To the universe belongs the danger.' 'Amen.'
'Who dances not, knows not what happens.' 'Amen' . . .

97 After dancing thus with us, my beloved, the Lord went out, and we, confused and asleep, as it were, fled one way and the other.

Sibylline Oracles

This work is a lengthy compilation in hexameters composed by Jewish and Christian authors in imitation of the pagan Sibylline Oracles. Alexandrian Jews of the second century BC were active in this respect already, and much of the present compilation is Jewish in origin although frequently reworked by Christian authors. The most thoroughly Christian section is Books VI through VIII. Book VI is a Gnostic Christian 'Hymn to Jesus', and Book VIII, excerpted here, opens with an apocalyptic description of pagan Rome's destruction. It appears to date from before 180 AD. The standard study of the *Sibylline Oracles* is Geffcken (1902).

39   *Sibylline Oracles* VIII, 113–21; *Geffcken*, 147–8

Among the features of Roman life to disappear are its sacrificial cult practices with their accompanying instrumental music. Although the passage
appears in a second century Christian portion of the work, Eric Werner
cites it as evidence of first century rabbinic attitudes towards musical
instruments (McKinnon, 1979–80).

They pour no blood on altars in sacrificial libations,
The tympanum sounds not nor does the cymbal,
Nor does the much pierced aulos with its frenzied voice,
Nor the syrinx, bearing the likeness of a crooked serpent,
Nor the trumpet, barbarous sounding herald of wars;
Neither are there drunkards in lawless carousals or in dances,
Nor the sound of the cithara, nor a wicked contrivance;
Nor is there strife, nor manifold wrath, nor a sword
Among the dead, but a new era for all.

40   *Sibylline Oracles* VIII, 487–500; *Geffcken*, 172–3

In place of the pagan sacrificial cults the Christian practices a 'spiritual
sacrifice' which includes sacred song. (See also VIII, 332–6). On the
relationship of 'spiritual sacrifice' to music, see Quasten (1930, pp. 51–7).

Never may we approach the temple sanctuaries,
Nor pour libations to images, nor honor them with vows,
Nor with the delightful fragrances of flowers, nor the glow
Of torches, nor yet adorn them with votive offerings;
Nor send up flames with incense smoke at the altar;
Nor pour the blood of slain sheep upon the libations of sacrificial
      bulls,
Glad to pay ransom as appeasement for earthly deliverance;
Nor with reeking smoke from the flesh devouring fire,
And foul vapors pollute the bright light of the ether.
But rejoicing with pure heart and cheerful spirit,
With abundant love and generous hands,
With propitiary psalms and chants beseeming God,
We are called upon to hymn thee, immortal and faithful
God, creator of all and understanding all.

The Letter of Pliny

The passage quoted here is clearly not from a Christian source, but no work on early
Christian music can avoid mention of it. It appears in a letter of Pliny the Younger
to the Emperor Trajan from the period when Pliny was governor of Bithynia and
Pontus (111–12). He seeks guidance in the letter on how to deal with lapsed
Christians. There is a large and diverse literature on the passage; here we cite but

one example of earlier speculation on the subject (Kraemer, 1934) and one example of more recent and cautious analysis (Quasten, 1954).

41   Letter x, xcvi; *LCL* II, 402–4

> The phrase *secum invicem* has occasioned much unguarded reference to the notion of antiphonal psalmody.

They affirmed, however, that this was the extent of their fault or error, that they were wont to assemble on a set day before dawn and to sing a hymn among themselves (*carmen . . . dicere secum invicem*) to the Christ, as to a god, and that they pledged themselves by vow not to some crime, but that they would commit neither fraud, nor theft, nor adultery, nor betray their word, nor deny a trust when summoned; after which it was their custom to separate and to come together again to take food – ordinary and harmless food, however.

CHAPTER 3

The Greek authors of the third century

It is puzzling in view of the vast Jewish community at Alexandria that Alexandrian Christianity was so slow to make its appearance upon the pages of history. When it did so in the late second century it had already achieved a status in keeping with the greatness of the city, and more than that it had taken on a character appropriate to the city's standing as a center of Hellenistic learning. In the so-called Catechetical School, whose first known head was Panthaenus (d. c.190), Clement and Origen developed an authentic Christian theology which not surprisingly took on a strongly Platonic cast. Origen in later life established a second school at Caesarea, and this school along with the original one helped to make the Alexandrian approach to theology dominant in subsequent Christian thought. As for musical references, perhaps the theoretical Alexandrian tendency can be blamed for the relative paucity of passages involving actual liturgical song. The area best represented is musical imagery, more specifically, the allegorical method of scriptural exegesis which was developed under Clement and especially Origen. Its fundamental tenet is that whether Scripture has literal meaning or not, its more important meaning is spiritual. Thus every verse, indeed every word, of the Bible has a divinely inspired hidden meaning. The principal result of this for our subject is that the musical instruments mentioned in the Bible – most notably in the Psalter – were given fanciful figurative interpretations while their historical use was by and large ignored.

Included also in this chapter is the church order commonly called the *Didascalia*.

Clement of Alexandria (c.150–c.215)

Possibly an Athenian by birth, he became head of the Catechetical School of Alexandria after the death of his teacher Pantaenus in c.190. In c.202 he left Alexandria for Asia Minor because of the persecution under Septimus Severus. His three principal works are related. First there is the *Proprepticus* or *Exhortation to the Heathen* and then the *Paedagogus*, which tells how the converted heathen is to conduct his everyday life. Finally the lengthy *Stromata* or *Miscellanies* ranges widely and deeply in an attempt to demonstrate the superiority of Christian over pagan learning. The first and last of these works are rich in musical allusion because of the corresponding richness of the Hellenic literature cited in them; while the *Paedagogus* contains a famous chapter on music at banquets. Clement attacks pagan musical excess, but he is largely sympathetic toward the intellectual strain in Hellenic culture. He is, moreover, an early exponent of the allegorical method and an advocate of a special Christian Gnosticism, that is, the belief that the truly learned and spiritual Christian will have perception beyond that of the simple believer. For a fuller representation of his musical imagery than that given here, see Skeris (1976, pp. 56–83).

42   *Protrepticus* I, 1–3; *PG* VIII, 49–53; *GCS* I, 3

> Clement opens the *Protrepticus* with a great rambling musical metaphor which rejects the musical mythology of Greece in favor of the New Song, Christ the Logos. About a third of the passage appears here in four excerpts; it is available in its entirety in *Strunk*. The first excerpt recounts the mythical power of music over animate and inanimate creatures.

Amphion the Theban and Arion the Methymnian were both fond of singing. There is a myth about them, told in a song which is sung to this day in the chorus of the Greeks, about how the one lured a fish with his musical art and the other built the walls of Thebes. And another ingenious musician, a Thracian – as told in another Greek myth – tamed wild beasts with nothing but his song, and transplanted trees, oaks no less, with his music. And I might tell you of another myth and song, kindred to these, about Eunomos the Locrian and the Pythian cricket . . . There was a competition and Eunomos was playing the cithara during the summer time when crickets warmed by the sun beneath the leaves were wont to sing along the hills. (They were not singing to a dead Pythian dragon, but rather the free song, one superior to the lays of Eunomos, to the all wise God.) Then one of the Locrian's strings snapped. The cricket climbed astride the yoke of the instrument and chirped there as if upon a twig, while the musician adapted to the song of the cricket and thus made up for the missing string.

43   *Protrepticus* I, 2, 4–I, 4, I; *PG* VIII, 53–7; *GCS* I, 4–5

> The figures of musical myth are rejected as the deceptive agents of idolatry. Note that Clement uses musical terminology by and large in its proper classical sense, for example 'harmony' as the Phrygian and Dorian harmonies of Plato's *Republic*.

What my Eunomos sings is not the strain (νόμον) of Terpander, nor of Capion, nor the Phrygian, nor Dorian, nor Lydian, but the eternal strain of the new harmony (ἁρμονίας) which bears God's name, the New Song . . . To me, then, that Thracian Orpheus, that Theban and Methymnian, men of a sort but not really men, appear to be deceivers, corrupting human life under the pretext of music, possessed by a kind of artful sorcery for purposes of destruction, outrageous in celebrating their orgies, deifying misfortune, the first to lead men by the hand to idols, indeed to construct an ill-omened wall about a nation with blocks of stone and wood, that is statues and images, and by means of their songs and incantations to subject to the most dire servitude the noble freedom of those who lived as citizens under heaven. But not such is my song which has come to depose soon the bitter oppression of the tyrannical demons. While leading us under the gentle and benign yoke of piety it calls back to heaven those cast down upon the earth. It alone tames man, the most intractable of all beasts . . .

44   *Protrepticus* I, 5, 1; *PG* VIII, 57; *GCS* I, 5–6

> The New Song presides over cosmic music.

It ordered the universe concordantly and tuned the discord of the elements in an harmonious arrangement, so that the entire cosmos might become through its agency a consonance. It let loose the rolling sea, yet checked it from advancing upon the earth. It stabilized the receding earth and established it as boundary to the sea. And indeed it even softened the raging fire with air as if tempering the Dorian harmony with the Lydian.

45   *Protrepticus* I, 5, 3–7, 3; *PG* VIII, 60–1; *GCS* I, 6–7

> The New Song is Christ, the Word, prefigured in David. This excerpt contains one of the earliest examples of instrumental allegory in the patristic literature.

He who is from David, yet before him, the Word of God, scorning the lyre and cithara as lifeless instruments, and having rendered harmonious by the Holy Spirit both this cosmos and even man the microcosm, made up of body and soul – he sings to God on his many voiced instrument and he sings to man, himself an instrument: 'You are my cithara, my aulos and my temple', a cithara because of harmony, and aulos because of spirit and a temple because of the word, so that the first might strum, the second might breathe and the third might encompass the Lord. Now this David whom we mentioned above, a king and citharist, urged people to the truth and dissuaded them from idolatry; indeed he was so far from hymning demons that they were actually put to flight by his music, when simply by singing he healed Saul who was plagued by them. The Lord made man a beautiful breathing instrument after his own image; certainly he is himself an all harmonious instrument of God, well tuned and holy, the transcendental wisdom, the heavenly Word ... This is the New Song, the shining manifestation among us now of the Word, who was in the beginning and before the beginning.

46   *Protrepticus* II, 15, 3; *PG* VIII, 76; *GCS* I, 13

> The tympanum and cymbal are among the absurd symbols employed in the mysteries of Demeter.

I know that the symbols of initiation into these rites when displayed to you in a moment of leisure will provoke you to laughter even if you are not inclined to laugh because of the disgrace involved. 'I have eaten from the tympanum, I have drunk from the cymbal, I have carried the Cernos, I have slipped into the bridal chamber.' Are not these symbols an outrage?

47   *Protrepticus* II, 24, 1; *PG* VIII, 89–92; *GCS* I, 18

> Clement approves of the execution of a Scythian citizen who displayed the
> effeminacy and musical symbols appropriate to the cult of Cybele.

All honor to the king of the Scythians, whoever this Archarsis was. That
citizen of his, who imitated among the Scythians the initiatory rites of the
Mother of the gods as practised by the Cyzicans, beating upon a tympanum
and like some priest of Cybele sounding a cymbal which hung from his neck
– him he shot with an arrow since he had become unmanly among the
Greeks and a teacher of the disease of effeminacy to the other Scythians.

48   *Protrepticus* VII, 75, 4; *PG* VIII, 184–5; *GCS* I, 57

> Clement quotes a passage from Menander which satirizes the apotropaic
> use of cymbals.

Again the same author of comedy, in his play *The Priestess*, expresses his
scorn for custom and attempts to refute this impious and foolish error,
sagely remarking:

> If indeed man leads a god
> Whither he will by cymbals,
> Doing this he is greater than the god.

49   *Protrepticus* XI, 116, 2–3; *PG* VIII, 236; *GCS* I, 82

> Possibly the first use of the metaphor of the Gospel as a trumpet.

If the clangorous trumpet when sounded assembles the soldiers and
announces the ensuing battle, will not Christ, breathing a melody of peace
unto the ends of the earth, assemble his own peaceful troops? He has
assembled then, O man, his bloodless army by his blood and his word, and
assigned the kingdom of heaven to them. The trumpet of Christ is his
Gospel: he has blown it and we have heard.

50   *Protrepticus* XII, 119, 1–2; *PG* VIII, 240; *GCS* I, 84

> The *Protrepticus* closes, as it began, with an extended passage of musical
> imagery. Perhaps its most vivid moment is that which contrasts Dionysian
> maenads with the 'daughters of God' in heaven.

This is the mountain beloved by God, not like Cithaeron given over to
tragedies, but dedicated to dramas of truth, a mount of temperance, thickly
shaded with sacred trees. The sisters of Semele the 'thunder-struck' do not
revel there, maenads who perform the unholy initiatory rite of the division
of flesh, but the daughters of God, the fair lambs who celebrate the august
rites of the Word, joining in a modest choral dance. The chorus is formed

by the righteous, the song is a hymn to the king of all creation. The maidens sing, the angels give praise, the prophets speak, the sound of music goes forth . . .

51   *Paedagogus* II, iv; *PG* VIII, 440–1; *GCS* I, 181–2

> Book II, iv of the *Paedagogus*, 'How to conduct oneself at banquets', is among the patristic musical passages of central importance. All but a few sentences of it is given here in five excerpts. The first condemns the use of musical instruments at banquets.

Let carousing be absent from our rational enjoyment, and also foolish vigils which revel in drunkenness . . . Let lust, intoxication and irrational passions be far removed from our native choir . . . The irregular movements of auloi, psalteries, choruses, dances, Egyptian clappers (κροτάλοις) and other such playthings become altogether indecent and uncouth, especially when joined by beating cymbals and tympana and accompanied by the noisy instruments of deception. Such a symposium, it seems to me, becomes nothing but a theatre of drunkenness. As the Apostle would have it: 'Let us then cast off the works of darkness and put on the armor of light; let us conduct ourselves becomingly as in the day, not in reveling and drunkenness, not in debauchery and licentiousness' (Rom 13.12–13).

Let the syrinx be assigned to shepherds and the aulos to superstitious men who are obsessed by idolatry. In truth these instruments are to be banished from the sober symposium; they are less suitable for men than for beasts and the bestial portion of mankind. For we are told that deer are lured by the syrinx and led by its melody into the traps when stalked by huntsmen. And when mares are being foaled, a sort of nuptial song is played on the aulos; musicians have called it the *hypothoron*.

52   *Paedagogus* II, iv; *PG* VIII, 441; *GCS* I, 182–3

> Quoting from Psalm 150, Clement proposes allegorical musical instruments in place of real ones.

The Spirit, distinguishing the divine liturgy from this sort of revelry, sings: 'Praise him with the sound of the trumpet', and indeed he will raise the dead with the sound of the trumpet. 'Praise him on the psaltery', for the tongue is the psaltery of the Lord. 'And praise him on the cithara', let the cithara be taken to mean the mouth, played by the Spirit as if by a plectrum. 'Praise him with tympanum and chorus' refers to the Church meditating on the resurrection of the flesh in the resounding membrane. 'Praise him on strings and the instrument' refers to our body as an instrument and its sinews as strings from which it derives its harmonious tension, and when strummed by the Spirit it gives off human notes. 'Praise him on the clangorous cymbals' speaks of the tongue as the cymbal of the mouth which sounds as the lips are moved. Therefore he called out to all mankind, 'Let every breath praise the Lord', because he watches over every breathing thing he has made.

53   *Paedagogus* II, iv; *PG* VIII, 441–4; *GCS* I, 183

> Musical istruments are associated with war, while man is an instrument of peace, and the theme of his banquets ought to be charity.

For man, in truth, is an instrument of peace, while the others, if one investigates them, he will find to be instruments of aggression, either inflaming the passions, enkindling lust, or stirring up wrath. The Etruscans, certainly, make use of the trumpet in their wars, the Arcadians the syrinx, the Sicilians the pektis, the Cretans the lyre, the Lacedaemonians the aulos, the Thracians the horn (κέρατι), the Egyptians the tympanum and the Arabians the cymbal. We, however, make use of but one instrument, the word of peace alone by which we honor God, and no longer the ancient psaltery, nor the trumpet, the tympanum and the aulos, as was the custom among those expert in war and those scornful of the fear of God who employed string instruments in their festive gatherings, as if to arouse their remissness of spirit through such rhythms. But let our geniality in drinking be twofold according to the Law: for if you love the Lord your God and then your neighbor, you should be genial first to God in thanksgiving and psalmody and secondly to your neighbor in dignified friendship.

54   *Paedagogus* II, iv; *PG* VIII, 444; *GCS* I, 183–4

> Here in a frequently quoted passage, 'if you should wish to sing and play to the cithara and lyre, this is not blameworthy', Clement seems to contradict all that goes before and to condone the use of these instruments. But surely the immediate context of the passage as well as Clement's views in general suggest that it is to be read allegorically. Note in particular the singling out of these two instruments in *Protrepticus* I, 5, 3: 'the Word of God, scorning the lyre and cithara as lifeless instruments'. On a matter of lesser detail, the 'element of the decad' refers to the first letter of Jesus' name, *iota*, which signifies ten.

The Lord is now our congenial guest, for the Apostle adds again, 'teaching and admonishing one another in all wisdom, singing psalms, hymns and spiritual songs with thankfulness in your hearts to God. And whatsoever you do, in word or in deed, do everything in the name of the Lord Jesus, giving thanks to God the Father through him' (Col 3.16–17). This is our grateful revelry, and if you should wish to sing and play (ψάλλειν) to the cithara and lyre, this is not blameworthy; you would imitate the just Hebrew king giving thanks to God. 'Rejoice in the Lord, O you righteous! Praise befits the upright' (Ps 32.1) says the prophecy. 'Praise the Lord on the cithara, make melody (ψάλατε) to him on the psaltery of ten strings!

Sing to him a new song' (Ps 32.2). And does not the psaltery of ten strings reveal Jesus, the Word, manifested in the element of the decad? Just as it is appropriate for us to praise the creator of all before partaking of food, so too is it proper while drinking to sing to him as the beneficiaries of his creation. For a psalm is a harmonious and reasonable blessing, and the Apostle calls a psalm a spiritual song.

55   *Paedagogus* II, iv; *PG* VIII, 445; *GCS* I, 184

> The chapter closes with a mixture of classical and psalmodic reference. Once again the Platonic 'harmonies' are invoked.

And among the ancient Greeks, at their drinking parties, a song called the scolion was sung over their brimming cups after the manner of the Hebrew psalms, as all together raised the paean in one voice, and sometimes passed around in order the toasts of song, while the more musical among them sang to the lyre. But let erotic songs be far removed from here; let hymns to God be our songs. 'Let them praise his name in dancing', it is said; 'let them play to him on tympanum and psaltery' (Ps 149.3). And who is this singing chorus? The Spirit will explain it to you. 'His praise is in the assembly of the faithful; let them rejoice in their king' (Ps 149.1–2). And again he adds, 'that the Lord takes pleasure in his people' (Ps 149.4). Now temperate harmonies (ἁρμονίας) are to be admitted, but the pliant harmonies are to be driven as far as possible from our robust minds. These through their sinuous strains instruct one in weakness and lead to ribaldry, but the grave and temperate melodies bid farewell to the arrogance of drunkenness. Chromatic harmonies, then, are to be left to 'colorless' carousals and to the florid and meretricious music.

56   *Paedagogus* III, xi; *PG* VIII, 660; *GCS* I, 280

> After services the faithful give themselves over to pagan music.

After reverently attending to the discourse about God, they left what they had heard within, while outside they amuse themselves with godless things, with the plucking of strings (κρουμάτων) and the erotic wailing of the aulos, defiling themselves with dancing (κρότου), drunkenness and every sort of trash. Those who sing thus and sing in response are those who hymned immortality before, but sing finally, wicked and wickedly, that vicious recantation: 'Let us eat and drink, for tomorrow we die.'

57   *Stromata* I, xvi, 76; *PG* VIII, 788–9; *GCS* II, 49–50

> In *Stromata* I, xvi there are several passages citing alleged musical discoveries of the Greeks, which are in reality attributable to chronologically anterior barbarians. One example is given here.

But concerning music, Olympus the Mysian practised the Lydian harmony, and those called the Troglodytes invented the sambuca (σαμβύκην), a musical instrument. They say that Satyrus the Phrygian invented the crooked syrinx and Hyagnis, a Phrygian also, invented the trichordon (τρίχορδον) and the diatonic harmony. They say that Olympus, likewise a Phrygian, invented instrumental music (κρούματα); and Marsyas, from the same region as those just mentioned, discovered the Phrygian harmony, the Mixophrygian and the Mixolydian; and Thamyris the Thracian discovered the Dorian.

58   *Stromata* v, iv, 19; *PG* ix, 37; *GCS* ii, 338

> Clement argues for allegorical interpretation: the unspiritual fail to understand just as the unmusical fail to perceive musically.

He who is still blind and deaf, lacking in understanding, and not perceiving with the fearless and keen vision of the soul, which the Savior alone grants, like the uninitiated at the mysteries or the unmusical (ἄμουσον) in choral dancing, neither pure nor worthy of the pure truth, discordant, disordered and material – he must remain standing outside the sacred chorus.

59   *Stromata* vi, xi, 88; *PG* ix, 309; *GCS* ii, 475–6

> The Christian Gnostic can cull from Hellenic erudition, including musical learning, information which is salutary, by the application of allegorical method. (See also *Stromata* i, i, 15–18 and vi, x, 80)

As a further example of music let us propose David, singing and prophesying at the same time, harmoniously hymning God. Now the enharmonic genus is very well suited to the Dorian harmony, as Aristoxenus says, and the diatonic to the Phrygian. Moreover, the harmony of the barbarian psaltery, which displays a sacral quality in its melody and happens to be the most ancient, served Terpander well as a model for the Dorian harmony when he hymned Zeus thus:

> Zeus, beginning of all, ruler of all,
> Zeus, to you I send this beginning of hymns.

The cithara, taken allegorically by the psalmist, would be according to its first meaning the Lord, and according to its second those who continuously pluck (κρούοντες) their souls under the musical direction of the Lord. And if the people who are saved are said to be the cithara, it is because they are heard to give honor musically through the inspiration of the Word and the knowledge of God, as they are played for faith by the Word. You might also wish to take music in another way, as the ecclesiastical symphony of the Law and the Prophets and the Apostles along with the Gospel . . .
    But, so it seems, most of those inscribed with the Name deal with the

Word clumsily, as did the companions of Odysseus, foolishly stopping their ears and thus missing the rhythm and the melody rather than the Sirens, since they know that once having lent their ears to Greek studies they could not subsequently find their way home. But he who culls what is necessary for the benefit of the catechumens, especially when they are Greek ('for the earth is the Lord's and all that is in it'), need not abstain from the love of learning, as do wild animals; rather he must gather as many aids as possible for his hearers. But by no means ought he to linger over these, except in so far as there is benefit from them, so that having taken this and secured it he can return homewards to the true philosophy . . .

60   *Stromata* VII, vii, 35; *PG* IX, 452; *GCS* III, 27–8

> The following two passages show how sacred song plays a part in the life of the Christian Gnostic.

Throughout our entire lives, then, we celebrate a feast, persuaded that God is present everywhere and in all things; we plough the fields while giving praise, we sail the seas while singing hymns, and on every other public occasion we conduct ourselves skillfully.

61   *Stromata* VII, vii, 49; *PG* IX, 469; *GCS* III, 37

His entire life is a sacred festival. His sacrifices are prayers and praise, converse with the Scriptures before the banquet, psalms and hymns at the banquet and before bed, and prayers again during the night. Through these he renders himself one with the sacred chorus, occupying himself by continual remembrance with a contemplation to be kept always in mind.

62   *Stromata* VII, xvi, 102; *PG* IX, 541; *GCS* III, 72

> A final reference to the New Song.

Would then that even these heretics, after studying these notes, would be chastened and turn to God the almighty. But if like 'deaf serpents' they do not give ear to the song which is called new, although most ancient, let them be chastised by God.

Origen (c.185–c.265)

He was born, probably in Alexandria, of Christian parents; indeed his father suffered martyrdom in the persecution of 202. When peace was restored he became head of the Catechetical School in place of Clement, who had fled. At this time he practised the most severe asceticism, going so far as to 'make of himself a eunuch for the sake of the kingdom of heaven' (Mt 19.12). Some find this extreme literalism ironic in view of his advocacy of allegorical exegesis. He spent much of his later life in Palestine, founding a school at Caesarea in 231. He was cruelly tortured during the persecution of Decius (251) and died not long afterwards. Origen was a thinker of comparable genius to Augustine and an author of prodigious energy although only a fraction of his output has been preserved. Certain of his views caused subsequent theologians to split into Origenist and anti-Origenist camps until they were officially declared heretical by the Second Council of Constantinople (553). His contribution to our subject lies chiefly in the area of musical imagery. The material is presented here after the order of his works as given in *PG*.

63   *Letter to Gregory* 1; *PG* xi, 88

> Origen advises his pupil Gregory Thaumaturgus to derive from Hellenic studies whatever serves Christian purposes.

I would wish that you take from Greek philosophy that which has the capacity, as it were, to become encyclical and propaedeutic studies for Christianity, and whatever of geometry and astronomy might be useful in the interpretation of the Holy Scriptures, so that just as the children of the philosophers speak of geometry and music, grammar, rhetoric and astronomy as being ancillary to philosophy, we too may say this of philosophy itself in relation to Christianity.

64   *On Prayer* II, 4; *PG* xi, 421; *GCS* II, 301–2

> It is difficult to tell whether Origen refers to actual or merely figurative music.

For our mind cannot pray unless the Spirit, within its hearing, as it were, first prays before it. Nor can it sing (ψάλαι) and hymn the Father in Christ with proper rhythm, melody (ἐμμελῶς), meter and harmony, unless the Spirit who searches all things, even the depths of God, has first searched the depths of the mind with praise and song (ὑμνήσει) and, as far as it is capable, has understood them.

65   *Against Celsus* VIII, 60; *PG* xi, 1605–8; *GCS* II, 276

> Origen quotes Celsus on the limitations of the chthonian demons. Subsequently he endorses the proposition that they are obsessed with physical desires, but expresses doubt about their ability to heal.

'It is necessary, presumably, not to doubt those wise men who say that the majority of earth demons are desirous of birth, are obsessed by blood, the savor of burnt sacrifice and melodies, and are addicted to other things of the sort. They can do no better than to heal the body and to tell in advance the fortunes of man and the city; they can know and do only such things as relate to mortal affairs.'

66   *Against Celsus* VIII, 67; *PG* XI, 1617; *GCS* II, 283

> We, along with the heavens, hymn God and his Son. This is clearly spiritual song, but not as clearly practical song.

For Celsus says that we would seem to honor the great god better if we would sing hymns to the sun and Athena. We, however, know it to be the opposite. For we sing (λέγομεν) hymns to the one God who is over all and his only begotten Word, who is God also. So we sing to God and his only begotten as do the sun, the moon, the stars and the entire heavenly host. For all these form a sacred chorus and sing hymns to the God of all and his only begotten along with those among men who are just.

67   *In librum Jesu Naue homilia* VII, 1; *PG* XII, 857; *GCS* VII, 327–8

> The trumpet as gospel is one of the more poetically apt examples of instrumental allegory.

First Matthew sounded the priestly trumpet of his gospel; and Mark too, and Luke and John played their own priestly trumpets. Peter also plays the two trumpets of his epistles, and likewise James and Jude. And John plays the trumpet yet again through his epistles and apocalypse, as does Luke in narrating the deeds of the Apostles. And finally he comes who said, 'I believe God has shown us as the last Apostles', and blasting forth on the trumpets of his fourteen epistles, he toppled the walls of Jericho to their very foundations and all the schemes of idolatry and the tenets of the philosophers.

68   Pseudo-Origen, *Selecta in psalmos* XXXII, 2–3; *PG* XII, 1304

> Instrumental allegory appears in the two following passages in its *locus classicus*, the psalm commentary. Actually this commentary, attributed to Origen, is largely the work of his spiritual descendant, Evagrius of Pontus. For further examples of instrumental allegory in this commentary, see XLII, 4; XLVIII, 5; LVI, 9; XCI, 4; CXXVI, 2; CXLIX, 3. For a general discussion of instrumental allegory see McKinnon (1968).

'Praise the Lord on the cithara, sing to him on the psaltery of ten strings, etc.' The cithara is the practical soul set in motion by the commandments of God; the psaltery is the pure mind set in motion by spiritual knowledge. The musical instruments of the Old Testament are not unsuitable for us if understood spiritually: figuratively the body can be called a cithara and the soul a psaltery, which are likened musically to the wise man who fittingly employs the limbs of the body and the powers of the soul as strings. Sweetly sings he who sings in the mind, uttering spiritual songs, singing in his heart to God. The ten strings stands for ten sinews, for a string is a sinew. And the body can also be said to be the psaltery of ten strings, as it has five senses and five powers of the soul, with each power arising from a respective sense.

'Sing to him a new song, etc.' He who is renewed after the interior man would sing the new song; he has put off the old man and put on the new, being made new in the image of the Creator.

69   Pseudo-Origen, *Selecta in psalmos* CL, 3–5; *PG* XII, 1684–5

> The term ὀργάνῳ is generally construed to mean the pipe organ in this passage. This is at variance, however, with both the original Hebrew (Finesinger, 1926, p. 52) and, even more to the point, the history of the term in patristic literature (AUGUSTINE, *In psalmum* CL, 7).

'Praise him in the sound of the trumpet, etc.' According to the spiritual meaning of what is said in Numbers on the construction of the trumpet, it is made so that in its sound we might praise God. These very trumpets, I would say, are indicated in this passage: 'For the trumpet will sound and the dead rise incorruptible' (1 Cor 15.52); and in this: 'In the voice of the archangel and in the trumpet of God, he will come down from heaven' (1 Thess 4.16). Then there is the feast of the new moon of the seventh month commemorated by trumpets; as it is written: 'Sound the trumpet at the new moon – on the well-omened day of our feast' (Ps 80.3).

Concerning the same. The trumpet is the contemplative mind, the mind which has accepted spiritual teaching.

'Praise him on the psaltery and cithara, praise him on the tympanum and in the dance, praise him with strings and the instrument (χορδαῖς καὶ ὀργάνῳ), praise him on the well sounding cymbals, praise him on the clangorous cymbals, etc.' The cithara is the practical soul activated by the commandments of Christ. The tympanum is the death of covetousness through goodness itself; the dance the symphony of rational souls speaking in unison and avoiding dissension. The strings are the harmony of the balanced sound of virtues and instruments. The instrument is the church of God, made up of contemplative and active souls. The well sounding cymbal is the active soul, fixed upon the desire for Christ; the clangorous cymbal is the pure mind made live by the salvation of Christ.

Concerning the same. The many strings brought together in harmony, each ordered musically in its proper place, are the many commandments and the doctrines concerning many things, which exhibit no discord among themselves. The instrument embracing all this is the soul of the man wise in Christ.

Concerning the same. He who speaks with the tongues of men and of angels, but does not have charity, is not a well sounding cymbal.

70   *Commentary on the Gospel of St Matthew* XIV, 1; *PG* XIII, 1181–8; *GCS* X, 271–7

> A lengthy play on the word συμφωνέω which means both to agree and to be in musical harmony. Numerous illustrations are adduced from both

Old and New Testaments. Something less than a third of the passage is
given here; it appears in its entirety in *ANF* x.

'Again I say to you, if two of you agree (συμφωνήσωσιν) on earth about anything they ask, it will be done for them' (Mt 18.19). The word symphony in
its proper sense is applied to the harmonies in the sounds of music. And
there are among musical sounds some which are consonant and others
dissonant. And the evangelic Scripture shows knowledge in this passage of
the word as used in music: 'He heard music and dancing' (Lk 15.15), for it
was fitting that coincident with the symphony through penitence toward
the father of the son who was delivered from destruction, one hears a symphony in the joyous celebration of the household. But the thoughtless
Laban showed ignorance of the term symphony in these words he spoke to
Jacob: 'If you had told me, I would have sent you away with mirth and song
(μουσικῶν), with tympana and cithara' (Gen 31.27). Related to this sort of
symphony is that written in the second book of Kings, where 'the brothers
of Abinidab went before the Ark, and David and his sons played before the
Lord on instruments tuned in power and in songs' (see 2 Sam 6.3–5). For
instruments tuned in power and in songs have within themselves the
musical symphony which has such power that when only two – joined in the
symphony of divine and spiritual music – bring a request to the Father who
is in heaven, whatever it might be, the Father grants their requests . . . Now
they were not in harmony (συνεφώνουν) who said, 'I am of Paul, I of
Apollos, I of Cephas and I of Christ' (1 Cor 1.12). Rather, there were
schisms among them, upon the dissolution of which they banded together
with the spirit in Paul and the power of the Lord Jesus Christ, so that they
would no longer bite and eat each other, as if to be consumed by one
another. For discord consumes just as concord brings together and makes
room for the Son of God to be present in the midst of those who are in
harmony.

Didascalia Apostolorum

The *Didascalia* is a church order, that is, a work containing ethical and liturgical
teaching of alleged apostolic origin. The earliest example is the *Didache*, from the
first half of the second century, and the most detailed the late fourth century *Apostolic
Constitutions*. The *Didascalia* was composed in Greek during the earlier third century
for a North Syrian congregation by its Jewish-Christian bishop. It exists in its
entirety in Syriac translation, with somewhat less than half in Latin translation,
while much of the Greek can be reconstructed because of its absorption into the
Apostolic Constitutions. One must exercize caution, however, in using the well-known
edition of Funk, which attempts such a reconstruction; there are passages of musical
interest there which seem not to belong to the original (for example v, 10 and VIII,
32). They will be quoted in the present work in a later chapter as part of the *Apostolic
Constitutions*. For now only what appears in the Syriac will be quoted – actually just
one passage of sufficient musical interest – translated, however, from the Greek
reconstruction rather than the Syriac.

71   *Didascalia* VI, 3–5; *Funk* , 15

> The Christian should avoid pagan writings, including lyric poetry, in place of which he has the Psalms of David.

What is lacking to you in the Law of God that you run after these myths of the gentiles? 4 If it is history that you wish to read, you have Kings; if it is wisdom and poetry, you have the Prophets, in which you will find sagacity beyond that of any wise man or poet, because they are the sounds of the Lord, the only wise. 5 If you yearn for songs, you have the Psalms; if antiquities, you have Genesis; if laws and precepts, you have the illustrious Law of the Lord.

CHAPTER 4

The western authors of the third and early fourth centuries: Carthage and Rome

The western authors of the period lack the Hellenizing tendency of their Alexandrian contemporaries. In their remarks about music this is reflected in the relative absence of musical imagery and the near total absence of reference to music as a liberal art. What they share with their eastern counterparts is an awakening mistrust of pagan instrumental music. Arnobius in particular, associates the playing of musical instruments with sexual immorality, in language of shocking vehemence. But the most important contribution of the third century western authors is in the positive realm of liturgical song. Two of the three extant pre-Nicene descriptions of the synaxis are from Tertullian; the most important contribution to the pre-history of vespers before Egeria is from the *Apostolic Tradition* of Hippolytus; and Cyprian favors us with a passage of singular warmth and sensibility on psalmody at Christian meals.

Tertullian (c.170–c.225)

A native and life-long resident of Carthage, he was the most powerful and original Christian author writing in Latin before Augustine. Prior to his conversion he was thoroughly schooled in literature and rhetoric. His work is brilliant and complex, more inclined to deal with questions of ethics and religious discipline than speculative theology. Above all it is intensely polemic. In his later years he embraced the rigoristic heresy of Montanism. With respect to music there are several important references to psalmody and hymnody scattered throughout his writings, and he was an early exemplar of the polemic against musical instruments. His rhetorical inclination assures us of the occasional musical image, one example of which – utilizing the hydraulis – is of particular interest. That he has left us no references to music as an encyclical study is not surprising in view of his attitude toward Greek learning expressed in the famous passage beginning: 'What has Athens to do with Jerusalem? What has the Academy in common with the Church?' His musical references are presented here according to the traditionally accepted chronological order as given in *CCL*, although a revised chronology has been proposed by Barnes (1971, p. 55).

72   *Ad nationes* II, v, 9; *PL* I, 592; *CCL* I, 49

> Tertullian uses a musical analogy to make the point that we should attribute divinity not to nature but to its maker.

Even in your amusements, after all, you do not award the crown as prize to the tibia or cithara, but rather to the performer (*artifici*) who wields the tibia or cithara with beguiling skill.

42

73   *Apologeticum* XXXIX, 1–4; *PL* I, 468–9; *CCL* I, 150

> Synaxis including prayer, reading and homily, but not psalms. On the term
> 'synaxis', see Cross (1974, pp. 1331–2).

I myself shall now set down the practices of the Christian community ... We
come together in an assembly and congregation to surround God with
prayer, as if in battle formation . . . We gather together to consider the
divine Scriptures . . . And at the same time there is encouragement, correc-
tion and holy censure.

74   *Apologeticum* XXXIX, 16–18; *PL* I, 474–7; *CCL* I, 152–3

> Description of *agape* with impromptu singing of individuals.

Our meal reveals its meaning in its very name; it is called that which
signifies love (*dilectio*) among Greeks . . . One does not recline at table without first savoring a prayer to God; and then one eats what the hungry would
take and drinks what would serve the needs of the temperate. They thus
satisfy themselves as those who remember that God is to be worshipped
even at night, and they converse as do those who know that God listens.
After the washing of hands and the lighting of lamps (*lumina*), each is urged
to come into the middle and sing to God, either from the sacred scriptures
or from his own invention (*de proprio ingenio*). In this way is the manner of his
drinking tested. Similarly the banquet (*conuiuium*) is brought to a close with
prayer.

75   *De spectaculis* X, 2; *PL* I, 642; *CCL* I, 236

> In *De Spectaculis* Tertullian points out the historical roots of the public
> games in pagan worship as well as their immorality. In the three passages
> given here musical instruments are cited. (See also XI, 3.)

The way to the theater leads from temple and altar with their dreadful mess
of incense and blood, amidst the sound of tibias and trumpets, under the
leadership of those two iniquitous arbiters of funeral and sacrifice, the
undertaker and the soothsayer.

76   *De spectaculis* X, 8–9; *PL* I, 643; *CCL* I, 237

Clearly Liber and Venus are the patrons of the theatrical arts. That
immodesty of gesture and bodily movement so peculiar and proper to the
stage is dedicated to them, the one god dissolute in her sex, the other in his
dress. While whatever transpires in voice, melody, instruments and writing
(*uoce et modis et organis et litteris*) is in the domain of Apollo, the Muses,
Minerva and Mercury. O Christian, you will detest those things whose
authors you cannot but detest!

77   *De Spectaculis* xxv, 3; *PL* i, 656–7; *CCL* i, 248

As the tragic actor loudly declaims, will one reflect upon the exclamations of a prophet, and as the effeminate tibicinist plays, will one call to mind a psalm, and as the athletes compete, will one say there must be no more blows?

78   *De oratione* xxvii; *PL* i, 1194; *CCL* i, 273

> Tertullian appears to describe the responsorial recitation of psalms, perhaps in a domestic context.

The more exacting in their prayer are accustomed to add to their prayers an Alleluia and that sort of psalm in which those present respond with the closing verses (*clausulis respondeant*).

79   *De oratione* xxviii, 4; *PL* i, 1194–5; *CCL* i, 273

> Tertullian mentions psalms and hymns at the 'altar of God' in a passage on spiritual sacrifice (*hostia spiritualia*).

This prayer . . . we must bring amid psalms and hymns to the altar of God, and it will obtain from God all that we ask.

80   *Ad uxorem* ii, viii, 8–9; *PL* i, 1304. *CCL* i, 394

> The pious husband and wife sing to each other. Some commentators see an allusion to antiphonal psalmody here.

Psalms and hymns sound between the two of them (*sonant inter duos psalmi et hymni*), and they challenge each other to see who better sings to the Lord. Seeing and hearing this, Christ rejoices. He sends them his peace. Where two come together, there is He also, and where He is, there the evil one is not.

81   *Aduersus Marcionem* v, viii, 12; *PL* ii, 490–1; *CCL* i, 688

> This passage casts considerable light upon *De anima* ix, 4, quoted below. It suggests that the 'psalms' referred to there are not biblical. See also i Cor 14.26.

So let Marcion display the gifts of his god – some prophets, who have spoken not from human understanding but from the spirit of God, who have both foretold the future and revealed the secrets of the heart. Let him produce a psalm, a vision, a prayer; only let it be of the spirit, while in ecstasy, that is, a state beyond reason, when some interpretation of tongues has come upon him. Let him also show me a woman of his group who has prophesied . . .

82   *De anima* IX, 4; *PL* II, 659–60; *CCL* II, 792

> A Montanist charismatic finds inspiration for her visions in the pre-
> eucharistic synaxis, which consists in readings, psalms, homily and prayer.

There is among us today a sister favored with gifts of revelation which she
experiences through an ecstasy of the spirit during the Sunday liturgy. She
converses with angels, at one time even with the Lord; she sees and hears
mysteries, reads the hearts of people and applies remedies to those who
need them. The material for her visions is supplied as the scriptures are
read, psalms are sung, the homily delivered and prayers are offered.

83   *De anima* XIV, 4; *PL* II, 669; *CCL* II, 800

> The unified diversity of the soul is like that of the hydraulis. The com-
> plexity of the hydraulis and its successor the pipe organ have always
> stirred the literary imagination.

Moreover, a single body is made up of various members, so that there is
unity and not a division. Observe that marvelous creation of Archimedes –
I speak of the hydraulis (*organum hydraulicum*) – with its many parts, sections,
connections, passages – such a collection of sound, variety of tone
(*commercia modorum*), array of pipes (*acies tibiarum*) – and yet it all constitutes
a single entity. So too the air, expelled from below by the agitation of the
water, is not thereby divided into parts because it is distributed into different places; rather it is one in substance though diverse in function.

84   *De carne Christi* XX, 3; *PL* II, 786; *CCL* II, 909

> Tertullian contrasts the psalms of David with those of the heretic
> Valentinus.

The psalms also come to our aid on this point, not the psalms of that
apostate, heretic and Platonist, Valentinus, but those of the most holy and
illustrious prophet David. He sings among us of Christ, and through him
Christ indeed sang of Himself.

85   *De corona* XI, 3–4; *PL* II, 92; *CCL* II, 1056–7

> Here Tertullian's quarrel is with pagan military custom rather than with
> the instrument cited.

Further, shall he be disturbed after death by the trumpet of a brass player
(*tuba aeneatoris*) who expects to be woken by the trumpet of an angel? Shall
a Christian be cremated according to military custom, who is not allowed to
burn sacrifice, and whom Christ spared the deserved fire of hell? How many
other offenses can be observed that are attributable to the aberrations of
military discipline!

Hippolytus (c.170–c.236)

There is much confusion about the facts of his controversial life. A presbyter of the church of Rome, he seems at one time to have set himself up against Pope Callistus (217–22), whom he considered a heretic and charlatan. He was exiled to Sardinia during the persecution of Maximin (235–8), where, apparently, he died. The important liturgical document, *The Apostolic Tradition*, has been established in this century as most probably his work.

86   *The Antichrist* II; *PG* x, 728–9; *GCS* I–II, 4–5

> The prophets were touched by divine inspiration as is a musical instrument by the plectrum.

For all these were furnished with the prophetic spirit and deservedly honored by the Word himself; they enjoyed an inner unity, like that of musical instruments, and had always within themselves the Word like a plectrum, by which the prophets were moved to proclaim what God willed.

87   *The Refutation of All Heresies* I, ii; *PG* xvi, 3024–5; *GCS* III, 5–7

> Hippolytus describes Pythagoras's doctrine of cosmic harmony and later indicates that he learned it from Zarates the Chaldean. On ancient conceptions of harmony see Lippman (1964).

Now Pythagoras, in his investigation of nature, combined astronomy, geometry, music [and arithmetic]. He thus declared that God is a monad; and, thoroughly schooled in the properties of number, he said that the world sings (μελῳδεῖν) and is made up of harmony. Moreover, he was the first to reduce the movement of the seven stars to rhythm and melody . . . But Diodorus the Eretrian and Aristoxenus the musician say that Pythagoras went to Zaratas the Chaldean, who explained to him . . . The world, he said, is like a musical harmony, and that this is why the sun makes its circuit in accordance with harmony.

88   *The Refutation of All Heresies* v, x; *PG* xvi, 3159; *GCS* III, 102

> In this reference to the Naassein Gnostics Hippolytus uses the term psalm to indicate a hymn of theirs.

This psalm was tossed off by them, in which they appear to hymn all the mysteries of their error in this manner:

> The generative law of all was the Primal Mind,
> While the second was the diffused chaos of the First Born . . .

89   *Apostolic Tradition* 25; *Botte*, 64–6

> At one time called the *Egyptian Church Order*, this important document is
> now considered to be the genuine work of Hippolytus or at least an authen-
> tic reflection of the Roman liturgy of his day. Its text transmission is
> extremely complex; it exists in Latin, Coptic, Arabic and Ethiopic trans-
> lations, while the original Greek is almost entirely lost. The one section
> which mentions music – the description of an agape celebration attended
> by the bishop – exists only in a problematic passage of the Ethiopic, itself
> a transation from Arabic. It appears, nevertheless, not to be an interp-
> olation and presents us therefore with testimony – probably accurate in
> substance if obscure in detail – to the singing of psalms with Alleluia
> refrain at the agape. The translation here is based upon Botte's Latin
> reconstruction. For bibliography and discussion see, in addition to *Botte*,
> Dix (1968) and Jones, Wainwright and Yarnold (1978, pp. 57–9).

And let them arise therefore after supper and pray; let the boys sing psalms,
the virgins also. And afterwards let the deacon, as he takes the mingled
chalice of oblation, say a psalm from those in which Alleluia is written. And
afterwards, if the presbyter so orders, again from these psalms. And after
the bishop has offered the chalice, let him say a psalm from those appropriate to the chalice – always one with Alleluia, which all say. When they
recite the psalms, let all say Alleluia, which means, 'We praise him who is
God; glory and praise to him who created the entire world through his work
alone.' And when the psalm is finished let him bless the chalice and give of
its fragments to all the faithful.

Novatian (d. c.258)

Although orthodox in doctrine, the Roman presbyter Novatian broke with the
Church in his rigorous attitude toward those who lapsed during persecution. The
adherents of his schism are referred to as Novatianists. He was martyred during the
Valerian persecution, 257–8.

90   *De spectaculis* III, 2–3; *PL* IV, 782; *CCL* IV, 170

> Novatian is now accepted as the probable author of this short treatise,
> formerly attributed to Cyprian. In the first passage quoted, he argues that
> musical instruments and dancing, which were used legitimately in the Old
> Testament, are to be condemned now in the pagan spectacles. Two of the
> instruments cited here, nabla and kinura, are transliterations from the
> Septuagint Greek of the Old Testament string instruments *nebel* and *kinnor*
> (see Finesinger, 1926, pp. 26–44).

That David led dancing in the sight of God is no excuse for the Christian
faithful to sit in the theatre, for he did not distort his limbs in obscene
gestures while dancing to a tale of Grecian lust. The nablas, kinuras, tibias,
tympana and citharas played for God, not an idol. It is not thereby per-

mitted that unlawful things be seen. By a trick of the devil sacred things have been transferred into illicit ones.

91   *De spectaculis* IV, 5; *PL* IV, 783; *CCL* IV, 172

> The central reason for this condemnation lies in their idolatrous association.

These Grecian contests, whether in poetry, cithara playing, voice or athletics (*cantibus*, *fidibus*, *uocibus*, *uiribus*), have various demons as their patrons. And whatever else catches the eye of the spectator or beguiles his ear, betrays at its source, if one enquires into its origin and organization, some idol, demon or dead person.

92   *De spectaculis* VII, 1–3; *PL* IV, 785; *CCL* IV, 175–6

> Idolatry aside, the music of the spectacles is a vain thing.

It is unlawful, I say, for the Christian faithful to be present; utterly unlawful even for those whom Greece, to please their ears, sends everywhere to all who have been schooled in her vain arts. One mimics the raucous, bellicose clangor of the trumpet; another forces his breath into the tibia to control its doleful sounds. In turn, yet another competes against the dance and the sonorous voice of man by playing on the holes of the tibia with his breath, drawn up with effort from his innards to the upper reaches of his body – checking the sound and holding it in, now pouring it out into the air by passing it through certain holes, now breaking it up into phrases, he labors to speak with his fingers, ungrateful to the Artificer who gave him a tongue. But why speak of the useless concerns of comedy? Why of those great rantings of the tragic voice? Why of strings set noisily vibrating? Even if these things were not consecrated to idols, faithful Christians ought not to frequent and observe them, for even if there were nothing criminal about them, they have in themselves an utter worthlessness hardly suitable for believers.

Cyprian (d. 258)

Born of wealthy pagan parents, and educated in rhetoric, he was converted in about 246 and elected bishop of Carthage in 248. An admirer of Tertullian, he lacked both his brilliance and his intemperateness. He is admired himself especially for the sage advice of his treatises and letters on practical subjects. He was martyred at Carthage during the persecution of Valerian in 258. His recommendation of psalm singing at Christian meals was cited in the introduction to this chapter; of at least indirect relevance to the subject of chant are remarks he made about the office of lector (*Epist.* XXXVIII and XXXIX).

93   *De habitu uirginum* xi; *PL* IV, 449–50; *CSEL* III–I, 195

> The gifts of God, including the voice, are not to be abused.

God gave man a voice, yet amorous and indecent songs ought not to be sung; God wished iron to be used in the cultivation of the earth, not in the commission of murder; and because the Lord provided incense, wine and fire, one must not therefore sacrifice to idols.

94   *Ad Donatum* xvi; *PL* IV, 222–3; *CSEL* III–I, 16

> Cyprian recommends the singing of psalms at the evening meal.

And since this is a restful holiday and a time of leisure, now as the sun is sinking towards evening, let us spend what remains of the day in gladness and not allow the hour of repast to go untouched by heavenly grace. Let a psalm be heard at the sober banquet, and since your memory is sure and your voice pleasant (*uox canora*), undertake this task as is your custom. You will better nurture your friends, if you provide a spiritual recital (*spiritalis auditio*) for us and beguile our ears with sweet religious strains (*religiosa mulcedo*).

Arnobius (d. c.330)

According to Jerome he was born at Sicca, Africa. His *Aduersus nationes* (c.303–10) was written shortly after his conversion in order to demonstrate his orthodoxy. He barely succeeds in this, however, as traces of pagan thought are mingled with his new found Christian beliefs. His emotional commitment, on the other hand, is beyond doubt, as evidenced in the vitriolic character of his attack upon pagan musical practice.

95   *Aduersus nationes* II, 42; *PL* V, 881–2; *CSEL* IV, 82

> Arnobius associates dancing, singing and playing musical instruments with sexual immorality. The scabellum is a foot clapper used by musical directors and the sambuca a type of harp.

Was it for this that he sent souls, that as members of a holy and dignified race they practise here the arts of music and piping (*symphoniacas agerent et fistulatorias hic artes*), that in blowing on the tibia they puff out their cheeks, that they lead obscene songs, that they raise a great din with the clapping of scabella (*scabillorum concrepationibus*); under the influence of which a multitude of other lascivious souls abandon themselves to bizarre movements of the body, dancing and singing, forming rings of dancers, and ultimately raising their buttocks and hips to sway with the rippling motion of their loins? Was it for this that he sent souls, that in men they become male prostitutes, and in women harlots, sambucists and harpists (*sambucistriae psaltriae*)?

96   *Aduersus nationes* VII, 32; *PL* V, 1262; *CSEL* IV, 265

> Arnobius mocks the belief that the instruments used in pagan cults have a
> tangible effect upon the gods. (See also VII, 36.)

Is the anger and outrage of the gods appeased . . . by the jangle of brass and
the clashing of cymbals? Or by tympana or other instruments (*symphoniis*)?
What effect has the clatter of the scabellum? That when the gods hear it they
consider themselves honored and set aside their seething wrath in forgetful-
ness? Or is it that as little boys are frightened by rattles (*crepitaculis*) to stop
their silly whimpering, so omnipotent deities are soothed by the whistling
of tibias and relax, their anger softened, to the rhythm of cymbals?

Lactantius (c.240–c.320)

He was a pupil of Arnobius. Diocletian appointed him to teach rhetoric in the new
eastern capital Nicomedia, but he lost the position upon his conversion in about
300. He is generally admired for his success in assimilating the style of Cicero, but
criticized for his inadequate assimilation of Christian doctrine. We last hear of him
when Constantine summons him to Trier in about 317 to tutor his son Crispus.

97   *Diuinae institutiones* VII, xiii; *PL* VI, 779; *CSEL* XIX–2, 627

> Aristoxenus denies the existence of the soul, fallaciously comparing the
> powers of perception to the tuning of cithara strings. (See also *De opificio Dei*
> XVI).

What of Aristoxenus who declared absolutely that there is no soul, even
while it lives in the body? He thought that just as a consonant sound or song
– what the musicians call harmony – is produced on citharas (*fidibus*) by
tension upon their strings (*ex intentione neruorum*), so too the power of
sentience exists in human bodies from the joining together of the viscera
and the vigor of the limbs. Nothing more senseless than this can be said.
Certainly this man had healthy eyes, but a heart that was blind, for with it
he failed to see that he lived and possessed a mind with which he had
thought that very thing.

CHAPTER 5

Fourth-century Alexandria and desert monasticism

The patristic authors of fourth-century Alexandria and the desert monks of Egypt are two distinct groups, but their chronological and geographic proximity, as well as personal relationships, make it convenient to bring them together into one chapter.

Before introducing them it is necessary first to make a few observations about the state of Christianity at the time. The great event which serves to define the period was Constantine's decision in 313 to tolerate the new religion. Its result was that Christianity would develop from a persecuted minority into the established religion by the end of the century. This is reflected in Christian literature by the remarkable proliferation of outstanding authors writing in both the traditional genres and in new ones such as the homily and the epistle. The period from 313 to roughly 450 is arguably the greatest in the history of Christian literature. But with the opportunities of the new situation there arose new problems. For one, mass conversions brought about the phenomenon of religious laxity and nominal Christianity, and for another, much of the polemical energy formerly devoted to combating paganism had now to be directed against the internal enemy of heresy. The majority of these heresies arose in the course of the great theological struggle to define the nature of Christ, more specifically, to spell out the relationship between the human and divine aspects of his person, and in turn the relationship of his person to the others of the Trinity.

The most persistent of these heresies was Arianism, which denied full divinity to Christ. Its father was the Alexandrian priest Arius (c.250–c.336), and its principal antagonist the Alexandrian bishop Athanasius, the first author quoted in this chapter. The Alexandrian literature of the period retained the highly speculative tendency of the previous century and perhaps for this reason is not particularly rich in references to liturgical chant. Of more importance to our subject is the literature of the monastic movement.

Tradition ascribes the origins of Christian monasticism to the Decian persecution (c.250), which sent many of the devout fleeing to the Egyptian deserts. Whatever the degree of truth in this, certainly the laxity and corruption of fourth century Christianity gave impetus to the movement, as it spurred thousands of idealistic men and women to seek a purer form of Christianity in the solitude of the desert. At first the predominant mode of existence was eremitic or anchoritic. The commanding figure of the period was Antony, whose edifying biography, written by an admiring Athanasius, is quoted below. Soon, however, the hermits became organized into regulated communities, and thus there developed the coenobitic mode, or monasticism in the proper sense. Here Pachomius was the great founder.

The attitude of the early monks to liturgical singing is to some degree in dispute. Quasten (1930, pp. 94–9) quotes passages expressing antagonism toward the musical elaboration of psalmody, and Dekkers (1960) claims that the early monks were antagonistic toward both psalmody and liturgy in general. But Veilleux (1968, pp. 162–3) argues convincingly that such issues were not consciously addressed by the early monks with their informal approach to liturgy. In any case, three relevant points emerge from the material presented below. (1) There are no expressions of antagonism toward psalmody from the earliest desert fathers; those passages quoted by Quasten, with their use of terms like kanōn, troparion and oktōēchos, are from a later period (but see Wessely, 1952). (2) Psalmody was a pervasive practice in early monasticism, but so far as one can guess, it appears not to have been an elaborately melodious affair like, say, the psalmody which moved Augustine in Milan, but rather an extended, chant-like exercise, which used the memorized Psalter as its vehicle. (3) Whatever its musical character at this early stage, the chanting of large portions of the Psalter, the so-called *cursus psalmorum*, was an innovation of early monasticism which was of immense importance in the eventual development of the sung Office.

For a basic bibliography of the texts and secondary literature of desert monasticism, see Ward (1980, pp. 154–7). The best general discussion of the phenomenon remains Chitty (1966), while an updated description of its liturgical practices is available in Taft (1982).

Athanasius (c.296–373)

He was probably educated at the famous Catechetical School of Alexandria, his native city. He accompanied Alexander, bishop of Alexandria, to the Council of Nicaea (325) as his secretary, and succeeded him as bishop in 328. For the rest of his life he was the most influential and consistent opponent of Arianism in all Christendom. He was repeatedly exiled from his see, generally through the influence of Arian factions upon sympathetic emperors, although he spent most of the last decade of his life at Alexandria observing the gradually strengthening status of the orthodox position.

In his references to music he was typically Alexandrian, with a pronounced penchant for engaging in musical imagery. There are occasional remarks, however, granting a glimpse of his attitude toward actual liturgical music, which would appear to be somewhat less generous than that of many of his contemporaries. The passages quoted here are presented as follows: first those from works relating to the psalms and then those from other works in alphabetical order.

98   *Epistula ad Marcellinum de interpretatione psalmorum* 27; *PG* XXVII, 37–40

Broadly considered, this work belongs to the genre of Psalter introduction. As such it makes the usual points that the Psalter contains in itself the virtue of all other Old Testament books, that it foretells the New Testament, and that it is a treasury of devotion. It differs, however, from comparable works by Basil, Chrysostom and Ambrose, as we read in the first passage quoted below, in that it gives short shrift to the notion that the Psalter is more effective than other books of Scripture because it adds ingratiating melody to doctrine. Instead Athanasius explains the musical aspect of the psalms according to the tenets of allegorical exegesis. This corresponds to the rather severe attitude toward psalmody attributed to him by Augustine in his *Confessions* x, 33.

Why are words of this sort sung with melody and song? We must not disregard this either. Some of the simple ones among us, even while believing the texts to be divinely inspired, still think that the psalms are sung melodiously for the sake of good sound and the pleasure of the ear. This is not so. Scripture has not sought what is sweet and persuasive; rather this was ordained to benefit the soul for every reason, but principally these two. First, because it was proper for Divine Scripture to hymn God not only with continuity but with expanse of voice. Recited with continuity, then, are such words as those of the Law and the Prophets, and all those of history, along with the New Testament; while recited with expanse are those of psalms, odes and songs. And thus it is assured that men love God with their entire strength and capability. Secondly, because as harmony creates a single concord in joining together the two pipes of the aulos, so . . . reason wills that a man be not disharmonious with himself, nor at variance with himself, so as to consider what is best but to accomplish with his inclination what is mean, as when Pilate says, 'I find no crime in him' (John 18.38), but concurs with the judgment of the Jews.

99   *Epistula ad Marcellinum* 28; *PG* XXVII, 40

> Again, the musical aspect of psalmody is justified as a sign of inner harmony.

Just as we make known and signify the thoughts of the soul through the words we express, so too the Lord wished the melody of the words to be a sign of the spiritual harmony of the soul, and ordained that the canticles be sung with melody and the psalms read with song.

100   *Epistula ad Marcellinum* 29; *PG* XXVII, 40–1

> To sing for the sake of pleasing sound rather than as a manifestation of inner harmony is blameworthy.

Those who do not recite the sacred songs in this manner, do not sing with understanding, but rather gratify themselves and incur blame, because 'Praise is not seemly in the mouth of a sinner' (Eccles 15.9). But those who sing in the manner described above – that is, with the melody of the words proceeding from the rhythm of the soul and its harmony with the spirit – such as they sing with the tongue and sing also with the mind, not only for themselves, but also to benefit greatly those who would hear them. Hence blessed David by singing in this manner for Saul, pleased God for his own sake and removed the confusion and manic passion from Saul, and made his soul be at peace. The priests sang in this manner, summoning the souls of the people to tranquility and to unanimity with the heavenly choir. Hence to recite the psalms with melody is not done from a desire for pleasing sound, but is a manifestation of harmony among the thoughts of the soul. And melodious reading is a sign of the well-ordered and tranquil condition of the mind.

101   *Expositio in psalmum lxxx*, 4; *PG* XXVII, 361–4

> Athanasius wrote a commentary on the psalms, substantial fragments of
> which are preserved in *catenae* of the eleventh century Nicetas of Heraclea.
> Typical passages of instrumental allegory appear at the expected places; a
> single example is given here.

'Blow the trumpet at the new moon' (Ps 80.4). Just as Israel in ancient times
took sensible trumpets and blew upon them at the new moon (an ordinance
given by God and a witness to their being freed from the Egyptian
servitude), so too the new people, using the Gospel trumpet, whose sound
has gone forth into the whole world, are called upon to blow a trumpet at the
new moon, that is, in the renewal of their mind, confessing and giving witness that it has been rescued from the figurative Egypt, that is, from the
power of darkness.

102   *Apologia pro fuga sua* 24; *PG* XXV, 673–6; *SC* LVI, 162

> This frequently cited incident presents a clear example of the responsorial
> performance of Psalm 135; how musical the performance was, however, is
> left open to question.

It was already night and some of the people were keeping vigil in antici-
pation of the synaxis, when suddenly the general Syrianus appeared with
more than 5,000 soldiers, heavily armed with bared swords, bows and
arrows, and cudgels, as I said above. he surrounded the church, stationing
his soldiers closely together, so that no one could leave the church and slip
by them. Now it seemed to me unreasonable to leave the people in such confusion and not rather to bear the brunt of battle for them, so sitting upon the
throne, I urged the deacon to read a psalm and the people to respond, 'For
his mercy endureth forever' (Ps 135.1) . . .

103   *Epistula de decretis Nicaenae synodi* 16; *PG* XXV, 441–4

> A certain heretical notion concerning the nature of Christ is found in the
> songs of Arius and in a specific composition, 'Thalia' (see also *Epistula de
> synodis Arimini et Seleuciae* 15, and Socrates, *Ecclesiastical History* I, ix).

But having come to naught here, and being constrained like those
adherents of Eusebius within dire straits, they have left to them this one
remaining argument, which Arius also fabricates as a last resort in his songs
and in his 'Thalia': 'God pronounces many words; which of them then do we
call the Son and Word, only-begotten of the Father?' They are fools and anything but Christians!

104   *Life of St Antony* 25; *PG* XXVI, 881

> This passage appears in Antony's famous address to the assembled desert
> monks; it refers to the demons who figure so prominently in the address
> and who subsequently exercized much influence upon the western
> religious and artistic imagination.

They are crafty and quick to change and to transform themselves into anything. Frequently, without appearing, they pretend to sing the psalms
melodiously (ψάλλειν μετ' ᾠδῆς), and they repeat passages from the
lections. Often, after we have read, they straightaway, like an echo, say precisely what has been read; and they arouse us to prayer when we are asleep,
doing so continuously, hardly allowing us to sleep at all.

105   *Life of St Antony* 44; *PG* XXVI, 908

> At the end of Antony's address, Athanasius provides a general description
> of the desert monks.

So there were monasteries in the mountains, like tabernacles, filled with
saintly choirs reciting psalms, devoutly reading, fasting, praying, rejoicing
in the hope of things to come, and laboring to give alms, while maintaining
love and harmony among themselves.

106   *Life of St Antony* 55; *PG* XXVI, 921

> Antony recommends morning and evening psalmody to his monastic
> followers.

To all monks, then, who came to him he always gave this instruction:
'Believe in the Lord and love him; guard yourselves against foul thoughts
and fleshly pleasures, and, as it is written in Proverbs, be not deceived by
"the feasting of the belly". Flee vainglory and pray continuously;
sing psalms before sleep and after sleep; store away the precepts of
Scripture . . . '

107   *Oratio contra gentes* 38; *PG* XXV, 76–7; *Thomson*, 104–6

> There are several figurative passages in this work involving the idea of har-
> mony (see also 37, 42 and 43).

Just as when one hears from afar a lyre, made up of many different strings,
and wonders at their harmonious symphony, that not only the low one produces a sound, not only the high one, and not only the middle one, but all
sound together in balanced tension; and one concludes from all this that the
lyre neither operates by itself nor is played by many, but rather that there
is one musician who by his art blends the sound of each string into a harmonious symphony – even though one fails to see him – so too, since there

is an entirely harmonious (παναρμονίου) order in the world as a whole, without things above being at odds with those below, and those below with those above, but one completed order of all; it follows that we know there is one leader and king of all reaction, not many, who illuminates and moves everything with his own light.

Synesius of Cyrene (c.370–c.414)

Born to noble pagan parents at Cyrene in Lybia, Synesius studied Neoplatonic philosophy at Alexandria with the renowned Hypatia. He married a Christian woman in 403, and in 410 was elected bishop of Ptolemais. He accepted the office reluctantly, under condition that he be allowed to continue living with his wife and not renounce certain of his philosophical beliefs such as the pre-existence of the soul and the eternity of matter. Never completely christianized, he stands unique among the church fathers in the degree of his attachment to the pagan past.

108   Hymn VII, 1–6; *PG* LXVI, 1161; *Terzaghi*, 48

> This hymn is the first of a trilogy addressed to Christ and composed in a new meter. The reference to the cithara in line six could be purely figurative or it could be taken to suggest that the hymns were actually recited to instrumental accompaniment – presumably in a domestic rather than liturgical setting (Quasten, 1983, p. 123). Hymn VIII opens with a similar reference, and Epistle 94 quotes from a poem about Nemesis which 'we sing to the lyre'.

> I was the first to invent this meter (νόμον)
> For thee, blessed, immortal,
> Illustrious offspring of the virgin,
> Jesus of Solyma,
> And with newly-devised harmonies (ἁρμογαῖς)
> To strike the cithara's strings (κιθάρας μίτους).

Pachomius (c.290–346)

Generally acknowledged to be the founder of coenobitic monasticism, Pachomius presided over a vast order of monks and nuns in nine monasteries and two convents in Upper Egypt. His achievement had a central influence upon subsequent monastic leaders like Basil, Cassian and Martin of Tours. A substantial body of literature by and about him, including his Rule and various versions of a biography, are conveniently available in English translation with excellent notes and apparatus in *Veilleux*.

109   *Precepts* 3; *Boon*, 14

> The Rule of Pachomius, originally compiled in Coptic, is preserved in its entirety only in Jerome's Latin translation of a Greek intermediary. His use

of the term *tuba* here in precept 3 and again in precept 9 is curious, as one
assumes the normal wooden gong of early monasticism. The Pachomian
monks referred to their twice daily gatherings for prayer and psalmody, in
the late afternoon and during the night, as the 'synaxis', and used the same
term to describe their meeting place; Jerome renders them *collecta* and
conventiculum respectively. On these and other points concerning the daily
life of the Pachomian monks, see Chitty (1966, pp. 22–7).

3 When one hears the sound of the trumpet (*tuba*) summoning [the monks]
to the synaxis (*collectam*), he will leave his cell immediately, meditating on
some passage from the Scriptures on the way to the door of the synaxis
(*conventiculi*).

110   *Precepta* 16–17; *Boon*, 17

At the Sunday daytime synaxis, only the elders may lead the psalmody.

16 On Sunday and in the synaxis in which the Eucharist (*oblatio*) is to be
offered, aside from the master of the house and the elders of the monastery
who are of some reputation, let no one have the authority to recite psalms
(*psallendi*).

17 If someone is absent, while anyone of the elders is chanting
(*psallente*), that is, reading the Psalter, he will immediately undergo the
order of penitence and reproach before the altar.

111   *Precepta* 127–8; *Boon*, 47

Two precepts deal with psalmody at the obsequies of a Pachomian monk.
From the biographies we know that there was a procession to a mountain
burying place (see *Vita Graeca prima* 103 and *Paralipomena* 6). The gist of the
regulation given here is that rather than singing psalms spontaneously the
monks should simply respond to the chanting of an appointed psalmist.

127 When a brother has died, the whole brotherhood should accompany
him [to the mountain]. No one should stay behind without the order of a
superior, nor sing psalms unless he has been ordered, nor add another
psalm to the one previously sung unless bidden by the master.

128 Two shall not sing together at the time of mourning, nor be clothed
in a linen mantle, nor shall anyone neglect to respond to the psalmist, but
they shall be united both in step and in consonant voice.

112   *Precepta* 140–2; *Boon*, 50–1

It is not clear from the wording of precept 140 whether the memorization
of the entire Psalter or only portions of it was required, although the former
was common from the fourth century on. The mention of a boat in precept
142 is explained by the fact that the monasteries of the Upper Nile used
boats to transport their produce. The reference to private psalmody in

precept 142, along with several similar references, would seem to argue against musically elaborate psalmody.

140 And there shall be absolutely no one in the monastery who does not learn to read and retain something from the Scriptures, at least the New Testament and the Psalter.

141 No one shall find pretexts for himself which prevent him from going to the synaxis, the psalmody and the prayer.

142 One shall not neglect the times for prayer and psalmody, whether on a boat, in a monastery, in the field, on a journey, or engaged in whatever duty.

113   *Vita Graeca prima* 103; *Halkin*, 68

> For other Pachomian references to funeral psalmody see *Precepta* 127–8, *Paralipomena* 6 and *Vita Bohaerica* 93.

At that time a certain brother died in the monastery. And after the preparation of the corpse, Pachomius would not allow the brethren to sing psalms before him on the way to the mountain as was the custom. Nor was the oblation (προσφερά) made over him. Rather he gathered his garments into the middle of the monastery and burned them, striking fear in all lest they take their way of life lightly.

Evagrius Ponticus (346–99)

Evagrius was ordained by Gregory of Nazianzus and became established as an outstanding preacher at Constantinople. He felt drawn to the more interior life, however, and in about 382 retired to the Egyptian desert, in the area of Nitria, where he was a disciple of Macarius the Great. With his intellectual background he became the first monastic figure to write extensively. Much of his work has not been preserved, probably because of its Origenist leanings, but what remains plays an important part in the history of monastic mysticism and spirituality. He appears, incidentally, to be the real author of the psalm commentary attributed to Origen (see Pseudo-Origen above).

114   *Praktikos* xv; *SC* CLXXI, 536–8

> The *Praktikos* is the first portion of a work called the *Monachikos*. It consists of one hundred sayings for the guidance of more simple monks, while the second portion, the *Gnostikos*, is directed to the more erudite.

Reading, keeping vigil (ἀγρυπνία) and prayer focus the wandering mind. Hunger, toil and solitude quell inflamed desire. Psalmody, patience and pity arrest seething anger. And these are to be practised at the appropriate time and in good measure, for what is excessive and ill-timed is not lasting, and what does not last is harmful rather than beneficial.

115   *De oratione* 82–3; *PG* XL, 1185

> This treatise, found among the writings of Nilus of Ancyra, is probably the
> work of Evagrius.

82 Pray with moderation and calm, and chant psalms with understanding
and proper measure (εὐρύθμως), and you will be raised on high like a young
eagle.

83 Psalmody lays the passions to rest and causes the stirrings of the body
to be stilled; prayer prepares the mind to perform its proper activity.

116   *Parainetikos*; Frankenberg, 561

> Some commentators might see this passage as hostile to psalmody, but its
> point is simply to express a preference for grace and inspiration over
> religious routine.

Again, if a beneficial thought should come to you, let it occupy you rather
than the psalms, and do not fend off the grace of God by maintaining
accepted practice ... Do not delight in the multitude of psalms while laying
a veil over your heart.

Palladius (c.364–425)

Born in Galatia and thoroughly educated in the classics, Palladius was drawn to
Egypt in about 388 by his admiration for the desert monks. He spent several years
as a disciple of various fathers, most notably Evagrius, but his delicate constitution
forced him to return to secular ecclesiastical life in about 400. He spent his last years
as bishop of Aspuna in Galatia. His most important work is the *Lausiac History*, a
central source for the history of early monasticism, so-called after Lausus, a
chamberlain at the court of Theodosius II, to whom it is dedicated. It is organized
in a series of biographies, consisting primarily in edifying, colorful and often
legendary anecdotes about the spiritual exploits of the fathers.

117   *Lausiac History* vii; *Butler*, 26

> This passage is from Palladius's eyewitness account of the great monastery
> on Mount Nitria. Egyptian monks occupied themselves for long hours in
> tasks such as making linen and plaiting ropes, indeed did so at the very
> times they were engaged in prayer and psalmody. Note too that on week-
> days they chanted psalms individually, but at the same time – not a prac-
> tice one associates today with the notion of psalmody.

They all make linen with their hands so that they are all without need.
Indeed one who stands there at about the ninth hour can hear the psalmody
issuing forth from each cell, so that he imagines himself to be high above in
paradise. They occupy the church on the Sabbath only and the Lord's Day.
Eight priests have charge of this church, in which, so long as the first priest

lives, no other celebrates (προσφέρει), or gives the homily, or judges, but rather they simply sit by him in silence.

118   *Lausiac History* xxii; *Butler,* 72–3

> On the 'twelve psalms' see Apophthegmata Patrum, *Anonymous Sayings* 229.

Again Antony arose and said twelve prayers and chanted twelve psalms. He lay down for his brief first sleep and arose once more in the middle of the night to chant psalms until it was day. And as he saw the old man eagerly following him in this regimen, he said to him: 'If you can do this every day, then remain with me'.

119   *Lausiac History* xxvi; *Butler,* 81–2

> The 'long' psalm is no doubt Psalm 118, while the 'fifteen', perhaps, are the Gradual Psalms, 119–33. Note how the recitation of psalms, presumably by heart, appears to be of a piece with the recitation of other Scripture.

Scetis was at a distance of forty miles from us, and during those forty miles we ate twice and drank water three times, while Heron tasted nothing, but went along on foot and recited the fifteen psalms, then the long one, then the Epistle to the Hebrews, then Isaiah and a portion of Jeremiah, then Luke the evangelist, and then proverbs.

120   *Lausiac History* xlviii; *Butler,* 142–3

> Again, the psalmody appears to be more a form of meditation than a self-consciously musical exercise.

He lived there for twenty-five years, partaking of food only on the Lord's Day and the Sabbath, standing throughout the night and reciting psalms ... One night as this Elpidius was chanting and we chanting along with him, a scorpion bit him; he stepped on it without altering his posture, paying no heed to the pain caused by the scorpion.

Isidore of Pelusium (d. c.435)

Born at Alexandria sometime in the third quarter of the fourth century, Isidore was a priest, and possibly abbot, at a monastery near Pelusium on the eastern estuary of the Nile. His literary heritage consists in more than 2,000 extant letters; indeed contemporaries credit him with nearly 3,000. This epistolary effort of some four decades, directed to high and low, and concerned chiefly with exegetical themes, but also with secular and administrative matters, marks him off from the simple desert fathers of earlier generations.

121 Epistle I, 90; *PG* LXXVIII, 244–5

> One sees in each of the three passages quoted here how Isidore's interests
> go beyond the confines of monasticism. His view on the singing of women
> in church is rigorous; on that subject see Quasten (1983, pp. 75–87).

The apostles of the Lord, who wanted to put an end to idle talk in the
churches, and who were our instructors in good behavior, wisely permitted
women to sing psalms there. But as every divine teaching has been turned
into its opposite, so this, too, has become an occasion of sin and laxity for
the majority of the people. They do not feel compunction in hearing the
divine hymns, but rather misuse the sweetness of melody to arouse passion,
thinking that it is no better than the songs of the stage. Thus it is necessary
– if we would seek what is pleasing to God and do that which is of public
benefit – that we stop these women both from singing in church, and also
from loitering in the city as if they were innkeepers to Christ, making a
divine gift into the wages of destruction.

122 Epistle I, 456; *PG* LXXVIII, 433

> Musical instruments play a central role in transforming the symposium
> into a shameful carousal.

A carousal, my dear friend, is the intoxicating aulos, together with prolonged drinking, which arouses one to sensuality, and makes of the symposium a shameful theater, as it bewitches the guests with cymbals and
other instruments of deception. It is written that they who frequent it stand
outside the kingdom, as they well know.

123 Epistle II, 176; *PG* LXXVIII, 628

> Isidore admired John Chrysostom and probably was influenced by his
> position on Old Testament instrumental usage; see CHRYSOSTOM, *In
> psalmum cl.*

If the Holy One tolerated blood and sacrifice because of the childishness of
men at that time, why do you wonder that the music of cithara and psaltery
was used, which, as some say, heals the passions of the soul and alleviates
pain, soothes anger and assuages grief through tears. For many, as they say,
by suppressing tears have succumbed to different afflictions.

Apophthegmata Patrum

Here with the *Sayings of the Fathers* we return to the heart and soul of desert monasticism. Anecdotes about the virtues and miracles of the fathers, preserved at first
orally in Coptic, one assumes, were set down in a number of Greek collections
toward the end of the fifth century. The most notable of these are the *Alphabetical
Collection*, organized according to the names of the fathers, and the *Anonymous Sayings*,
consisting in material which cannot be attributed to particular individuals. Their
content holds a curious charm for the modern reader; in addition to the awesome

austerity of the desert fathers' lives, one perceives much compassion, occasional wit, and even a touch of mischief.

On technical questions about the collections, see Bousset (1923) and Guy (1962).

124   *Apophthegmata Patrum*, Epiphanius 3; *PG* LXV, 164

> This incident occurs when Epiphanius, now bishop of Cyprus, visits the monastery he had founded near his birthplace in Palestine. He is displeased with the new practice of observing the day hours as separate services, which seems to him contrary to the Egyptian ideal of continual prayer and psalmody.

It was explained to the blessed Epiphanius, bishop of Cyprus, by the abbot of the monastery he had in Palestine: 'In accordance with your instructions we have not neglected our rule, but diligently discharge Terce, Sext and None'. However, Epiphanius corrected them and made it clear to them, saying: 'You obviously neglect the other hours of the day when you refrain from prayer, for the true monk must have prayer and psalmody in his heart without ceasing.'

125   *AP*, Ioannes Curtus 35; *PG* LXV, 216

> Prayer, meditation and psalmody are linked.

It was said of the same Abba John that, while returning from the harvest or from meeting with the elders, he devoted himself to prayer, meditation and psalmody until he had restored his mind to its original order.

126   *AP*, Serapion 1; *PG* LXV, 413–16

> The reader should know that this woman does find a suitable convent where she lives in holiness for the rest of her days.

Once Abba Serapion was passing through a certain Egyptian village, and he saw a prostitute standing in her cell, and the old man said to her, 'Expect me later today; I wish to come to you and spend the night next to you'. She replied, 'Very well, Abba'. And she prepared herself and made ready the bed. When it was evening the old man came to her, went into the cell, and asked her, 'Have you made ready the bed?' And she replied, 'Yes, Abba'. He closed the door and said to her, 'Wait a moment, since we have a regulation which I must first fulfill'. So the old man began his synaxis – beginning the Psalter, he said a prayer after each psalm, beseeching God for her that she repent and be saved. And God heard him. And the woman stood trembling and praying by the old man, and as the old man completed the entire Psalter, the woman fell to the ground. Then the old man began the Epistle, reciting a considerable portion of it, and thus completed the synaxis. Now the woman was filled with compunction, and realizing that he did not come to her to sin but to save her soul, she prostrated herself before him and said, 'Do an act of charity, Abba, and lead me to where I can please God'.

127   *AP, Anonymous Sayings* 150; *Nau*, 51

> Another instance of the entire Psalter's recitation in one night.

Another old man came to one of the fathers, who, after boiling a few lentils, said to him: 'Let us perform a little synaxis'. He completed the entire Psalter, while the brother recited the two great prophets. And when morning came the old visitor went away and they forgot the food.

128   *AP, Anonymous Sayings* 229; *Nau*, 361

> There are frequent references to the 'twelve psalms' in the literature of desert monasticism. Apparently, it is not a matter of simply twelve psalms but an extended series of prayers, each section of which closes with a psalm. Possibly it has a direct bearing on the eventual shape of matins; see Veilleux (1968, pp. 324–9).

Some brethren went from their monastery into the desert to visit an anchorite. He received them with joy, and according to the custom of the hermits, seeing that they were weary, he prepared a table before the usual hour, offered them whatever he had, and provided rest for them. And late in the day they recited the twelve psalms, and did likewise throughout the night.

CHAPTER 6

Fourth-century Asia Minor: the Cappadocians

Although Arianism was condemned at the Council of Nicaea (325), it flourished subsequently in Asia Minor, particularly under its champion, the emperor Constantius II (337–61). This may help to account for the paucity of orthodox Christian literature in the earlier part of the century. The last third of the century, however, saw the emergence of the three outstanding church fathers of Cappadocia, a region of eastern Asia Minor; they were Basil, his friend Gregory of Nazianzus and his brother Gregory of Nyssa. Theological descendants of Athanasius, they played a key role in the fight against Arianism, which was effectively suppressed by the time of the Council of Constantinople (381). They also contributed much to the development of eastern monasticism and helped to shape the Christian compromise with pagan learning. In the area of musical reference Basil is especially important, ranking with figures like John Chrysostom, Ambrose and Augustine.

Basil the Great (c.330–379)

He came of an exemplary Christian family that contributed several saints to the Church including his brother, Gregory of Nyssa. He was schooled in rhetoric, first at his native Caesarea and then at Constantinople and Athens; upon his return home to Caesarea in about 356, he taught rhetoric there as his father had before him. Within a short time, however, he renounced his career and devoted himself entirely to the religious life. He journeyed throughout Egypt, Palestine, Syria and Mesopotamia to observe the most famous ascetics and then established a monastic retreat on the Iris River near Neocaesarea in Pontus. In about 365 the bishop of Caesarea, Eusebius, persuaded him to come there as his aide. When Eusebius died in 370, Basil succeeded him and distinguished himself as a bishop, particularly as a builder of charitable institutions and a bold foe of Arianism. Basil is sometimes called a 'Roman among the Greeks' because he manifested a greater degree of interest and ability in practical matters than did the typical speculatively inclined eastern theologian. His monastic writings, for example, perform a roughly analogous function in the east to Benedict's *Rule* in the west. His role in the formation of the eastern liturgy, however, while undeniable, is not quite so clearly defined. Contemporaries attest to his penchant for liturgical innovation, but the so-called 'Liturgy of St Basil', still in use on certain occasions in the eastern Church, achieved its definitive form many centuries after his death. Only its anaphora is likely to owe much to him personally.

Basil has left us several important references to music, among them a discussion of monastic office hours and a vivid description of nocturnal psalmody. The references are given here in the following order; those from the homilies on the psalms, the monastic rules, the letters, and the remaining works presented alphabetically.

For bibliography and authoritative discussion on various aspects of Basil's life and works, see the appropriate articles in Fedwick (1981).

129   *Homilia in psalmum i; PG* XXIX, 209–12

> Thirteen of the eighteen homilies on individual psalms preserved under
> Basil's name are considered to be genuine. The first two capitula of the
> homily on Psalm 1 serve as an introduction to the entire Psalter in similar
> fashion to Ambrose's exposition of Psalm 1. Such fourth century eulogies
> on the psalms, incidentally, suggest their widespread use in the contem-
> porary liturgy. Five excerpts of the passage in question are given here in an
> attempt to present its more important individual points. The first claims
> that the psalms have within them the benefits of all other categories of
> Scripture.

All Scripture is inspired by God for our benefit; it was composed by the
Spirit for this reason, that all we men, as if at a common surgery for souls,
might each of us select a remedy for his particular malady. 'Care', it is said,
'makes the greatest sin to cease'. Now the Prophets teach certain things, the
Historians and the Law teach others, and Proverbs provides still a different
sort of advice, but the Book of Psalms encompasses the benefit of them all.
It foretells what is to come and memorializes history; it legislates for life,
gives advice on practical matters, and serves in general as a repository of
good teachings, carefully searching out what is suitable for each individual.

130   *Homilia in psalmum i; PG* XXIX, 212

> The melodiousness of the psalms is an effective tool for teaching weak
> humans.

What did the Holy Spirit do when he saw that the human race was not led
easily to virtue, and that due to our penchant for pleasure we gave little heed
to an upright life? He mixed sweetness of melody with doctrine so that
inadvertently we would absorb the benefit of the words through gentleness
and ease of hearing, just as clever physicians frequently smear the cup with
honey when giving the fastidious some rather bitter medicine to drink.
Thus he contrived for us these harmonious psalm tunes, so that those who
are children in actual age as well as those who are young in behavior, while
appearing only to sing would in reality be training their souls. For not one
of these many indifferent people ever leaves church easily retaining in
memory some maxim of either the Apostles or the Prophets, but they do
sing the texts of the Psalms at home and circulate them in the marketplace.

131   *Homilia in psalmum i,* 2; *PG* XXIX, 212

> The psalms foster charity in particular.

A psalm is tranquility of soul and the arbitration of peace; it settles one's
tumultuous and seething thoughts. It mollifies the soul's wrath and
chastens its recalcitrance. A psalm creates friendships, unites the separated
and reconciles those at emnity. Who can still consider one to be a foe with

whom one utters the same prayer to God! Thus psalmody provides the greatest of all goods, charity, by devising in its common song a certain bond of unity, and by joining together the people into the concord of a single chorus.

132   *Homilia in psalmum i*, 2; *PG* XXIX, 213

> A similar point to that made in the second excerpt.

O the wise invention of the teacher who contrives that in our singing we learn what is profitable, and that thereby doctrine is somehow more deeply impressed upon our souls! What is learned under duress tends not to be retained, but what suavely ingratiates itself somehow abides within our souls more steadfastly.

133   *Homilia in psalmum i*, 2; *PG* XXIX, 213

> The final excerpt tells how the Psalter bears a spiritual resemblance to its namesake among musical instruments, the psaltery.

While there are many musical instruments, the Prophet adapted this book to that called the psaltery, which, as it seems to me, displays resonating within itself the grace of the Spirit from on high, because it alone among musical instruments has the source of its sound in its upper parts. While the brass of the cithara and lyre respond to the plectrum from below, this psaltery has the source of its harmonious strains (ἁρμονικῶν ῥυθμῶν) from above, so that we too might be anxious to pursue higher things, and not brought down to the passions of the flesh by the pleasure of song (μέλους).

134   *Homilia in psalmum xxviii*, 7; *PG* XXIX, 304

> The psalm is mentioned here as one of several Scripture readings, perhaps in connection with a pre-eucharistic synaxis.

You have a psalm, you have a prophecy, you have the gospel precepts and the pronouncements of the Apostles. While your tongue sings, let your mind search out the meaning of the words, so that you might sing in spirit and sing also in understanding.

135   *Homilia in psalmum lix*, 2; *PG* XXIX, 464

> This psalm is of more relevance to the Christian convert than the ancient Jew.

So the psalm was not written for the Jews of that time, but for us who are to be transformed, who exchange polytheism for piety and the error of idolatry for the recognition of him who made us, who choose moderation under the law in place of illegitimate pleasure, and who substitute psalms, fasting and prayer, for auloi, dancing and drunkenness.

136 *Homilia in psalmum cxiv,* 1; *PG* xxix, 484

Basil arrives late at a vigil service just as Psalm 114 is being sung.

Long since have you arrived at this sacred shrine of the martyrs, and from the middle of the night you have propitiated their God with hymns, persevering to the middle of this day, awaiting my arrival. Now is the reward at hand for you who have preferred the veneration of the martyrs and the worship of God to sleep and relaxation ... So as not to distress you by detaining you any longer, I will first discourse briefly upon the psalm you were singing as I came upon you, nourishing your souls with words of consolation so far as in me lies, and then dismiss you all for the care of your bodies. Now what was it that you sang? 'I have loved', he says, 'because the Lord will hear the voice of my prayer' (Ps 114.1).

137 *Regulae fusius tractatae, Interrogatio* xxxvii, 3–5; *PG* xxxi, 1013–16

There are two works of Basil referred to commonly as monastic rules; actually they are collections of answers to questions put to him by monks he had visited. One work consists of 313 brief replies, while that quoted here, the so-called 'Long Rules', consists of fifty-five discursive replies. In answer to question thirty-seven Basil argues first that prayer and psalmody must not be used as an excuse to shirk manual labor and then goes on to detail the times set aside for prayer and psalmody. They appear to correspond to the medieval office hours although the distinctions among morning, evening and night offices is not altogether clear (Mateos, 1963). Note Basil's appeal for 'variety' (ποικιλία) in psalmody.

Daybreak is a set time for prayer so that we dedicate the first stirrings of soul and mind to God, and take up no other consideration until made joyous by the thought of God; as it is written: 'I remembered God and was delighted' (Ps 76.4); and so that the body will busy itself with no work before accomplishing that which was written: 'For to thee will I pray, O Lord, in the morning thou shalt hear my voice. In the morning I will stand before thee, and will see' (Ps 5.4–5). Again at the third hour the brethren must come together and assist at prayer, even if they each happen to be occupied in different tasks. They must remember the gift of the Spirit, granted to the Apostles at the third hour, and worship all together in one accord ... We judge prayer to be necessary at the sixth hour in imitation of those holy ones who said: 'Evening and morning and at noon, I will speak and declare; and he shall hear my voice' (Ps 54.18). And so that we might be safe from misfortune and the midday demon, the ninetieth psalm is recited at this time. That we must pray at the ninth hour is related to us by the Apostles themselves in their Acts, where it says that Peter and John went up to the Temple 'at the hour of prayer, the ninth' (Acts 3.1). At day's end thanksgiving should be offered for those things given us in its course as well as those things done rightly, and confession should be made of any lapses, deliberate or inadvertent . . . And again as night begins, we must ask that our rest will be free from sin and evil phantasy; again the ninetieth psalm must be recited at this hour. For the middle of the night Paul and Silas have told us that prayer is necessary, as the account in their Acts narrates: 'But about midnight Paul and Silas were singing hymns to God' (Acts 16.25); and as the Psalmist says: 'In the middle of the night I arose to praise thee for the judgments of thy righteousness' (Ps 118.62). And finally it is necessary to anticipate the dawn and rise for prayer so that one is not caught by the day asleep in bed, according to the saying: 'My eyes have woken before daybreak, that I might meditate on thy words' (Ps 118.148).

Not one of these times is to be overlooked by those who have earnestly dedicated their lives to the glory of God and Christ himself. Moreover I think it useful to have diversity and variety in the prayer and psalmody at these appointed times, because somehow the soul is frequently bored and distracted by routine, while by change and variety of the psalmody and prayer at each hour its desire is renewed and its concentration restored.

138 Letter II, 2; *PG* XXXII, 225–8; *LCL* I, 12

> Basil, writing to Gregory of Nazianzus in about 358, recommends the attractions of his monastic retreat in Pontus.

What is more blessed than to imitate the chorus of angels here on earth; to arise for prayer at the very break of day and honor the Creator with hymns and songs; and then when the sun shines brightly to turn to our work, and, with prayer as an everpresent companion, to season our tasks with hymns, as if with salt? For the consolation of hymns favors the soul with a state of happiness and freedom from care.

139 Letter CCVII, 3; *PG* XXXII, 764; *LCL* III, 186–8

> Basil, in the year 375, answers the criticism of the Neocaesarean clergy against the psalmody practised by his monks at vigils. (That the term λαός refers to his monastic community rather than to lay people is clear from the context of the whole letter.) This important passage offers a rare description of dual-choir psalmody, commonly referred to as antiphonal psalmody, and a particularly clear description of responsorial psalmody. On the problem of antiphonal psalmody, see Hucke (1953, pp. 153–71) and Leeb (1967, pp. 18–23).

Concerning that complaint about psalmody, with which our accusers have intimidated the simpler souls especially, I have this to say: that our customs as now established are in full accord and harmony with all the churches of God. Among us the people (λαός) arise at night and go to the house of prayer; in pain, distress and anguished tears they make confession to God, and finally getting up from prayer they commence the singing of psalms. At first they divide themselves into two groups (διχῇ διανεμηθέντες) and sing psalms in alternation with each other (ἀντιψάλλουσιν ἀλλήλοις), at once intensifying their carefulness over the sacred texts, and focusing their attention and freeing their hearts from distraction. And then they entrust the lead of the chant (κατάρχειν τοῦ μέλους) to one person, while the rest sing in response. After thus spending the night in a variety of psalmody with interspersed prayer, now that the light of day has appeared, all in common as if from one mouth and one heart offer the psalm of confession to the Lord, while each fashions his personal words of repentance. Now if you shun us because of these practices, you will shun the Egyptians, you will shun the Libyans as well, and the Thebans, Palestinians, Arabians, Phoenicians, Syrians, and those who live by the Euphrates; and indeed all those among whom vigils, prayers and common psalmody are esteemed.

140 *Exhortation to Youths as to How They Shall Best Profit by the Writings of Pagan Authors* vii; *PG* xxxi, 581–4; *LCL* iv, 418

> Youths are reminded of the edifying uses of music among the ancients and warned against contemporary music.

The passions born of illiberality and baseness of spirit are naturally occasioned by this sort of music. But we must pursue that other kind, which is better and leads to the better, and which, as they say, was used by David, that author of sacred songs, to soothe the king in his madness. And it is said that Pythagoras, upon encountering some drunken revellers, commanded the aulete who was leading their song (κώμου) to change the mode (ἁρμονίαν) and to play the Dorian for them. They were so sobered by this music (μέλους) that tearing off their garlands they returned home ashamed. Others dance to the aulos in the manner of Corybantes and Bacchantes. Such is the difference in filling one's ears with wholesome or wicked tunes! And since the latter type now prevails, you must have less to do with it than with any utterly depraved thing.

141 *Homilia dicta tempore famis et siccitatis* iii; *PG* xxxi, 309

> Adults assist distractedly at prayer and psalmody, while young boys, freed from their studies, join in with gusto.

You men, with the exception of a few, devote yourselves to business; while you women serve them in the work of mammon. There are few left with me to pray, and they are faint and yawning, and they turn to one another constantly and watch for the psalmodist to finish the verses, when they shall be released, as if from prison, from church and the obligation to pray. Yet these boys, these little ones here, after stowing away their writing tablets at school, roar along with us, performing this task as if it were play and fun, making a holiday of our sadness, because they are free for a while from the oppression of the teacher and the mental exertion of being students.

142   *Homilia in ebriosos* i; *PG* XXXI, 445

> Women defile the martyrs' shrines by their unseemly behavior at the Easter vigil.

These licentious women . . . having cast the veils of modesty from their heads, showing contempt for God and for his angels, shamelessly in the sight of every man, shake their hair, as with wanton eye and excessive laughter they are driven madly to dance . . . they form a dancing troop in the martyrs' shrines before the city, making of those holy places a workshop of their characteristic indecency; they defile the air with their harlot's songs (ᾄσμασι πορνικοῖς), they defile the ground with their unclean feet.

143   Pseudo-Basil, *Commentary on Isaiah* v, 158; *PG* xxx, 376–80

> Recently some have advocated this work's authenticity, although most continue to deny it (Quasten, 1950–60, vol. III, pp. 218–19). The passage vividly associates the public lyre playing of a young woman with immorality. Note the place in Isaiah which inspires the observation. Note further the listing of useful and useless arts.

'Woe', it is written, 'unto them who drink wine to the accompaniment of cithara, aulos, tympanum and song' (Is 5.11–12). You place a lyre ornamented with gold and ivory upon a high pedestal as if it were a statue or devilish idol, and some miserable woman, rather than being taught to place her hands upon the spindle, is taught by you, bound as she is in servitude, to stretch them out upon the lyre. Perhaps you pay her wages or perhaps you turn her over to some female pimp, who after exhausting the licentious potential of her own body, presides over young women as the teacher of similar deeds. Because of her you will meet with a double punishment on the day of judgment, since you are yourself immoral, and since you have estranged this poor soul from God through evil teaching. So she stands at the lyre and lays her hands upon the strings, her arms bare and her expression impudent. The entire symposium is then transformed, as the eyes of all are focused upon her and the ears upon her strumming; the crowd noise dies down, as the laughter and the din of ribald talk are quieted. All in the house are silenced, charmed by the lascivious song. (While he who is silent here is not silent in the church of God, nor does he listen quietly to the words of the Gospel. Not surprisingly! For that enemy who enjoins quiet there, advocates a disturbance here.) What a sorry sight for sober eyes that a woman weaves not but rather plays the lyre . . . Now among the arts which are necessary to life, the goal of which is plain to see, there is carpentry and the chair, architecture and the house, ship building and the boat, weaving and the cloak, forging and the blade; among the useless arts are cithara playing, dancing (ὀρχηστικῆς), aulos playing and all others whose product disappears when the activity ceases.

Gregory of Nazianzus (c.329–389)

Born the son of the bishop of Nazianzus, also named Gregory, he was a close contemporary and associate of Basil. His schooling at both Caesarea and Athens coincided at least partially with the time Basil spent in each location, and later he joined him in his monastic retreat in Pontus. He lacked Basil's energy, however, and although he was a brilliant orator, his ecclesiastical career was checkered. He moved back and forth between retirement and brief periods of exercizing authority, most notably as successor to his father at Nazianzus and as bishop of Constantinople in 381. His writings provide us with a number of interesting references to psalmody as well as to pagan musical excess. They are quoted here in their order of appearance in orations, letters and poems.

144   Oration IV, *Contra Julianum* I, 70; *PG* XXXV, 589–92

> Among a long series of shameful pagan practices, Gregory lists the self-castration of Phrygian votaries inspired by aulos music. See also Gregory's *Carmina* II, II, vii (*Ad Nemesium*) 262, and Lucian, *De dea syria* 50.

You will not honor these things, but rather despise them . . . and those castrations which the Phrygians perform, bewitched at first by the aulos, and afterwards made arrogant . . .

145   Oration V, *Contra Julianum* II, 35; *PG* XXXV, 708–12

> In a passage contrasting pagan and Christian celebration, Gregory alludes to music. He closes with an intriguing remark on Christian dance. Its phrase 'and if you must dance' poses analogous problems of interpretation to CLEMENT OF ALEXANDRIA's 'and if you wish to sing and play to cithara and lyre' (Paedagogus II, iv).

First, brethren, let us celebrate the feast, not with carnal rejoicing, nor with extravagance and frequent changes of clothing, nor with carousing and drunkenness, nor surrounded by the sound of auloi and percussion (συναυλίαις καὶ κρότοις); for this is the manner of the monthly Grecian rites . . . Let us take up hymns rather than tympana, psalmody rather than shameful dances (λυγισμάτων) and songs, a well-rendered applause of thanksgiving rather than theatrical applause, meditation rather than debauchery. And if you must dance, as one who attends festivals and loves to celebrate, then dance; but not that dance of the shameful Herodias, which resulted in the death of the Baptist, but rather that of David as the Ark was being brought to its resting place, which I consider to be a sign of lithe and agile walking in God.

146   Oration VIII, *In laudem sororis suae Gorgoniae* 14; *PG* xxxv, 805

> Among a series of austerities practised by the nuns in question is lengthy
> nocturnal psalmody.

O sleepless nights, with the singing of psalms, and with standing which
lasts from one day to the next; O David, only for these faithful souls, have
you not sung (μελῳδήσας) too long!

147   Oration XL, *In sanctum baptisma* 46; *PG* xxxvi, 425

> A rare reference to psalmody at Baptism.

The place before the great sanctuary (βήματος), where you will stand after
Baptism, is a sign of future glory; the psalmody with which you will be
received is a foreshadowing of future hymnody.

148   Oration XLIII, *In laudem Basilii Magni* 52; *PG* xxxvi, 561

> The Emperor Valens is greatly impressed upon entering Basil's church at
> Caesarea.

He entered the temple with his entire retinue about him – it was the day of
the Epiphany, and there was a great crowd – and he took his place among
the people, thus making a profession of unity (which should not be lightly
dismissed). When he got inside, he was struck by the thunderous sound of
the psalmody; he saw the sea of people, and everywhere good order, more
angelic than human, both throughout the sanctuary (βῆμα) and all the
adjoining area.

149   Epistle CCXXXII, *Diocli*; *PG* xxxvii, 376; *GCS*, 166

> Proper decorum at Christian weddings excludes frivolous entertainment
> and music.

Among good things, one is the presence of Christ at weddings (for where
Christ is, there is good order), and the changing of water into wine, which
represents the changing of everything for the better, so that what cannot be
mixed is not combined or identified; neither bishops with jesters, nor
prayers with dancing (κρότους), nor psalmody with aulos-playing
(συναυλίας).

150   *Carmina* II, I, lxxxviii, *Ad suam animam carmen anacreonticum* 87–92;
         PG xxxvii, 1438

> Gregory addresses his soul and asks what it desires, giving a long series of
> luxuries among which music figures.

Do you desire the striking of hands upon barbitons and the way it excites?

Do you want the breaking voices (?, κλάσεις) of pretty boys moving effeminately?

And the indecent convolutions of naked maidens?

Gregory of Nyssa (c.330–c.395)

He was educated by his older brother Basil, and at an early age entered upon an ecclesiastical career, serving first as a lector in his native Caesarea. After a worldly interlude of a few years in which he taught rhetoric and married, he was persuaded to join Basil and Gregory of Nazianzus at Basil's monastic retreat in Pontus. In about 371 he was named bishop of Nyssa, an obscure town in his brother's metropolitan district of Caesarea. Although in his later years he appeared occasionally at Constantinople as a preacher or participant in councils, he had neither Basil's administrative skill nor Gregory's oratorical ability. He was, however, the deepest thinker and the most generally successful author of the three great Cappadocians. As for musical reference, he has less to contribute than most other major patristic figures, although there are a few noteworthy remarks in the popular biography of his sainted sister Macrina. Perhaps further material will be uncovered when his works are thoroughly indexed.

151   *Life of Macrina* 3; *PG* XLVI, 961–4; *SC* CLXXVIII, 150

> The child Macrina (one is reminded of Jerome's correspondence to Laeta concerning her daughter Paula) was educated with great scruple. She was shielded from the classics and led instead to Scripture, especially Proverbs and the Psalter. Her daily routine with the Psalter is clearly modelled after the typical monastic practice.

And by no means was she ignorant of the Book of Psalms (ψαλμῳδουμένης γραφῆς), completing each portion of psalmody at the appropriate times; and upon rising from her bed, when taking up her chores and leaving off from them, when beginning to eat and leaving the table, when going to bed and arising for prayers – everywhere she had with her the Psalter (ψαλμῳδίαν), like a good companion which one forsakes not for a moment.

152   *Life of Marcina* 33; *PG* XLVI, 992–3; *SC* CLXXVIII, 246–8

> Here Gregory tells of the singing at Macrina's funeral rites, when the assembled laity joined the psalmody of monks and nuns.

While we were involved in these activities, and as the psalmody of the virgins, mingled with lamentation, was heard about the place – the rumor of her death, I know not how, having circulated everywhere – all those who lived in the area gathered for the sad event, so that the forecourt was not adequate to house all those assembled. At day-break, when the hymnic vigil (παννυχίδος ἐν ὑμνῳδίαις) in her honor was completed after the manner of martyrs' celebrations, the crowd of men and women who had come together for the entire region, broke in on the psalmody with their loud wailing. But I, though my spirit was in so sorry a state because of my misfortune, contrived as much as possible from the circumstances that nothing befitting a funeral of this sort be omitted. So I separated the assembled people according to sex, and mixed the crowd of women with the choir of virgins and the male population with the band of monks, thus bringing it about that one coordinated (εὐρυθμόν) and harmonious psalmody resulted, like that of a practiced chorus (χοροστασίᾳ), blended from the graceful common song of all.

153   Anonymous, *De uirginitate* xx; *TU* xxix, 55–6

> This undated treatise, formerly attributed to Athanasius, is no longer considered by most to be his work; Taft (1984, pp. 150–3) identifies its liturgical content as Cappadocian. The passage quoted here describes the night and morning offices.

In the middle of the night arise and hymn the Lord your God, for at that hour our Lord arose from the dead and hymned the Father, for which reason he has enjoined us to hymn God at that hour. After rising say first this verse: 'I rose at midnight to give praise to thee: for the judgments of thy righteousness' (Ps 118.62) and pray, and begin to say the entire fiftieth psalm until you finish; and these things have been prescribed for you to carry out each day. Say as many psalms as you can while standing, and after a psalm pray and make a prostration, with tears acknowledging your sins to the Lord and asking that he forgive you. And with each three psalms say the Alleluia. And if there are virgins with you, let them also sing the psalms and perform the prayers one by one. At dawn say this psalm: 'O God my God, to thee do I watch at break of day: for thee my soul has thirsted' (Ps 62.2); and at daybreak: 'All ye works of the Lord, bless the Lord, sing hymns' (Dan 3.57); 'Glory to God in the highest' (Lk 2.14); and what follows.

CHAPTER 7

Palestine, Antioch and Syria

The authors of this chapter have in common only a rough geographic proximity; they are none the less among the most important of the period. Indeed John Chrysostom ranks first among all church fathers in the quantity of his musical reference. What he has to say, moreover, is at least comparable in interest to that of any of his contemporaries. The significance of Ephraem is of an altogether different sort: writing in Syriac rather than Greek or Latin, his importance lies in his singularity. The typical patristic polemical reflex seems absent from his works and the hackneyed allegorizing as well; in their place is a rich and original musical imagery that tempts one to think his attitudes toward practical music might be more friendly than those of his Greek and Latin colleagues.

Cyril of Jerusalem (c.315–386)

Cyril was appointed bishop of Jerusalem in about 349 and held the position until his death, although banished a number of times by his Arian superiors. The principal work attributed to him is a set of twenty-four catechetical lectures, rich in liturgical allusion. There is an opening lecture, the *Procatechesis*, and eighteen subsequent lectures, the *catecheses* proper, delivered in Lent of c.350 to the catechumens at Jerusalem who were to be baptized on Holy Saturday. These are followed by five lectures, the *Mystagogical Catecheses*, addressed to the newly baptized during Easter week. There has, however, been considerable doubt since the sixteenth century about the authenticity of the *Mystagogical Catecheses*, and in recent decades several scholars, indeed those most closely associated with Cyril's work, have argued that manuscript evidence, style and liturgical content make it likely that they were written toward the end of the century by Cyril's successor, John, bishop from 387 to 417. Still, many remain satisfied with the traditional attribution (see *SC* CXXVI, pp. 18–40, for a summary of the controversy). The issue has musical significance since it affects the date of key references to both the Sanctus and the communion psalm.

154   *Procatechesis* xiv; *PG* XXXIII, 356

> As they await the rite of exorcism, the men and the women catechumens are strictly separated and engage in the following activities.

The men, then, ought to sit and occupy themselves with some useful book: let one read and another listen. If there is no book, let one pray and another say something of benefit. The assembly of virgins, however, should be gathered together, quietly reciting psalms or reading, so that their lips move, but the ears of others do not hear – 'For I do not permit that a woman speak in the Church' (1 Cor 14.34). And the married woman should do likewise: she should pray and move her lips, while not allowing her voice to be heard.

155   *Procatechesis* xv; *PG* xxxiii, 360

It is suggested that Psalm 31 was sung at Baptism.

Even now let there ring in your ears that sweet sound which you desire to hear the angels sing (ἐπιφωνήσουσι) after you have been saved: 'Blessed are they whose iniquities are taken away and whose sins are covered' (Ps 31.1), when you enter in, as if stars of the Church, shining in body and luminous in soul.

156   *Catechesis* xiii, 26; *PG* xxiii, 804–5

There is some confusion in the secondary literature about this passage. It is, for example, cited as the earliest extant use of the Greek term for cantor, ψάλτης; whereas the term appears only in the Latin translation of *PG*, not in the original, which has the more general ψαλμῳδός.

They divide the cloak and cast lots for the tunic. Is this not also written? The Zealous singers (ψαλμῳδοί) of the church know, who imitate the angelic hosts and hymn God at all times; they are found worthy to sing on this Golgotha and say: 'They parted my garments among them, and for my clothing they cast lots' (Ps 21.9, quoted in Jn 19.24).

157   *Mystagogical Catechesis* v, 6; *PG* xxxiii, 1113; *SC* cxxvi, 154

The faithful sing the Sanctus in the Eucharist as do the Seraphim in heaven.

We call to mind the Seraphim also, whom Isaiah saw in the Holy Spirit, present in a circle about the throne of God, covering their faces with two wings, their feet with two, and flying with two, and saying: 'Holy, holy, holy is the Lord of hosts' (Is 6.3). Therefore we recite this doxology transmitted to us by the Seraphim, in order to become participants in the hymnody of the super terrestrial hosts.

158   *Mystagogical Catechesis* v, 20; *PG* xxxiii, 1124; *SC* cxxvi, 168–70

If the *Mystagogical Catecheses* are genuine, this is the earliest extant reference to psalmody at the distribution of communion. Note also that it cites Psalm 33.9.

After these things, listen to the singer (ψάλλοντος), who invites us with a sacred melody to communion in the holy mysteries, and says: 'Taste and see that the Lord is good' (Ps 33.9).

Diodore of Tarsus (d. c.390)

Although he was condemned as a Nestorian about a century after his death, Diodore was a champion of orthodoxy during the years he spent as a teacher and monastic superior in his native Antioch. He vigorously opposed the Arian authorities and the Emperor Julian as well. He was a central figure in establishing the Antiochene exegetical method, which insists upon a literal and historical reading of the Bible at the expense of the more generally favored allegorical method of the Alexandrian school. Among his students were John Chrysostom and Theodore of Mopsuestia. In 378 he became bishop of Tarsus, where, apparently, he lived out the remainder of his life.

159 *In psalmum xxxii*, 1–2; *CCG* VI, 186–7

> Only in recent years has this commentary been established as the work of Diodore. It may be the earliest extant Antiochene commentary on the psalms and hence important for our subject as a forerunner of the commentaries of John Chrysostom and Theodoret of Cyrus. The excerpt given here is typical in its terse, matter of fact, historical approach; the 'marvellous event' it refers to is a victory over the Assyrians. (See Bibliography, Texts, under *Devreese* for a related commentary, not quoted here, that of Theodore of Mopsuestia.)

'Rejoice, ye just, in the Lord; praise befits the upright' (Ps 32.1). He calls the Israelites 'just' in comparison with the Assyrians and similarly he calls them 'upright'. Thus he encouraged them to hymn God after the marvellous event which happened to them.

'Praise the Lord upon the cithara, sing to him on the psaltery of ten strings' (Ps 32.2). Having said above that it is necessary for them to hymn God, he adds then that they must do this with instruments.

Epiphanius of Salamis (c.315–403)

Born near Gaza in Palestine, Epiphanius became interested in the monastic movement at an early age; he visited the most famous Egyptian settlements and in about 335 established a community of his own near his birthplace, over which he presided for some thirty years. In 367 the bishops of Cyprus, attracted by his zeal and learning, elected him to their metropolitan seat of Salamis. Epiphanius is best known as an intransigent foe of Origenism and the allegorical method. His chief work is the *Panarion* (medicine chest), purporting to offer a remedy for some eighty heresies, which are described in detail. (For an incident with musical significance from Epiphanius's monastic career, see APOPHTHEGMATA PATRUM, Epiphanius 3.)

160   *Panarion* xxv, 4; *PG* XLI, 325–8; *GCS* I, 272

> The aulos resembles the devil in the form of a serpent.

In fact the aulos itself is an imitation of the serpent through which the Evil One spoke and tricked Eve. For it was in imitation of that type that the aulos was made, for the purpose of deceiving mankind. And observe the type, which he who plays the aulos represents upon the instrument. For the player throws his head back, then bows forward; he inclines to the right, then similarly to the left. Now the devil has used the same gestures in order to flaunt blasphemously at the inhabitants of heaven, and to bring utter destruction to things on earth, at once encompassing the entire world, causing ruin right and left to those persuaded and charmed by his treachery, as if by the deceptive tones of a musical instrument.

161   *Panarion* li, 22; *GCS* II, 285–6

> The nightly rites described here took place in the temple of Core at Alexandria.

They remain awake the entire night celebrating the idol in song and with aulos playing, and at the cockcrow, their vigil completed, they descend with lamps in hand to a certain underground shrine, and they bring up a naked wooden image which sits upon a litter and has a kind of cruciform gold signet upon its forehead, and on each hand another such signet, and on the two knees another two – in all, five signets fashioned from gold. And they carry the image about, encircling the innermost temple seven times, amid the sound of auloi, tympana and hymns; and after their revelry they carry it down again to the subterranean place. When asked 'What is this mystery', they reply: 'Today at this hour Core, that is the virgin, has begotten the Aion'.

John Chrysostom (c.347–407)

Perhaps the greatest preacher of Christian antiquity, hence the sobriquet 'golden mouth', John Chrysostom was born to a wealthy Christian family at Antioch and thoroughly educated in rhetoric. Having felt drawn to the monastic life from an early age, he finally left home in 373 to become a hermit, and while in solitude practised such austerity that his health was permanently damaged. After returning to Antioch in 381 he was ordained a deacon and then in 386 a priest by Bishop Flavian, who charged him with preaching in the principal church of the city. He did so with great success for more than a decade, and it is to this period that the bulk of his exegetical homilies dates. In 398 he was persuaded to accept consecration as the Patriarch of Constantinople, an event which proved a sad turning point in his life. His personal holiness and outspoken moralism were a reproach to both clergy and court, and in 404 he was exiled to Cucusus in Armenia, not far from Antioch. Here eventually the people of Antioch flocked to their former spiritual guide so that in 407 the Emperor

Arcadius, at the urging of jealous factions in Antioch, had him sent to a remote spot on the Black Sea. The saint died from the rigors of the journey.

The vivid anecdotal style of his preaching along with the sheer quantity of it assures us of a wealth of interesting references to music, both in the context of the liturgy and of everyday life. Indeed this makes it necessary to be more selective with him than with most other authors represented in this volume, and therefore it seems appropriate to add at the end of this section a paragraph of citations to passages of lesser interest perhaps – yet comparable – to those quoted. For exhaustive citation of references to liturgical chant, as well as extended discussion, see Paverd (1970) and Kaczynski (1974).

The material presented here appears in the following order: first references from the homilies on the psalms, then from the other exegetical homilies, and finally the remaining works – all homilies themselves – in alphabetical order.

162   *In psalmum vii*, 15; *PG* LV, 104

> Just as God did not need the sacrifices of the Jews, he does not need the hymns of Christians.

Just as he accepted sacrifices while not needing sacrifices – 'If I were hungry,' he says, 'I would not tell you' (Ps 49.12) – but rather to lead men to honor him, so too does he accept hymns while not needing our praise, but rather because he desires our salvation.

163   *In psalmum xli*, 1; *PG* LV, 155

> The first two capitula of the commentary to Psalm 41 contain Chrysostom's often quoted encomium of psalmody. Before launching into it he reveals that the first verse of the psalm was used that day as a response. The phrase 'into the middle' is obscure in meaning; perhaps it is meant to evoke the topos of David in the midst of his four companion musicians (see, for example, EUSEBIUS, *In psalmos*).

As I said, then, when the wolves attack the flock, the shepherds set aside the pipe (σύριγγα) and take the sling in hand. So now, with the Jewish festivals at an end, we who are bitter enemies of all wolves should in turn set the sling aside and return to the pipe. Further, let us desist from contentious discourse and engage in other, more truthful things, taking in hand the cithara of David, and leading into the middle (εἰς μέσον) the refrain which we all sang today in response. What is this refrain, then? 'As the hart longs for flowing streams, so longs my soul for thee, O God' (Ps 41.1).

164   *In psalmum xli*, 1; *PG* LV, 156

> This is perhaps the richest and most eloquent of the patristic encomiums of psalmody. It is translated in its entirety in *Strunk*; here five of the more apposite passages are given. The first enunciates the commonplace that in the psalms God made Scripture more accessible by joining it to music (for

the same thought see *In psalmum cxxxiv*, 1; *In Colossenses*, Cap. III, Hom. IX, 2
and BASIL, *In psalmum i*, 1).

When God saw that the majority of men were slothful, and that they
approached spiritual reading with reluctance and submitted to the effort
involved without pleasure – wishing to make the task more agreeable and to
relieve the sense of laboriousness – he mixed melody with prophecy, so that
enticed by the rhythm and melody, all might raise sacred hymns to him with
great eagerness. For nothing so arouses the soul, gives it wing, sets it free
from the earth, releases it from the prison of the body, teaches it to love wisdom, and to condemn all the things of this life, as concordant melody and
sacred song composed in rhythm.

165   *In psalmum xli*, 1; *PG* LV, 157

> After citing the many occasions in which song is employed in everyday life,
> Chrysostom warns that the singing of psalms is necessary to crowd out the
> singing of immoral songs.

Since this sort of pleasure is natural to our soul, and lest the demons introduce licentious songs and upset everything, God erected the barrier of the
psalms, so that they would be a matter of both pleasure and profit. For from
strange songs, harm and destruction enter in along with many a dread
thing, since what is wanton and contrary to the law in these songs settles in
the various parts of the soul, rendering it weak and soft. But from the
spiritual psalms can come considerable pleasure, much that is useful, much
that is holy, and the foundation of all philosophy, as these texts cleanse the
soul and the Holy Spirit flies swiftly to the soul who sings such songs.

166   *In psalmum xli*, 2; *PG* LV, 157

> The occasion at which one especially needs protection from licentious
> song is mealtimes.

I say these things, not so that you alone sing praise, but so that you teach
your children and wives also to sing such songs, not only while weaving or
while engaged in other tasks, but especially at table. For since the devil
generally lies in wait at banquets, having as his allies drunkenness and
gluttony, along with inordinate laughter and an unbridled spirit, it is
necessary especially then, both before and after the meal, to construct a
defense against him from the psalms, and to arise from the banquet
together with wife and children to sing sacred hymns to God.

167   *In psalmum xli*, 2; *PG* LV, 158

> Again one notes the emphasis upon domestic, specifically mealtime,
> psalmody here with only an indirect reference to church. The beginning of
> the passage, incidentally, has a quasi-liturgical character.

And let us stand together and say: 'Thou has made us glad, Lord, in thy work, and in the works of thy hands we will rejoice' (Ps 91.5). And after the psalmody prayer is to be offered, so that we might also sanctify the house itself along with the soul. Just as those who introduce actors, dancers and prostitutes into banquets, also summon there demons and the devil, and fill their homes with every manner of discord – instances of jealousy, adultery, fornication and numerous other dread things – so those who call upon David with his cithara, call upon Christ inwardly through him. Where Christ is, no demon would dare enter, indeed none would even dare peep in there; rather would peace, love, and all good things flow as from fountains. Those others make a theatre of their house; you must make a church of your home. For where there is a psalm, prayer, the dance (χορεία) of prophets, and a pious attitude among the singers, one would not err in calling such a gathering a church.

168   *In psalmum xli*, 2; *PG* LV, 158

> There follow some thoughts on the proper disposition of the Christian singer of psalms. The 'rough voice' (δασύφονος) of this passage might remind one of the '*kakophonos*' of JEROME, *in epistolam ad Eph.* III, v, 19.

And even if you do not understand the meaning of the words, for the time being teach your mouth to say them, for the tongue is sanctified by the words alone whenever it says them with good will. Once we have become confirmed in this custom, we will not neglect this congenial duty (λειτουργίαν) either deliberately or through indifference, as custom will compel us to fulfill this grateful service (λατρείαν) every day, even if unwilling. Nor will any complaint concerning this singing arise, even if one has grown old, is still a child, has a rough voice, or is altogether ignorant of rhythm. This is because what is sought here is a sober soul, an alert mind, a contrite heart, sound reason and a clear conscience. If having these, you enter into the holy choir of God, you will be able to stand beside David yourself.

169   *In psalmum xli*, 2; *PG* LV, 158

> Chrysostom gives a particularly clear example of instrumental allegory.

Here there is no need of the cithara, nor taut strings, nor the plectrum and technique, nor any sort of instrument; but if you wish, make of yourself a cithara, by mortifying the limbs of the flesh and creating full harmony between body and soul. For when the flesh does not lust against the spirit, but yields to its commands, and perseveres along the path that is noble and admirable, you thus produce a spiritual melody

170   *In psalmum cxvii*, 1; *PG* LV, 328

> The people sing '*Haec dies*' as a response, perhaps to the Easter gradual psalm.

The passage of the psalm which the people are accustomed to sing in response (ὑποψάλλειν) is this: 'This is the day which the Lord has made, let us rejoice in it and be glad' (Ps 117. 24). It arouses many, and the people are especially accustomed to respond (ὑπηχεῖν) with it at that spiritual assembly and heavenly banquet. We however, if you will, shall pursue the entire psalm from the beginning, not from the verse of the response (ὑπηχήσεως), making our commentary from the very introduction. Now the fathers ruled that the multitude sing this verse in response (στίχον . . . ὑπηχεῖν), since it is sonorous and contains sublime doctrine, and because they do not know the whole psalm, in order to receive perfect teaching from it.

171   *In psalmum cxl*, 1; *PG* LV, 426–7

> In a passage which argues that the sense of the psalms is the important consideration, it is revealed that Psalm 140 is sung every evening, possibly by heart, and that an analogous situation exists for Psalm 62 in the morning.

Virtually all know the words of this psalm and they continue to sing it at every age, without knowing, however, the sense of what has been said. This is not a small charge, to sing something every day, putting forth words from the mouth, without searching out the meaning of the thoughts residing in the words . . . But pay strict attention. I do not think simply that the fathers assigned this psalm to be read every evening because of the one expression that says: 'The lifting of my hands as an evening sacrifice' (Ps 140.2). This is because there are other psalms which have the same expression, as that which reads: 'Evening, morning and noon I describe and announce' (Ps 54.18) . . . And so is it with the morning psalm . . . 'O God, my God, I awake to thee; my soul thirsts after thee' (Ps 62.1).

172   *In psalmum cxliv*, 1; *PG* LV, 464

> It would appear from this passage that Psalm 144.5 was sung as a response during Communion at Antioch.

It is worth paying special attention to this psalm. For this is the psalm containing the words that initiates into the mysteries continuously sing in response, saying: 'The eyes of all look to thee, and thou givest them their food in due season' (Ps 144.15).

173 *In psalmum cxlix*, 2; *PG* LV,. 494

> John first cites the conventional instrumental allegories, but then, as a representative of the Antiochene school of exegesis, offers an historical explanation. Just as God allowed the Jews to sacrifice he permitted them the use of instruments as a concession to their weakness. This view, in addition to its musical significance, raises the question of John's attitude toward Jews: on that see Wilken (1983).

Some also take the meaning of these instruments allegorically and say that the tympanum calls for the death of the flesh and that the psaltery looks to heaven. And indeed this instrument is moved from above, not from below like the cithara. But I would say this: that in ancient times, they were thus led by these instruments due to the slowness of their understanding, and were gradually drawn away from idolatry. Accordingly, just as he allowed sacrifices, so too did he permit instruments, making concession to their weakness.

174 *In psalmum cl*; *PG* LV, 497–8

> The argument of the previous passage is taken up again.

He allowed those instruments, then, for this reason: because of their weakness, and because he wanted to temper them in love and harmony, to raise their understanding through enjoyment to do what accrues to their benefit, and to lead them to great zeal through enticement of this sort. For knowing their thoughtlessness, laziness and carelessness, God wished to arouse them by this stratagem, blending the sweetness of melody in with the effort of paying attention.

175 *Homilia habita in magnum hebdomadam* 2; *PG* LV, 520–1

> In a homily prepared for Palm Sunday, Chrysostom says that Psalm 145.2 was sung as a response on that day. One might go so far as to say that in passages like this we have an incipient Proper of the Mass.

They went out at that time holding palm branches, and they cried out and said: 'Hosanna in the highest! Blessed is he who comes in the name of the Lord' (Mt 21.9). Let us also go out, and displaying in place of palm branches blossoming good intentions, let us cry out as we sang today in response: 'Praise the Lord, O my soul! I will praise the Lord as long as I live' (Ps 145.2) . . . But let us see what he says. 'Praise the Lord, O my soul!' Let us also sing these words today along with David.

176 *In caput XXIX Genesim*, Hom. LVI, 1; *PG* LIV, 486

> In commenting on the wedding of Jacob and Leah, John cites the lascivious wedding music of his time. See also Hom. XLVIII, 6 on the wedding of Isaac

and Rebecca and *In illud propter fornicationes uxorem* 2 for similar passages not quoted in this volume.

Do you not see with what dignity weddings were celebrated in antiquity? Hear this, you who flutter after Satan's pomp and who from the very start dishonor the nuptial solemnities. Were there auloi there? Were there cymbals, or diabolical dances? For what reason, tell me, do you straightway bring such shame into your house, and summon people from the stage and orchestra pit, so that with extravagant expense you spoil the modesty of the maiden and make the groom more wanton.

177   *In Isaiam* v, 5; *PG* LVI, 62

> In commenting upon Isaiah 5.11–12, which excoriates drunken feasting, John cites a similar passage, Amos 6.5–6, and then goes on to remark:

This is a sign of ultimate insensibility and a dissolute soul, to make a theater of one's own house and to give oneself up to such songs. And what drunkenness accomplishes by obscuring, the same does music as it slackens the taughtness of the mind, enfeebles the vigor of the spirit, and leads it to greater licentiousness.

178   *In Matthaeum*, Hom. XI, 7; *PG* LVII, 200

> The responsorial singing of two or three psalms at a church service, possibly the Eucharist, is mentioned.

For we would establish as your teachers in each church the prophets, apostles, patriarchs and all righteous men. Yet nothing more is accomplished by this. Rather, when you are dismissed, after singing the response to two or three psalms and saying the accustomed prayers superficially and in an indifferent manner, you consider this to be enough for your salvation.

179   *In Matthaeum*, Hom. XXXI, 2; *PG* LVII, 373

> In commenting on Matthew 9.23–4, John notes with sarcasm the use of instruments at a wake.

'And when Jesus came to the ruler's house, and saw the aulos players, and the crowd making a tumult, he said, "Depart; for the girl is not dead but sleeping". And they laughed at him' (Mt 9.23–4). Noble tokens, these, of the rulers of the synagogue – auloi and cymbals raising a dirge in the hour of her death.

180 *In Matthaeum*, Hom. LXVIII, 3; *PG* LVIII, 644

> The 'Gloria in excelsis' is mentioned as part of the morning monastic office. The passage continues at some length beyond the portion quoted here, eventually comparing the monastic psalmody with the lurid music of secular society. The entire passage should be compared with *In I Timotheum*, Hom. XIV, 3–4, quoted below.

These that are the light of the world, when the sun is up, or rather long before its appearance, rise from bed, healthy, alert and sober . . . arising, then, straightway from their beds, radiant and cheerful, they form one choir, and all together in unison (συμφώνως) and with clear conscience, they sing, as if from one mouth, hymns to the God of all, honoring him and giving him thanks for every benefit, whether individual or common. So, if it seems proper . . . we will ask what is the difference between a choir of angels and this choir of men on earth singing the words, 'Glory to God in the highest, and on earth peace, good will among men' (Lk 2.14).

181 *Homilia nova in Matthaeum* IX, 37; *PG* LXIII, 519

> John mentions a series of four scriptural passages, including a psalm, which was heard, presumably, at a pre-Eucharistic synaxis, and decides to base his homily on the last, that from the Gospel of St Matthew. This is the sort of passage liturgical historians adduce to demonstrate that psalms were sung between the lessons, the so-called *Zwischenpsalmodie* (Paverd, 1970, pp. 438–40), but actually the passage seems more to treat the psalm as a scriptural equal.

Just as there are various flowers in the meadow and, since all in a row are exceedingly lovely, each draws the eye of the beholder to look upon them, so too can one view the Holy Scriptures. For blessed David attracts our understanding to himself, so too the apostolic passage concerning Timothy which was read, and further the bold Isaiah philosophizing on human nature, and their Lord Jesus, speaking to the disciples and saying, 'The harvest is plentiful, but the laborers are few' (Mt 9.37). Come then, if we may, let us concentrate upon this verse and explain its sense.

182 *In Acta Apostolorum*, Hom. XLII, 3; *PG* LX, 301

> Another of John's several passages railing against the musical abuses at marriages.

It is not the marriage of which I speak – one would hope not – but what accompanies it. Nature indulges in Bacchic frenzy then, those present become brutes rather than men; they neigh like horses and kick like asses. There is much dissipation, much dissolution, but nothing earnest, nothing high-minded; there is much pomp of the devil here – cymbals, auloi and songs full of fornication and adultery.

183   *In I Corinthios*, Hom. XII, 5; *PG* LXI, 103

> This passage makes the same point as the preceding; it is exceptional,
> however, in the vehemence of its language. The theme is taken up again
> later in the same homily.

For marriage appears to be an honorable thing, both to us and to those without it; and it is indeed honorable. But when weddings are performed, there
take place the sort of absurd practices of which you will now hear. For the
majority are bound and misled by custom, since they do not discern the
unnaturalness of these things, but instead require others to teach them. For
then they introduce dancing, cymbals, auloi, shameful words and songs,
drunkenness and carousing, and much such rubbish of the devil.

184   *In I Corinthios*, Hom. XXXVI, 5–6; *PG* LXI, 313–15

> John contrasts the decorum of the primitive church with the unruliness of
> his own time. Eventually he describes properly conducted pre-Eucharistic
> synaxis, with a particularly clear reference to responsorial psalmody.

All came together in earlier times and sang psalms in common. We do this
now also, but then there was but one heart and soul among all, while now
one could not see such unity even in a single spirit, but much dispute on
every side . . . Then the houses themselves were churches, while now the
church is a house, or rather worse than any house. For in a house one might
see considerable good order since the mistress of the house is seated on her
chair with total propriety, the handmaidens weave in silence, and each of
the servants has his appointed task in hand. Here, however, there is much
noise, much confusion, nothing to distinguish our assemblies from a tavern;
there is such laughter, such disorder, as when all cry out and clamor in the
baths and the market places . . . And indeed there must always be but one
voice in the church, as there is but one body. Thus the reader alone speaks,
and he who holds the episcopacy sits and maintains silence, and the singer
(ψάλλων) sings psalms alone, and, while all respond (ὑπηχῶσιν), the sound
issues as if from one mouth, and only he preaches who gives the homily.

185   *In Colossenses*, Hom. I, 5; *PG* LXII, 306

> At one point in a long passage contrasting the table of the dissolute rich
> with that of the devout poor, music is mentioned.

There, indeed, are auloi, citharas and syrinxes, but here no discordant
melody. What then? Hymns and psalmody. There the demons are hymned,
but here God, the ruler of all. Do you see with what gratitude this table
abounds, and with what thoughtlessness and insensibility that? Tell me
now, when God has nourished you with his good things, and when after eat-
ing you ought to give thanks to him, do you introduce demons? For these
songs accompanied by the pektis are nothing else but those of demons.

186   *In Colossenses*, Hom. IX, 2; *PG* LXII, 362–3

> In commenting upon Colossians 3.16, John invokes a number of standard
> patristic themes. The last given here, the exegetical distinction between
> psalms and hymns, actually two categories of Davidic psalm, tends to con-
> fuse modern commentators.

'Teach', he says, 'and admonish one another with psalms, with hymns and
spiritual songs' (Col 3.16). Observe also the considerateness of Paul. Since
reading is laborious and very tiring, he did not lead you to histories but to
psalms, so that you could by singing both delight your spirit and lighten the
burden. 'With hymns', he says, 'and spiritual songs'. Now your children
choose satanical songs and dances, as if they were cooks, caterers and
chorus dancers (χορευταί); while no one knows a single psalm, which seems
rather to be a thing of shame even, to be laughed at and ridiculed . . . The
psalms contain all things, but hymns in turn have nothing human. When
one is instructed in the psalms, he will then know hymns also, as a more
divine thing. For the powers above sing hymns, they do not sing psalms.

187   *In I Timotheum*, Hom. XIV, 3–4; *PG* LXII, 575–6

> Three key excerpts are given here from an important passage in the history
> of the early monastic office. The first describes the rising of the monks for
> the night office and contrasts their singing with musical instruments. For
> discussion of the passage, see Mateos (1963).

It is daybreak, or rather the cock has crowed before daybreak. And it is not
as in a house, with the servants snoring, the doors shut, and everyone sleeping like the dead, while the mule driver rings his bells. There is nothing like
that here, rather straightway, as the prefect arouses them, all stand forming
a sacred choir, and at once extending their hands they sing the sacred
hymns . . . As soon as they are up, they immediately stand and sing the
prophetic hymns with great harmony, and well ordered (εὐρύφμων)
melody. Neither cithara, nor syrinx, nor any other musical instrument
emits such sound as is to be heard in the deep silence and solitude of those
holy men as they sing.

188   *In I Timotheum*, Hom. XIV, 4; *PG* LXII, 576

> The second excerpt suggests the actual content of the night office. Given
> here are only the beginning and end of a long series of psalm verses; inter-
> vening are Psalms 8.5; 143.4; 48.17; 67.7; 118.164; 118.62; 48.16; 22.4;
> 90.5–6; and 43.22.

And these songs themselves are appropriate and full of love for God. 'In the
nights', he says, 'lift up your hands to God' (Ps 133.2). And again, 'My spirit
rises up early to thee from the night, O God, so that the light of thy commandments will be upon the earth' (Is 26.9). And the songs of David cause

great fountains of tears, whenever he sings these words, 'I am weary with my moaning; every night I flood my bed with tears, I drench my couch with weeping' (Ps 6.7). And again, 'Because I have eaten ashes like bread' (Ps 101.10 . . . Again when they sing with the angels (for the angels also sing at that time), saying, 'Praise the Lord from the heavens' (Ps 148.1); as we are yawning, scratching, snoring, or else just flat on our backs, planning myriad empty schemes. What a thing it is for them to spend the entire night in this manner.

189   *In I Timotheum*, Hom. XIV, 4; *PG* LXII, 576–7

> The third excerpt cites six additional times for prayer and psalmody so that all told only prime is omitted.

When the day is about to begin, they finally leave off from their activity, and as we begin our tasks, they have a period of rest . . . Again after they have completed their morning prayers and hymns, they turn to the reading of the Scriptures (while some have also been educated in the copying of books). Each occupies a single allotted cell, he practises silence throughout, no one speaks frivolously, no one says anything at all. Then they observe the third, the sixth, the ninth hours, and the evening prayers, dividing the day into four parts, with each part filled, as they honor God with psalmody and hymns. So while all others are lunching, laughing, playing, and bursting from gluttony, they are patiently occupied with their hymns. Then after sitting for a short while, or rather concluding everything with hymns, each goes to bed upon a straw pallet made up for rest only, not luxury.

190   *In Hebraeos*, Hom. IV, 5; *PG* LXIII, 43

> In criticizing wailing at Christian funerals, John cites specific psalms sung there. (See also *De sanctis Bernice et Prosdoce* 3, quoted below.)

Why do we have hymns? Do we not glorify God and give him thanks that he has at last crowned the departed, that he has freed him from his burdens, and with fear cast aside taken him to himself? Is not this why there are hymns? Is not this why there is psalmody? All these are the acts of those who rejoice. 'For is anyone cheerful', it says, 'then let him sing psalms' (Jas 4.13) . . . Know what it is that you sing on that occasion. 'Return, O my soul, to your rest; for the Lord has dealt bountifully with you' (Ps 115.17). And again, 'I will fear no evil, for thou art with me' (Ps 22.4). And again, 'Thou art my refuge from the trouble which has encompassed me' (Ps 31.7). You should consider what these psalms mean, but you pay no attention; instead you are intoxicated with your grief.

191   *In Hebraeos*, Hom. xv, 4; *PG* LXIII, 122

> In the course of a passage condemning excessive laughter John indicates
> that Psalm 6 is sung everyday.

Do you not hear Christ saying, 'Woe to those who laugh, for they shall weep'
(Lk 6.25)? You sing these things everyday. What is it that you say? Tell me.
That you laughed? By no means. What then? 'I labored in my groaning'
(Ps 6.7).

192   *De sanctis Bernice et Prosdoce* 3; *PG* L, 634

> Psalms are sung at Christian funerals as a sign of joy.

Hence in the beginning there was wailing and lamentation over the dead,
but now there are psalms and hymnody. The Jews, in any case, mourned
Jacob for forty days and Moses for a similar number; they grieved because
death at that time was death indeed. Now, however, it is not so; rather, there
is hymnody, prayer and psalms, as all reveal that there is an element of
pleasure in the matter. For psalms are a sign of good cheer; as it is written,
'Is anyone among you cheerful? Let him sing psalms' (Jas 5.13).

193   *Homilia I in Oziam seu de Seraphinis* 1; *PG* lvi, 97

> This comparison of angelic and human choirs suggests that both Gloria
> and Sanctus form part of the earthly liturgy.

Above, the hosts of angels sing praise; below, men form choirs in the
churches and imitate them by singing the same doxology. Above, the
Seraphim cry out in the Tersanctus (τρισάγιον ὕμνον); below, the human
throng sends up the same cry. The inhabitants of heaven and earth are
brought together in a common solemn assembly; there is one thanksgiving,
one shout of delight, one joyful chorus.

194   *Homilia II dicta postquam reliquiae martyrum* 3; *PG* LXIII, 472

> The empress Eudoxia, leading a procession of relics in which psalms are
> sung in many languages, is compared to Miriam (Ex 15.20–1).

Miriam led the people then, carrying the bones of Joseph and singing a
song. Now, she did this after the Egyptians had been immersed in the sea,
while you acted as the demons were being suffocated; she after Pharoah had
been drowned, you after the devil had been toppled; she holding cymbals,
you with the mind and spirit sounding over the trumpet; she after the Jews
had been freed, you while the church was being crowned; she after leading
out one people of uniform tongue, you with many people of diverse tongues.
Indeed you have led out many choirs from among us, those of the Roman

tongue, of the Syrian, of the barbarians, and of the Greek, striking up the songs of David.

195   Pseudo-Chrysostom, *De poenitentia*; *PG* LXIV, 12–13

> Since the time of Gerbert (1774, vol. 2, p. 64) this attractive passage has been widely quoted, curiously without reference to its spuriousness which is clearly indicated in the editions.

In the churches there are vigils, and David is first and middle and last. In the singing of early morning hymns David is first and middle and last. In the tents at funeral processions David is first and last. In the houses of virgins there is weaving, and David is first and middle and last. What a thing of wonder! Many who have not even made their first attempt at reading know all of David by heart and recite him in order (ἀποστιχίζουσιν). Yet it is not only in the cities and the churches that he is so prominent on every occasion and with people of all ages; even in the fields and deserts and stretching into uninhabited wasteland, he rouses sacred choirs to God with greater zeal. In the monasteries there is a holy chorus of angelic hosts, and David is first and middle and last. In the convents there are bands of virgins who imitate Mary, and David is first and middle and last. In the deserts men crucified to this world hold converse with God, and David is first and middle and last. And at night all men are dominated by physical sleep and drawn into the depths, and David alone stands by, arousing all the servants of God to angelic vigils, turning earth into heaven and making angels of men.

> Additional references: *In psalmum viii*, 1; *In Mattheum*, Hom. II, 10; *In I Corinthios*, Hom.xxxv, 3; *In I Corinthios*, Hom. xxxvi, 4; *In Colossenses*, Hom. XII, 5; *In Ephesios*, Hom. xix, 2; *Ad populum Antiochenum*, Hom. xv, 1; *Contra ludos et theatra* 2; *Laudatio sancti martyris Juliani* 4; *Sermo post reditum a priore exilio* 1.

Nilus of Ancyra (d. c.430)

Nilus, a disciple of John Chrysostom, spent several decades as abbot of a monastery near Ancyra, present-day Ankara. He mentions psalmody on a number of occasions, usually as a prominent item within a series of practices and virtues which define the monastic ideal. (For additional references see Epistles II, 77, 140, 161 and III, 125, 127.)

196   Epistle, III, 126, to Philagrius, bishop; *PG* LXXIX, 441–4

> The monastic ideal is recommended to a bishop acquaintance.

Mortify for me, I beseech you, the limbs of your body; subjugate everything, if possible, to the spirit. Do not shrink from walking upon that narrow way which is passable to but few. Be humble yet uplifted, mortal yet immortal, of this earth yet of heaven, an heir of God and a joint heir with Christ. Let there be continuous prayer, psalmody that is pleasant, grave and harmonious, attentiveness to the divine sayings, a deep bending of withered knees, and wakefulness of soul, and of body too, while tears wipe away, as it were, the dirt which penetrates through the senses; let there be succor for the oppressed, and solicitude, nourishment, clothing and drink for the needy. If these and things like them inhere in you, and grow each day and increase, they will show you to be neither slothful nor unproductive to Christ, the God of all, at the day of retribution.

197   Epistle, III, 58, to Murianus, monk; *PG* LXXIX, 417

If monks faithfully pursue their ideal, God will see to their material wants.

If we maintain silence, and remain steadfast in prayer and psalmody in the monastery, and do not trouble ourselves with worldly concerns, God, providing and caring for us, will bring those people to us, and will compel them to meet our corporal needs willingly. For God has a care for us, since we also have a care for the work of the spirit.

198   Epistle, II, 159, to Gaudentius, deacon; *PG* LXXIX, 276

The typical monastic practices are recommended to Gaudentius, the deacon, as a bulwark against the demon of fornication.

The demon of fornication, in the manner of a licking puppy, is wont to cling to the one he tempts, so as not to be cast out. But it is possible for you – it is a matter of your prerogative and intention – either to nourish him with the work of dishonor or vigorously to put him to flight with prayer and psalmody, with fasting and vigils, and with sleeping on the ground.

199   Epistle, III, 38, to Callinicus, monk; *PG* LXXIX, 405

In a somewhat obscure comparison involving the stag, psalmody is closely linked with contemplation in leading one to the highest spiritual attainment.

'The high mountains are for the stags' (Ps 103.18). And again, 'The voice of the Lord prepareth the stags' (Ps 28.9). If, then, by the teaching of the Lord and the sacred canons of asceticism you become as a stag, and stripped bare of the graves of evil, having become emboldened against the figurative serpents, you kill them; do not remain at this level, but strive to ascend to the high mountains through continuous psalmody, through the practice of perfection, and through that blessed contemplation than which nothing is higher. Thus, 'Blessed are the pure in heart, for they shall see God' (Mt 5.8); and, 'The Lord has set me upon high places' (Ps 17.34) . . .

Callinicus (fl. mid-fifth century)

He wrote an important biography of his mentor, St Hypatius (d. 446), who was abbot of a monastery near Chalcedon.

200   *Life of Hypatius* xxvi, 2–3; *SC* CLXXVII, 180–2

> During Lent Hypatius chanted one hundred psalms every day, each followed by a prayer. The editor of the *Life* translated ὀρφρινά as prime, but this appears unlikely on linguistic as well as historical grounds. The first unequivocal references to prime do not appear until the time of St Benedict.

And during Lent he ate every second day, confining himself, and chanting psalms and praying at daybreak (ὀρφρινά), the third hour, the sixth, the ninth, the lighting of lamps (λυχνικά), late evening (πρωθύπνια), and the middle of the night, according to the saying, 'Seven times a day I have praised thee for the judgments of thy righteousness' (Ps 118.164). 3 Chanting psalms, then, seven times in the course of the day and night, he completed one hundred psalms and one hundred prayers.

Ephraem Syrus (c.306–73)

Born at Nisibis, Ephraem was ordained a deacon sometime before 338 and maintained that office until his death. In 363, when the Persians occupied Nisibis, he moved west to Edessa and lived out the rest of his life there, much admired for both his learning and exemplary life.

He was in a sense too much admired. By the sixth century his biography had become richly ornamented with legend and his oeuvre interlarded with *spuria*. Indeed the standard edition of his works by J. S. Assemani, consisting of three volumes of Syriac works (Rome, 1737–46) and three volumes of Greek works (Rome, 1732–46), contains less authentic material, particularly among the Greek titles, than it does misattributed and substantially altered works. The situation was not much improved by nineteenth- and early twentieth-century editors, but in recent decades Edmund Beck has edited the majority of the authentic Syriac works in the *CSCO* series. The same author, joined by two other specialists, has produced an article for the *Dictionnaire de Spiritualité* that may be the best overview of Ephraem's achievement presently available (Beck, 1960).

The general difficulties involved in Ephraem scholarship apply also to his musical significance, where at least four issues are to be distinguished. First, the notion that Ephraem was a typical participant in the Greek and Latin patristic polemic against pagan musical practice and instruments (Quasten, 1930, pp. 134, 175) must be questioned now in view of the dubiousness of the sources that established it. Secondly, the biographical tradition that Ephraem trained choirs of virgins and boys to sing his hymns, purportedly in answer to a similar practice by the heretic Bardesanes, remains plausible enough; and that he employed a cithara in doing so (Werner, 1959, p. 218), while somewhat less plausible, it not out of the question. Still, both points require a very careful analysis of the sources involved. The third issue – the actual liturgical usage of Ephraem's poetic works – is related to the second. Most of

Ephraem's authentic works are cast in two poetic genres: metrical sermons called *mimre* and strophic hymns called *madrāshe*. The latter in particular are widely considered to be practical liturgical compositions, set to music, moreover, by Ephraem himself (Husmann, 1980, p. 479). Yet a measure of scepticism seems justified until one produces external evidence of their precise placement within a contemporary liturgical order. Finally there is the fourth issue – Ephraem's musical imagery. The few examples presented here in literal translation will show it is striking, if obscure, and altogether different from the routine allegorical exegesis of his Greek and Latin contemporaries. They are offered as an invitation to qualified scholars to undertake a more adequate treatment.

Thus the presentation of Ephraem here differs from the approach taken in the volume as a whole: it is not an attempt to consolidate previous research but to point out the need for further work.

201   *Hymns of Eastertide* II, 7–9; *CSCO* CCXLVIII, 84

> There is more than images involved here. After invoking the historical Palm Sunday (Mt 9.5–9), Ephraem goes on to describe the contemporary feast day. Note that virgins do in fact sing *madrāshe*, whether trained by Ephraem or not.

Beautiful and eloquent blossoms
  the children scattered before the king.
The foal was crowned with them
  the path filled with them.
They scattered praise like blossoms
  and songs like lilies.
Even now, my Lord, during this festival
  the band of children scattered before thee my Lord
Alleluias like flowers.
  Blessed be the one who was praised by the children.

Lo, our hearing, like one's lap
  is filled with the voices of children;
Again, my Lord, the recesses of our ears are filled
  with the musical strains of virgins.
Let every one gather all the blossoms,
  mingling what is his own with them,
Flowers which have sprouted in his land,
  for this great festival –
Let us plait a magnificent crown for him;
  Blessed is the one who has called us to his crowning.

The bishop weaves into it
  his biblical exegesis as his flowers;
The presbyters their martyr stories,
  the deacons their lections,

The young men their alleluias,
    the boys their psalms,
The virgins their *madrāshe*,
    the rulers their achievements,
And the lay people their virtues.
    Blessed be the one who has multiplied victories for us.

202   *Hymns against Heresies* II, 7; *CSCO* CLXIX, 7

Musical dissonance is invoked as an image of contentiousness among
heretical factions. Note that Ephraem uses the Hebrew cognate kinnor for
cithara (Finesinger, 1926, pp. 27–36), while the ODES OF SOLOMON uses the
Greek cithara.

The evil one made them
    in the image of pipes
And played songs on them –
    agitated songs of contention.
This is a kinnor
    whose litigious
Strings with their songs
    do not sound together in one
Note of unity.
    Its maker is accursed.

203   *Hymns on Virginity* XXV, 3; *CSCO* CCXXIII, 89

Ephraem's use of kinnor as metaphor is pervasive, and at times puzzling,
as in this example. Proper names are substituted for pronouns to make the
translation intelligible. The passage is addressed to Mary standing at the
foot of the cross with the disciple John.

Jesus suckled visible milk from your breast,
John hidden mysteries from Jesus' breast.
Jesus drew near to your breast trustingly,
John drew near and inclined upon Jesus' breast.
Because you paid heed to him he gave you his kinnor
That it might console you.

204   *Hymns of Virginity* XXIX, 1–9; *CSCO* CCXXIII, 105–8

The entire poem is a complex of kinnor metaphors, the meaning of which
is barely suggested by the portions given here. The two kinnors held in the
hands of the Word appear to stand for the Old and New Testaments.

The Word of the Most High came down and put on
A frail body with hands.
He set two kinnors in balance,
To his right and to his left.
A third one he set before himself
To be a witness for them both.
For this middle kinnor was to demonstrate
That their Lord was playing upon them.
5 For thy hands, O Savior, there are two kinnors,
The temporal kinnor and the kinnor of truth . . .
He played what was the New and the Old . . .

9 Who has ever seen two kinnors –
The one silent the other eloquent?
And the silence of the one was not heard;
The announcement of him was from the eloquent one.
For the silent one persuaded by deeds,
But the eloquent one by its song.
In word and in deeds they both
Announced the Lord of all.

CHAPTER 8

The Greek historians

If one notes a manifestation of the historical impulse in the Gospels and Acts of the Apostles, this quality is substantially lacking in the patristic writings of the second and third centuries. It reasserts itself, however, in the person of Eusebius of Caesarea (d. 339), perhaps because he was a firsthand witness to the momentous events of the early fourth century. In about 325 he completed his famous *Ecclesiastical History*. It is not only the first church history, but the inspiration of most of those to follow; indeed subsequent church histories, east and west, were essentially continuations of his work. The three most notable eastern examples are those of Socrates, Sozomen and Theodoret of Cyrus; they all bear the title *Ecclesiastical History* and run along parallel lines, extending the story to the first half of the fifth century. Considered historiographically, these works, along with that of Eusebius, have the virtue of maintaining a rough chronology while presenting many valuable primary sources. Needless to say they are apologetic in purpose and cannot be expected always to meet modern standards of objectivity. The four of them, in any case, leave us a number of interesting passages on liturgical music.

Eusebius of Caesarea (c.260–c.340)

He is unique among church fathers in the way he straddles two eras, somewhat reminiscent of Monteverdi in music. He is also unique in that beyond the more conventional sort of patristic subject matter, he wrote the first history of the Church. Thus, while finding place here among the Greek church historians, he might have appeared in any of several chapters.

In about 315 he was appointed bishop of Caesarea and for the rest of his career sought to occupy something of a theological middle ground between the Arians and the Athanasian opposition. For many years he enjoyed a close association with the Emperor Constantine which may help to explain his interest in history. His works display a fair quantity of musical imagery, and his celebrated *Ecclesiastical History* has several remarks about actual psalmody and hymnody. The references appear here as follows: those from his psalm commentary, from the *History*, and from other works.

205   *In psalmos*; *PG* XXIII, 72–3

> There are a number of introductory items preceding the Eusebian psalm commentary in *PG* XXIII. Their overlapping subject matter makes it improbable that all – if indeed any – are authentic. A long portion of the most musically interesting is quoted here. It deals with two important topoi, first the four-fold exegetical distinction among psalm, canticle, psalm of a canticle and canticle of a psalm, and then the colorful scene of David with psaltery, surrounded by his four musical associates. The

former has occasionally confused musicologists, while the latter has inspired many beautiful frontispieces in early medieval psalters (see Steger, 1961). Whether genuine or not, this passage appears to be the earliest extant source of the material.

It seems that the word psalm derives from its similarity to the word psaltery. The psaltery, in turn, is defined as a kind of musical instrument which differs from the cithara in shape: the song played upon it is called a 'psalm', while a 'canticle' (ᾠδήν) is musical speech proclaimed in melody without an instrument. There is said to be a 'psalm of a canticle' whenever the same melody of the preceding canticle is played on the psaltery, and a 'canticle of a psalm' when the reverse obtains.

As is written in the historical books of Kings and Chronicles, David, king after the death of Saul, brought up the Ark of the Lord's Covenant – it had been in the house of Obedom for twenty years, when it had been taken from the Azotians – installed it in Jerusalem, and chose by lot four musicians (ψαλτῳδούς) from the tribe of Levi as leaders of song, to play and sing (ψάλλειν καὶ ᾄδειν) before the Ark of the Lord, and to raise a voice of joy in confession and praise upon harmonious instruments and in song – upon kinuras (κινύραις), nablas (νάβλαις), tympana, cymbals, psaltery and keratin (κερατίνῃ). [These four were] Asaph, Heman, Ethan and Jeduthun, to whom a certain number of songs was assigned along with two hundred and eighty-eight singers, seventy-two to each, thirty-two from the family of Ham, twenty-five from Shem, and fifteen from Japhet. These [four] stood before the Ark of the Lord's Covenant and played and sang to the Lord, one on the kinura, one on the cymbals, one on the cithara, one on the psaltery; and in their midst stood the blessed David, leading the leaders of song, grasping in his hands the psaltery. Each sang and played hymns to God, in an order set by the Holy Spirit. And when the Spirit fell upon one of the chief musicians, the others stood by in silence and then responded in unison (ὑπακούοντες συμφώνως) to the psalmist, 'Alleluia'.

206　*In psalmum xci*, 4; *PG* XXIII, 1172–3

It is known that Eusebius wrote a psalm commentary late in his life, and it is generally accepted that the material appearing in *PG* XXIII for Psalms 50–95 is an authentic part of it. It is more discursive in style and complex in thought than most later commentaries. A portion of the commentary on Psalm 91.4 is quoted as an example.

When formerly the people of the circumcision worshipped through symbols and types, it was not unreasonable that they raised hymns to God on psalteries and cithara, and that they did this on the days of the Sabbath, thus clearly violating the required rest and transgressing the law of the Sabbath. We, however, maintain the Jewish law inwardly, according to the saying of the Apostle: 'For he is not a real Jew who is one outwardly, nor is real circumcision something external and physical, but he is a Jew who is one inwardly, and real circumcision is a matter of the heart, spiritual and not literal' (Rom 2.28–9); and it is upon a living psaltery and an animate cithara and in spiritual songs that we render the hymn. And so more sweetly pleasing to God than any musical instrument would be the symphony of the people of God, by which, in every church of God, with kindred spirit and single disposition, with one mind and unanimity of faith and piety, we raise melody in unison (ὁμόφωνον μέλος) in our psalmody.

207   *In psalmum cxlii*, 8; *PG* xxiv, 49

> The singing of Psalm 62 at the morning office is suggested. On the morning office in general, see Taft (1984).

'Make thy mercy heard to me in the morning' (Ps 148.2). Amid temptations we need God's mercy, and in our prayers we vigilantly devote ourselves to its arrival, especially at the early morning hour, so that it can be said: 'God, my God, to thee do I watch at the break of day' (Ps 62.2).

208   *Ecclesiastical History* II, xvii, 22; *PG* xx, 181–4; *SC* xxxi, 77

> There are several incidental references to psalmody in Eusebius's *Ecclesiastical History*. In a long passage he recapitulates Philo of Alexandria's description of the Jewish Therapeutai (*De vita contemplativa* 64–90) and identifies them as Christians, a chronological impossibility. Here, in paraphrasing Philo's narration of the group's singing, Eusebius gives a clear description of responsorial psalmody.

The above mentioned man has given a description of all this in his own writing – which agrees precisely with the manner observed up to now by us alone – of the vigil celebrations on the great feast, the practices associated with them, the hymns we are accustomed to recite, and how as an individual sings in comely measure (ἑνὸς μετὰ ῥυθμοῦ κοσμίως ἐπιψάλλοντος), the rest listen in silence and join in singing only the refrains (ἀκροτελεύτια) of the hymns; how on certain days they sleep on the floor on straw pallets, abstain entirely from wine . . .

209   *Ecclesiastical History* III, xxxiii, 1; *PG* xx, 285; *SC* xxxi, 145

> Eusebius reports on the famous LETTER OF PLINY. In doing so he replaces the ambiguous term *carmen* with the less problematic ὑμνεῖν.

Such was the persecution brought to bear against us then in so many places, that Pliny the Younger, one of the most outstanding governors, was troubled by the great number of martyrs. He informed the Emperor of the number of those put to death for their faith, and declared at the same time that they practised nothing profane or outside the law, but only that they arose at dawn to sing a hymn (ὑμνεῖν) to Christ, as though to God, that they not only renounced adultery, murder and similar godless crimes, but also did everything pursuant to the laws.

210   *Ecclesiastical History* v, xxviii, 5; *PG* xx, 512–13; *SC* xli, 75

> Eusebius speaks of non-biblical psalms and songs written by Christians 'from the beginning'. The context of the remark is a defense of the divinity of Christ against Paul of Samosata.

For who does not know the books of Iranaeus, Melito and the others which pronounce Christ to be both God and man, and all the psalms and songs written from the beginning (ἀπ᾽ ἀρχῆς) by faithful brethren, which hymn Christ as the Word of God, and address him as God?

211   *Ecclesiastical History* vii, xxx, 10; *PG* xx, 713; *SC* xli, 217

> Once again Paul of Samosata is the musical malefactor.

He put a stop to singing those psalms addressed to our Lord Jesus Christ, on the grounds that they were new or composed by recent authors, and instead trained women to sing (ψαλμῳδεῖν) to himself in the middle of the church on the great day of the Pascha – anyone hearing them would shudder.

212   *Ecclesiastical History* ix, viii, 11; *PG* xx, 817; *SC* lv, 59

> Secular funeral rites are accompanied by auloi.

And so all places were filled with the sound of wailing; in every street, square and avenue, there was nothing to observe but lamentation with the accustomed auloi and breast beating.

213   *Ecclesiastical History* x, iii, 3; *PG* xx, 848; *SC* lv, 80

> After the 'Peace of the Church commences in 313, churches are con-
> structed everywhere and solemn rites are held. The language of this
> passage has a rich hieratic quality that contrasts with the more matter of
> fact language usually employed in liturgical description. It is redolent
> perhaps of the Old Testament Temple, and possibly even pagan imperial
> rites.

Yea, verily, the unblemished rites (ἐντελεῖς θρησκεῖναι) [were conducted] by the leaders and the services (ἱερουγίαι) and godly ordinances of the Church [were fulfilled] by our priests – here with psalmody and other utterances of the voices which speak to us from God – there with the accomplishment of sacred and mystical ministrations (διακονίαις) – also present were the ineffable symbols of the passion of our Savior.

214   *Ecclesiastical History* x, iv, 5–6; *PG* xx, 849; *SC* LV, 82

> Now Eusebius speaks of the dedication of a specific church, the basilica at
> Tyre, as he quotes an address given on the occasion, probably by himself.
> He seems almost to speak of Scriptural reading followed by psalmodic
> response, but it is difficult to sustain this interpretation upon closer read-
> ing. (For additional references to liturgical song in the *History*, see VII, xxiv,
> 4; VIII, ix, 5; IX, i, 11; x, ix, 7.)

'Formerly, when we learned the miraculous signs of God and the benefits
secured for men by the wondrous deeds of the Lord by hearing the divine
Scriptures being read, we could raise hymns and canticles to God and say
as we were taught: "We have heard with our ears, O God; our fathers have
told us what work thou didst perform in their days, in the days of old"
(Ps 43.1). But now as we learn of the uplifted arm and heavenly right hand
of our all-gracious and sovereign God, not from hearsay or word of mouth,
but by observing in deeds, as one might say, and with our very eyes what
before had been recorded as faithful and true, we can raise a second hymn
of triumph, and sing out clearly, saying: "As we have heard, so have we
seen, in the city of the Lord of hosts, in the city of our God" (Ps 47.8).'

215   *Preparatio euangelica* IV, 11–12; *PG* XXI, 260. *SC* CCLXII, 140–2

> Eusebius quotes Porphyry who, in turn, quotes the Neopythagorean
> Apollonius of Tyana (up to the break). The point of the passage is that to
> the supreme Neoplatonic being only a hymnody of absolute interior
> silence is appropriate, while to the second highest order of deities
> hymnody in the ordinary sense is fitting. The passage has significance in
> view of what authors like Quasten have had to say on Christian 'spiritual
> sacrifice' (Quasten, 1930, pp. 51–7).

'To the god who is above all, as a certain wise man has said, we must offer
nothing sensible, nor incense, nor anything articulate; for there is nothing
material which is not straightway impure to the immaterial being. Hence no
speech is appropriate to him, whether spoken or uttered within, if the soul
happens to be defiled by some disturbance; rather we must worship him
with pure silence and unsullied thoughts. It is necessary, then, once we have
been brought into contact with and made like him, for us to offer up to God
the ascent of our souls as a holy sacrifice; it is this that is both a hymn and
our salvation . . . However to those gods born of him, the intelligible gods,
we must direct a hymnody of speech . . .

216   *Tricennial Oration* XIV, 5; *PG* xx, 1409; *GCS* I, 242

> Eusebius addressed a panegyric to Constantine in 335, the thirtieth year of
> his reign. There are a number of extended musical metaphors in it, the
> most interesting of which perhaps is the following.

A Greek myth tells us that Orpheus charmed every sort of animal and mollified the savagery of wild beasts by plucking on the strings of an instrument with a plectrum. Moreover, this is celebrated in a Greek chorus and it is believed that a lifeless lyre tamed these beasts and that even trees (they were oak) moved in response to music. But the all-wise and panharmonious Word of God, applying every sort of remedy to the souls of men afflicted with manifold vices, takes the work of his wisdom, his human nature, into his hands as if it were a musical instrument and with it plays odes and epodes for rational beings, not mindless beasts, and thus, with the medication of his inspired doctrine, he cures all kinds of savages, Greek no less than barbarian, of their wild passion and bestiality of soul.

Socrates (c.380–450)

A native of Constantinople and a lawyer, his *Ecclesiastical History* is the best among several continuations to the work of Eusebius. It was written in seven books covering the years 305 to 439 with each book corresponding to the life span of one of the seven emperors who reigned during the period. What we have today is a second edition of the original work. Socrates had relied greatly upon Rufinus, and after learning of the many mistakes in Rufinus from studying the writings of Athanasius, he substantially revised his work. This gives an indication of his historical objectivity – rare for his time – as does also his extensive citation of numerous contemporary documents. His most important contribution to music history is a description of antiphonal psalmody at Constantinople among both Arians and the orthodox.

217   *Ecclesiastical History* v, 22; *PG* LXVII, 636–7

> *PG* translates ὑποβολεῖς, literally 'prompters', as *psaltae*, cantors. There is a degree of plausibility in this since in the commonly practised responsorial psalmody of the time, the cantor sang the refrain before its repetition by the people.

In the same city of Alexandria readers and cantors (ὑποβολεῖς) are created regardless of whether they are catechumens or faithful, while the churches everywhere else promote only the faithful to this office.

218   *Ecclesiastical History* VI, 8; *PG* LXVII, 688–92

> This is the central patristic source for the thorny question of antiphonal psalmody. Note that the 'antiphonal hymnody' of this passage is not associated here with the notion of alternate or dual choir psalmody as it is in the secondary sources. (For a cognate passage see SOZOMEN, *Ecclesiastical History* VIII, 8; and for recent, more critical, secondary sources on the question of antiphonal psalmody, see Hucke, 1953, pp. 152–71, and Leeb, 1967, pp. 18–20.)

The Arians, as I have said, conducted their assemblies outside the city. Each week when the festivals took place – I refer to the Sabbath and the

Lord's Day on which the synaxes were accustomed to be held in the churches – they gathered within the gates of the city about the porticoes and sang antiphonal songs (ᾠδὰς ἀντιφώνους) composed in accordance with Arian doctrine. This they did for the greater part of the night. At dawn, after reciting the same sort of antiphona (ἀντίφωνα), they passed through the middle of the city and went out through the gates and came to the places where they were wont to assemble. Now since they did not cease to speak in provocation of those who held the homoousian position – often they even sang some song such as this: 'Where are they who tell of the three as one power?' – John, concerned lest any of the more simple be drawn away from the church by such songs, set in opposition to them some of his own people, so that they too, by devoting themselves to nocturnal hymnody, would obscure the efforts of others in this regard, and render their own people steadfast in their faith. But while John's purpose appeared to be beneficial, it ended in confusion and peril. Since the homoousian hymns proved to be more splendid in their nightly singing – for John devised silver crosses, bearing light from wax tapers, provided at the expense of the Empress Eudoxia – the Arians, numerous as they were and seized by jealousy, resolved to avenge themselves and to instigate conflict. Due to their inherent strength, they were anxious to do battle and despised the others. Without hesitation, then, they struck one night and threw a stone at the forehead of Briso, a eunuch of the Empress, who was leading the singers (ὑμνῳδούς) at the time. A number of people from both sides were also killed. The Emperor, moved by these occurrences, forbade the Arians to perform their hymnody in public. And such were the events narrated.

It must further be told whence the custom of antiphonal hymns had its beginning in the Church. Ignatius of Antioch in Syria, the third bishop after the Apostle Peter, and an acquaintance of the Apostles themselves, saw a vision of angels, hymning the Holy Trinity with antiphonal hymns, and passed on to the church of Antioch the manner of singing he saw in the vision. Whence the same tradition was handed down to all the churches. This then, is the account of antiphonal hymns.

Sozomen (fl. second quarter of fifth century)

Like his near contemporary Socrates he was a lawyer who worked in Constantinople, although born at Bethelia, near Gaza in Palestine. Little else is known of his life. His *Ecclesiastical History*, written in nine books covering the period 323 to 425, is superior to that of Socrates in literary style, but inferior in historical grasp. The two works are clearly interdependent, and it is generally assumed that Sozomen follows Socrates.

219   *Ecclesiastical History* III, 20; *PG* LXVII, 1101; *GCS* 135

The various factions of Antioch manifest their Christological positions in the doxologies sung at the close of their hymns.

As was their custom, they assembled in choruses when singing hymns to God, and at the end of the songs they declared their individual positions. Some praised the Father and Son as equally worthy of honor, while others praised the Father in the Son, indicating by the insertion of the preposition that the Son played a secondary role.

220   *Ecclesiastical History* IV, 3; *PG* LXVII, 1113; *GCS* 141

> Martyrius and Marcian, the so-called Holy Notaries, were martyred at Constantinople in about 350. Note the term ψάλτης.

Martyrius was a subdeacon, while Marcian was a cantor (ψάλτης) and a reader of Holy Scripture.

221   *Ecclesiastical History* V, 19; *PG* LXVII, 1276; *GCS* 226

> The Emperor orders the body of the martyr Babylas to be removed from the area of the oracle at Daphne. The Christians translate the relics amid psalm singing. The manner described is responsorial, but the refrain is non-biblical.

They say that at that time the men and women – both youths and maidens, old people and children – who pulled the casket kept encouraging each other by singing psalms all along the way. This was done under pretext of lightening their exertions, while the truth is that they were moved by zeal and enthusiasm for that particular view of the divinity which the Emperor did not share with them. Those who knew the psalms better than the others began them, while the crowd echoed in symphony, adding this refrain (ῥῆσιν): 'Confounded are all they who worship sculpted things, who glory in idols'.

222   *Ecclesiastical History* VII, 19; *PG* LXVII, 1476; *GCS* 330

> Sozomen makes this reference to the Alleluia in the course of listing the peculiarities of various churches. He appears to be wrong, but see Bailey (1983, pp. 8–9).

Moreover, they sing the Alleluia at Rome only once each year, on the first day of the Paschal festival . . .

223   *Ecclesiastical History* VIII, 7; *PG* LXVII, 1536; *GCS* 360

> Sozomen records precisely the same events as does SOCRATES in his *Ecclesiastical History* VI, 8. Only the beginning of the Sozomen passage is quoted to show his different terminology for the supposed antiphonal psalmody. Note the refrains that suggest a formal similarity to responsorial psalmody.

Since those who follow the Arian heresy had been deprived of their churches in Constantinople during the reign of Theodosius, they held their assemblies outside the city wall. First they gathered at night in the public porticoes, and dividing themselves into groups, they sang (ἔψαλλον) according to the manner of antiphons (τῶν ἀντιφώνων τρόπον), divising refrains (ἀκροτελεύτια) composed in conformity with their doctrine.

Theodoret of Cyrus (c.393–c.466)

Born in Antioch and educated in its monasteries, he was elected bishop of Cyrus in 423, a small town near Antioch, and held the position with distinction for most of his life. The one blot on his reputation was his siding with Nestorius against the Christological decrees of the Council of Ephesus (431). At the Council of Chalcedon (451), however, he relented and maintained orthodoxy for the rest of his life. He is categorized here as an historian, although his other works establish him equally as the last great exegete and theologian of the Antiochene school. His remarks about music are extremely valuable, surpassed in quantity and interest only by those of Chrysostom, Basil, Ambrose and Augustine. They appear here in the following order: first those from the historical works, and then those from the remaining works beginning with the psalm commentary. The latter group of quotations, as it happens, all deal with the question of why instruments were allowed in the worship of the Old Testament, but not that of the New.

224   *Ecclesiastical History* II, 24, 8–9; *PG* LXXXII, 1060; *GCS* 154

> Theodoret's work, treating the period 323 to 428, may be the weakest of the three Greek continuations of Eusebius. It is criticized for its over-zealous assault on all heresies and its unreliable chronology. It has, nonetheless, a number of interesting remarks about music. The first quoted here is one of only a handful from the patristic period which bear on the question of antiphonal psalmody. Note that while the practice of dual choir alternation is indicated the term antiphonal is not employed.

That remarkable pair, Flavianus and Diodorus, though not yet engaged in their priestly ministry and still numbered among the laity, urged on all, night and day, in the pursuit of piety. They were the first to divide in two (διχῆ διελόντες) the choruses of psalm singers, and to teach them to sing the Davidic song (μελῳδίαν) in alternation (ἐκ διαδοχῆς). And what was introduced at Antioch spread everywhere, reaching to the ends of the earth. They gathered lovers of holy things into the shrines of the martyrs and spent the entire night with them singing hymns to God.

225   *Ecclesiastical History* III, 19, 1–4; *PG* LXXXII, 1109–12; *GCS* 197–8

> Julia, a respected widow of Antioch, established a convent there. She is remembered for this anecdote in which she has her choir of virgins taunt the idolatrous Julian with selected verses from the Psalter.

As the Emperor passed by, they sang together more loudly than usual, since they looked upon this 'destroying angel' as an object of contempt and derision. They sang especially those songs which satirize the impotence of idols, declaiming in the words of David that: 'The idols of the nations are silver and gold, the work of men's hands' (Ps 113B.4). And after this declaration of the idols' insensibility they added: 'Let those who make them be like them, and so too all who trust in them' (Ps 113B.8). When the Emperor heard these things, he was greatly upset and commanded them to keep silent at the time of his passing by. Publia, however, having little respect for his laws, instilled greater enthusiasm in her chorus, and when he came by again bade them sing: 'Let God arise, let his enemies be scattered' (Ps 67.1). Angered by this, he ordered the leader of the chorus to be brought before him, and while recognizing that her advanced age was most worthy of respect, he neither took pity on the grey hairs of her body nor honored the virtue of her soul, but ordered some of his personal guard to box her ears and to redden her cheeks with their blows. But she took this outrage as a great honor, and after returning home, she took up her accustomed assault upon the Emperor in spiritual song (μελῳδίαις), after the manner of that author and teacher of song who quieted the evil spirit which was troubling Saul.

226 *Ecclesiastical History* IV, 29, 1–3; *PG* LXXXII, 1189; *GCS* 269

> Theodoret tells how Ephraem adapted to orthodox purposes the gnostic hymnody of Harmonios. (For additional references to liturgical song from this work, see II, 13, 4–7; III, 10, 3; V, 21, 15; V, 35, 4; V, 36, 4.)

And Ephraem, using the Syrian tongue, shed beams of spiritual grace. Although lacking experience in Hellenic learning, he exposed the multifarious schemes of the Greeks, and lay bare the weakness of every heretical artifice. And since Harmonios, the son of Bardesanes, had composed some songs long ago, and by mixing the sweetness of melody with his impiety had beguiled his audience and led them to their destruction, Ephraem took the music for his song (τὴν ἁρμονίαν τοῦ μέλους), mixed in his own piety, and thus presented his listeners with a remedy both exceedingly sweet and beneficial. Even now these songs render the festivals of the victorious martyrs more splendid.

227 *Haereticarum fabularum compendium* IV, 7; *PG* LXXXIII, 425

> Theodoret describes the practices of the Melitians, schismatics who were active at Alexandria during the first half of the fourth century.

Therefore, as if not bound by law, they contrived the following absurd practices: to cleanse the body with water on alternate days, to sing hymns accompanied by hand-clapping and a sort of dance, to shake a group of bells attached to a rope, and other things similar to these.

228   *Historia religiosa* xx, Maris; *PG* LXXXII, 1429; *SC* CCLVII, 64–6

> The *Historia religiosa*, Theodoret's earliest historical work, gives the biographies of twenty-eight monks and three women ascetics from Antioch and its environs. This passage tells how Maris maintained his purity despite his youthful participation in martyrs' vigils. It suggests a curiously suspicious attitude toward these popular Christian celebrations.

And this he himself clearly indicated to me, teaching that his body remained undefiled, just as it had come from his mother's womb. And this even though, while still young, he had celebrated many festivals of the martyrs, and charmed the people with his pleasant voice (εὐφωνίᾳ). For he spent much time singing (ψάλλων), and was also physically striking. But neither his corporeal beauty, nor his splendid voice, nor his mingling with the crowd, spoiled his beauty of soul.

229   *Interpretatio in psalmos* 150; *PG* LXXX, 1996

> As a representative of the Antiochene exegetical school, Theodoret explains the instruments of Psalm 150 in similar fashion to JOHN CHRYSOSTOM. The same line of thought is represented in the next three passages quoted here.

'Praise him on psaltery and cithara. Praise him with tympanum and dance. Praise him on strings and instrument. Praise him on well-sounding cymbals, praise him on loud-clashing cymbals' (Ps 150. 4–5). The Levites employed these instruments long ago as they hymned God in his holy Temple, not because God enjoyed their sound but because he accepted the intention of those involved. That the Deity does not take pleasure in singing and playing we hear him saying to the Jews: 'Take away from me the sound of your songs; to the voice of your instruments I will not listen' (Amos 5.23). He allowed these things to happen because he wished to free them from the error of idols. For since they were fond of play and laughter, and all these things took place in the temples of the idols, he permitted them and thereby enticed them, thus avoiding the greater evil by allowing the lesser, and teaching perfect things through the imperfect.

230   *Graecarum affectionum curatio, de sacrificiis* 16; *PG* LXXXIII, 996; *SC* LVII, 300

> In this work Theodoret pursues the argument at length. He explains first how the Jews acquired their addiction to sacrifice and its musical accessories during their sojourn in Egypt.

The people of Israel spent a long time in Egypt and were introduced to the shameful customs of the inhabitants; they were taught by them to sacrifice to idols and demons, to play, to dance, and to take pleasure in musical instruments. God, wishing to free them from their inclination to these things, allowed them to make sacrifice, but not every sort of sacrifice, certainly not to sacrifice to the false gods of the Egyptians, but rather to offer the Egyptian gods themselves to him alone. For the Egyptians at that time deified the cow, the sheep, the goat, the pigeon, the dove ...

231   *Graecarum affectionum curatio, de sacrificiis* 34–5; *PG* LXXXIII, 1001–2; *SC* LVII, 305

> In the course of his argument Theodoret devotes more space to the animals involved in sacrifice than the instruments, but in his summarizing statement instruments are emphasized again. (He had also mentioned instruments more briefly in paragraphs 21 and 22.)

What he ordained in the Law, then, concerning these things, was because of their weakness, not their need or their intention. And he says this elsewhere: 'Your burnt offerings are not acceptable, nor your sacrifices pleasing to me' (Jer 6.20). And again he cries: 'Take away from me the sound of your songs; to the voice of your instruments I will not listen' (Amos 5.23). And there are many other such passages to be found, which show clearly that God prescribed these practices not because he had need of sacrifices, nor because he enjoyed their smoke, their savor, or the musical instruments, but because he was considering a remedy for them.

232   *Quaestiones et responsiones ad orthodoxos* CVII; *PG* VI, 1353; *Otto* V, 164

> This pseudo-Justinian work is now generally accepted as Theodoret's. The passage quoted here, while allied to the preceding in its general sense, makes the distinction between song and instrumental music more explicit.

Question 107   If songs were invented by unbelievers as a ruse, and introduced to those under the Law because of their simple mindedness, while those under Grace have adopted better practices, unlike those customs just mentioned, why have they used these songs in the churches as did the children of the Law?

    Response   It is not singing as such which befits the childish, but singing with lifeless instruments, and with dancing and finger clappers (κροτάλων); wherefore the use of such instruments and other things appropriate to those who are childish is dispensed with in the churches and singing alone has been left over.

CHAPTER 9

The Apostolic Constitutions, Egeria, and the eastern councils

This last eastern chapter consists of a miscellany of crucially important material. The *Apostolic Constitutions* give a detailed description of the liturgy in late fourth-century Antioch; Egeria's celebrated diary presents a service by service description of the liturgical week in early fifth-century Jerusalem; and the Councils of Laodicea offer a scattering of specific information about liturgical song in later fourth-century Asia Minor. The so-called Canons of Basil are of more dubious significance because of their uncertain date.

Apostolic Constitutions

This compilation of legislative and liturgical material is the longest of the church orders. It appears to have been written in about 380 by a Syrian of Arian tendencies, quite possibly the author of the interpolated Ignatian epistles. It incorporates large portions of earlier church orders: the *Didascalia* in books one through six, the *Didache* in book seven and the *Apostolic Tradition* in book eight. Still the material is so reworked or expanded that virtually all the musical references reflect the time of compilation. Of particular significance among these are passages citing the gradual psalm, the Sanctus and the communion psalm. The material is presented here in the following order: that dealing with the Eucharist, the daily offices, and other occasions and circumstances.

233   *Apostolic Constitutions* II, lvii, 3–7; *Funk,* 159–63

> This important passage first sets the architectural context of the liturgy with considerable precision, the only significant omission being the *cancelli* (on the architectural setting of early eastern liturgy see Mathews, 1971). Then it describes the readings of the pre-eucharistic synaxis in detail; it is significant that psalms are distinguished from Scripture which is merely read. Note the use of the first person in connection with the New Testament books, indicating the purported Apostolic origin of the passage.

3 And first of all the building should be oblong, directed toward the rising sun, with sacristies (παστοφόρια) on each side toward the east, so that it resembles a ship. 4 Let the throne of the bishop be placed in the middle, the presbytery to sit on either side of him, and the deacons to stand nearby, neatly dressed in their full garments, resembling the sailors and officers of a ship. Relative to them the lay men are to sit toward the other end in complete quiet and good order, and the women are to sit alone and they too are to maintain silence. 5 In the middle the reader is to stand upon something

high (ὑψηλοῦ τινος) and read the books of Moses, of Joshua the son of Nun, of Judges and Kings, of Chronicles and those from after the return, and in addition those of Job, of Solomon and of the sixteen Prophets. 6 After two readings let someone else sing the hymns of David, and let the people respond with verses (ἀκροστίχια). 7 After this let our Acts be read and the epistles of Paul our fellow worker, which he sent to the churches under the guidance of the Holy Spirit; and after these let a deacon or priest read the Gospels, which I, Matthew, and John have transmitted to you, and which the co-workers of Paul, Luke and Mark, have received and passed on to you.

234 *Apostolic Constitutions* VIII, xii, 27; *Funk*, 504–6

> The people join with the angels in singing the Sanctus; see also CYRIL OF JERUSALEM, *Mystagogical Catechesis* IV, 6. Contemporary sources, particularly in the west, are by no means unanimous in attesting to the presence of the Sanctus in the Eucharist.

'The Cherubim and six-winged Seraphim, their feet covered with two, their heads with two, and flying with two', saying together with thousand times thousands of archangels and ten-thousand times ten-thousands of angels, without ceasing and in a loud voice; and let all the people say with them, 'Holy, holy, holy, Lord of Sabaoth, heaven and earth are full of his glory; blessed be he for ever; Amen'.

235 *Apostolic Constitutions* VIII, xiii, 14–17; VIII, xiv, 1; *Funk*, 516–18

> There are two points of musical significance here: Psalm 33 with its highly relevant verse 8, 'O taste and see that the Lord is good', is sung during the distribution of Communion; and the cantor (ψάλτης) is listed among the clerical orders receiving. The term ψάλτης appears several times throughout the *Apostolic Constitutions* in similar lists (see, for example, VIII, xxviii, 7–8 and VIII, xlvii, 26), while on two occasions a different term, ψαλτῳδός, is used (II, xxviii, 5 and VI, xvii, 2).

14 And after this let the bishop receive, then the priests, and the deacons, and the subdeacons, and the readers, and the cantors (ψάλται), and the ascetics; and among the women the deaconesses, and the virgins, and the widows; then the children, and then all the people in good order with reverence and piety and without commotion. 15 And let the bishop give the oblation (προσφοράν) saying, 'Body of Christ', and let the one receiving say, 'Amen'. And let the deacon take the chalice and in giving it say, 'Blood of Christ, the chalice of life', and let the one drinking say, 'Amen'. 16 Let the thirty-third psalm be sung while all the rest receive. 17 And when all have received, men and women, let the deacon take what remains and carry it into the sacristies. xiv, 1. And when the singer (ψάλλοντος) is finished, let the deacon say . . .

236   *Apostolic Constitutions* II, lix, 1–3; *Funk*, 171

> Morning and evening public prayer is enjoined for both clergy and laity,
> and Psalm 62 is specified as a morning psalm and Psalm 140 as a vesper
> psalm. Compare with VIII, xxxiv, where six office hours are cited; the differ-
> ence might be accounted for by the mention of the laity here or perhaps by
> chronology. (On the subject of specific material for morning and evening
> offices, see the head note to VII, xxxv, 2, below.)

As you teach, O bishop, order and exhort the people always to assemble in
the church, morning and evening of each day ... For it is said not only of
priests, but rather each of the laity must hear it and consider it for himself
... But you must assemble each day, morning and evening, singing psalms
and praying in the houses of the Lord, saying the sixty-second psalm in the
morning, and in the evening the one hundred and fortieth, 3 especially on
the day of the Sabbath; and on the day of the Lord's Resurrection, the
Lord's Day, meet still more earnestly ...

237   *Apostolic Constitutions* VIII, xxxiv, 1, 8, 10; *Funk*, 540–2

> Six public offices are enjoined, the medieval eight minus prime and
> compline. In troubled times (a reference to the reign of Julian?), the hours
> should be observed privately.

1 Discharge your prayer offices (εὐχάς) in the morning, and at the third
hour, and at the sixth, and at the ninth, and in the evening, and at cockcrow
... 8 If it is not possible to come to church because of the faithless, gather
at a house, O bishop, so that the righteous may not enter into the assembly
of the ungodly ... 10 If it is not possible to meet in either home or church,
let each sing psalms, read and pray by himself, or together with two or three,
'For where two or three are gathered in my name', says the Lord, 'there am
I in the midst of them' (Mt 18.20).

238   *Apostolic Constitutions* VIII, xxxv, 2; *Funk*, 544

> At the vesper service a '*lucernarium* psalm' is mentioned. The passage con-
> tinues with a series of specific prayers quoted. See also VII, xlviii, where
> additional material including the *Nunc dimittis* is cited, presumably for the
> evening service, but not explicitly indicated as such. (The previous
> capitulum had quoted the Gloria in excelsis – analogously part of the
> morning service – one again presumes.) On the morning offices in general,
> see Taft (1984) and on the evening office, Winkler (1974).

When it is evening, O bishop, you will assemble the congregation, and after
the singing (ῥηθῆναι) of the *lucernarium* (ἐπιλύχνιον) psalm, the deacon
will pronounce [prayers] on behalf of the catechumens, and the distressed,
and the enlightened, and the penitents, as we said above.

239 *Apostolic Constitutions* VI, xxx, 2; *Funk*, 381

> The faithful are to avoid the Jewish and pagan practice of purgations associated with the dead and instead celebrate the Eucharist and sing psalms. (On funerals, see also VIII, xlii, 1.)

Unencumbered [by such practices] you must gather in the cemeteries, holding a reading of the sacred books and singing (ψάλλοντες) for the martyrs who have fallen asleep and all those sainted from of old and your own brethren who have fallen asleep in the Lord; and offer the acceptable Eucharist, the representation of the royal body of Christ, in both your churches and in the cemeteries; and at the departure of those who have fallen asleep lead them out with singing, if indeed they are faithful in the Lord.

240 *Apostolic Constitutions* VIII, xxxii, 9; *Funk*, 534

> Given here is the musically relevant portion of a long passage listing occupations and forms of behavior which, if not renounced, disqualify a candidate for baptism. Such lists of proscribed occupations are common in early Christian legislation, but musicians are not always mentioned.

If one of those who work upon the stage approaches, either man or woman, or charioteer, or gladiator, or runner, or wagerer, or athlete, or aulos player (χοραύλης), or cithara player, or lyre player, or one who performs the pantomime, or a hukster, let them desist or be rejected.

241 *Apostolic Constitutions* V, x, 2; *Funk*, 265

> The passage shows clearly the typical mingling of motivation in the polemic against pagan music – idolatry and obscenity are linked. (For musical references in the *Apostolic Constitutions* neither quoted nor cited here, see I, v, 2; II, liv, 1; II, lvi, 3; II, lviii, 4; III, vii, 7; V, xix, 3.)

Even your rejoicings must be conducted with fear and trembling. For the Christian who is faithful ought to sing neither a heathen hymn (ᾠδήν) nor an obscene song, since he will be obliged by that hymn to mention the demonic names of idols, and in place of the Holy Spirit the evil one will enter into him.

Egeria

In 1884 G. F. Gammurrini announced the discovery – in an eleventh-century manuscript at Arezzo – of the diary of an early Christian woman on pilgrimage to the Holy Land. He attributed it to a St Silvia of Aquitaine, sister-in-law of the late fourth century Rufinus, a Roman prefect. Subsequently, and more plausibly, it has been attributed to Aetheria (the preferred spelling of whose name is Egeria), a Spanish nun of approximately the same period. The precise date of her pilgrimage cannot be determined, but internal evidence – quotations from contemporary literature and the state of the Jerusalem liturgy – suggest the beginning of the fifth century.

It is a document of great importance to liturgical history, closing as it does with a lengthy description of the liturgy at Jerusalem. This begins with the weekday and Sunday services and continues, after a break in the manuscript of one folio, with the yearly services from Epiphany to Pentecost. In the present work only the former section is translated; this because of its general significance as opposed to the more localized relevance of the festival services which are adapted to the various holy places in Palestine. Just two short passages from the latter material are selected for translation here because of their interesting musical terminology. For those wishing to read the entire work there are several English translations, two of which are quite recent and have useful introductions: *Gingras* and *Wilkinson*. *Gingras* – more carefully literal than *Wilkinson* – is especially recommended for its excellent notes with their detailed references to the copious secondary literature.

The present translation of Egeria's curious, perhaps primitive, Latin is more scrupulously literal than usual, particularly in dealing with the frequent references to 'psalms', 'hymns' and 'antiphons'. These can be puzzling to those looking for light on the performance practice of early Christian psalmody, but of great benefit to those seeking a broad view of psalmody as it functioned within the context of an integrated monastic and cathedral office, with the various contributions of monks, clergy and people quite clearly defined.

242   *Itinerarium Egeriae* xxiv, 1; *CCL* clxxv, 67

> The weekday night office is first described. The psalmody is performed by monks and nuns, while there is only a small representation of the local clergy to say the interspersed prayers. At least that is the apparent meaning of the last sentence; if the word order is observed more scrupulously, however, the nice distinction between the function of monks and clergy is obscured: 'For two or three priests, and deacons also, take turns each day along with the monazontes, who say prayers with every hymn and antiphon'. For a secondary source, incidentally, that presents a particularly cogent summary of the distinction between monastic and cathedral office, see Jones, Wainwright and Yarnold (1978, pp. 358–69).
>
> Note the perplexing distinction among 'hymns', 'psalms' and 'antiphons'. Note also the verb *dicere* which Egeria uses consistently to indicate their performance; it will be translated here with similar consistency by the appropriate form of the English 'to sing'.

Each day before cockcrow, all the doors of the Anastasis are opened, and all the *monazontes* and *parthenae*, as they are called here, come down, and not only they, but also those lay people, men and women, who wish to keep vigil at so early an hour. From that hour until it is light, hymns are sung (*dicuntur*) and psalms responded to, and likewise antiphons; and with every hymn there is a prayer. For two or three priests, and likewise deacons, who say these prayers with every hymn and antiphon, take turns to be there each day with the *monazontes*.

243   *Itinerarium Egeriae* xxiv, 2; *CCL* clxxv, 67–8

> Secondly the morning office, the later lauds, is described. Here the bishop
> and his clergy play a central role, suggesting that lauds was part of the
> original cathedral versus monastic office. Note the term *cancelli*, literally
> lattice work, used to designate the waist-high chancel barriers or railings
> of the fourth century, the ancestors of the eastern iconostasis and the west-
> ern choir screen.

As soon as it begins to grow light, they start to sing the morning hymns. And
behold the bishop arrives with the clergy and immediately enters the cave.
First he says a prayer for all from within the railings (*cancellos*); he himself
commemorates the names of whomever he chooses and then blesses the
catechumens. Similarly he says a prayer for the faithful and blesses them.
After this the bishop comes out from within the railings, and all approach
him to [kiss] his hand; as he leaves, he blesses them one by one, and thus is
the dismissal (*missa*) given as it is already light.

244   *Itinerarium Egeriae* xxiv, 3; *CCL* clxxv, 68

> The sixth and ninth hours consist in monastic psalmody followed by an
> episcopal blessing. Prime is omitted as one would expect, but the absence
> of terce is somewhat surprising.

Again at the sixth hour all come down to the Anastasis in the same way,
and sing psalms and antiphons until the bishop is called. He likewise comes
down and does not sit, but immediately enters within the railings of the
Anastasis, that is within the cave where he was earlier; and again he first
says a prayer, then blesses the faithful, and as he goes out from behind the
railings they again approach him to kiss his hand. And at the ninth hour
they do the same as at the sixth.

245   *Itinerarium Egeriae* xxiv. 4–6; *CCL* clxxv, 68

> The final daily service is the forerunner of vespers, a service characterized
> by the lighting of the evening lamps and hence called λύχνικον in Greek
> and *lucernare*, or more commonly *lucernarium*, in Latin. It is generally con-
> sidered to be, along with the morning office, an essential component of the
> cathedral office. Note, however, the monastic psalmodic prelude before
> the advent of the bishop. The adjective *infinitae*, referring to the voices of
> the children who respond to the litany, is construed here to refer to volume,
> but it could just as well be a redundant reference to the number of voices.

But at the tenth hour – what they call here *licinicon*, and what we call *lucernare*
– the entire throng gathers again at the Anastasis, and all the lamps and
candles are lit, producing a boundless light. The light, however, is not
carried in from outside, but brought from the inner cave, that is from within
the railings, where night and day a lamp burns always. And the *psalmi*

lucernares, as well as antiphons, are sung for a long time. And behold the bishop is called and comes down and takes the high seat, while the priests also sit in their places, and hymns and antiphons are sung. And when these have been finished according to custom, the bishop arises and stands before the railings, that is before the cave, and one of the deacons makes the commemoration of individuals as is customary. And as the deacon pronounces the individual names, a great number of children, whose voices are very loud (*infinitae*), stand there and respond *Kyrie eleison*, or as we say, *miserere Domine*. And when the deacon has finished all that he has to say, the bishop first says a prayer, praying for all, and then all pray, both faithful and catechumens at the same time. Then the deacon calls out that every catechumen, wherever he stands, should bow his head, and then the bishop stands and recites the blessing over the catechumens. Then follows a prayer and again the deacon calls out and admonishes everyone of the faithful to stand and bow his head; again the bishop blesses the faithful and thus the dismissal is given at the Anastasis. And everyone begins to approach the bishop to kiss his hand.

246   *Itinerarium Egeriae* xxiv, 7; *CCL* CLXXV, 68

> Immediately after vespers there is a ceremony unique to Jerusalem, a visit to the site of the Crucifixion, in a corner of the large courtyard adjoining the Anastasis to the east. Given here is only the first sentence of the passage which mentions the procession to the site; the procession resembles virtually every one subsequently described by Egeria in that it is accompanied by singing.

And afterwards the bishop is led from the Anastasis to the Cross accompanied by hymns (*cum ymnis*), and all the people go at the same time . . .

247   *Itinerarium Egeriae* xxiv, 8; *CCL* CLXXV, 69

> The description of Sunday services begins. In place of the weekday monastic vigil there is a rather informal vigil in which the laity take part. It is held in the courtyard between the Anastasis and the Martyrium church. The term basilica is not entirely inappropriate in view of the portico surrounding the courtyard.

On the seventh day, however, that is the Lord's Day, all the people gather before cockcrow, as at Easter, as many as is possible in that place, the basilica, which is located next to the Anastasis, yet out of doors, where lamps are hung for the occasion. Since they fear they might not arrive before cockcrow, they come early and sit there. Hymns are sung and also antiphons, and there are prayers with each hymn and antiphon. For priests and deacons are always prepared for vigils in that place because of the crowd which gathers, and because it is customary that the holy places not be opened before cockcrow.

248 *Itinerarium Egeriae* xxiv, 9–11; *CCL* clxxv, 69

> Next there is a service involving the bishop from the outset. Its classification is controversial, with some seeing it as Sunday lauds and others as a vigil before lauds. If it is lauds, the three psalms mentiioned could be Psalms 148–50, but unfortunately Egeria rarely specifies which psalms are sung.

As soon as the first cock crows, straightway the bishop comes down and enters the cave in the Anastasis. All the gates are opened, and the entire throng enters the Anastasis, where already countless lamps are burning, and when the people are within, one of the priests sings a psalm and all respond, after which there is a prayer. Then one of the deacons sings a psalm, similarly followed by a prayer, and a third psalm is sung by some cleric, followed by a third prayer and the commemoration of all. When these three psalms have been sung and the three prayers said, behold censers (*thiamataria*) are brought into the cave of the Anastasis, so that the entire Anastasis basilica is filled with the smell. And then as the bishop stands behind the railings, he takes the Gospel book and goes to the gate and the bishop himself reads the Resurrection of the Lord. When the reading of it has begun, there is such moaning and groaning among everybody and such crying, that even the hardest of hearts could be moved to tears because the Lord has suffered so much for us. When the Gospel has been read, the bishop leaves and is led with hymns to the Cross, accompanied by all the people. There, again, one psalm is sung and a prayer said. Then he blesses the people, and the dismissal takes place. And as the bishop goes out, all approach to kiss his hand.

249 *Itinerarium Egeriae* xxiv, 12; *CCL* clxxv, 69–70

> After the previous service there is a period of monastic psalmody with interspersed clerical prayer. Some see this as Sunday lauds, unlikely in view of the bishop's absence, while others speculate that lauds, not mentioned by Egeria, was absorbed into the beginning of the synaxis which is described next.

As soon as the bishop withdraws to his house, the monks right from that very hour return to the Anastasis and psalms and antiphons are sung until it is light; and with every psalm and antiphon a prayer is said, for the priests and deacons take turns in keeping daily vigil with the people at the Anastasis. Also those of the laity who wish, men and women, remain at the place until it is light, while those who do not, return to their homes to take some sleep.

250   *Itinerarium Egeriae* xxv, 1; *CCL* CLXXV, 70

> At dawn the pre-eucharistic synaxis is held. Unfortunately Egeria omits
> the typical events and cites only the peculiarity of protracted preaching.
> The description is controversial in that some take it to refer only to the
> synaxis, while others assume the Eucharist is completed before the dis-
> missal from the church, which is, incidentally, the great Constantinian
> basilica called the Martyrium. Much significance is attached to the term
> *proceditur* by liturgical historians; see *Gingras* pp. 220–1.

When it is light, however, because it is the Lord's Day, they go (*proceditur*)
to the greater church, which Constantine built, the church on Golgotha
behind the Cross, and all is done according to custom as maintained everywhere on the Lord's Day. Indeed, since the custom here is such that as many
of the priests sitting in attendance preach (*predicent*) as wish to, and after all
of them the bishop preaches – and this preaching, moreover, always takes
place on the Lord's Day, so that the people are always educated in the Scriptures and in the love of God – while this preaching is going on a great deal
of time elapses until the dismissal from the church, and so the dismissal
takes place before the fourth or perhaps even the fifth hour.

251   *Itinerarium Egeriae* xxv, 2–4; *CCL* CLXXV, 70

> Whether or not the Eucharist had been celebrated in the previous service
> at the Martyrium basilica, the exclusion of catechumens here at the
> Anastasis implies that it is now. The phrase *aguntur gratiae Deo* would seem
> also to suggest this, but some who find it insufficient add the phrase *et sic
> fit oblatio*, with little apparent justification. (On the Sunday order of
> services, see also xxvii, 2–3).

But when the dismissal from church has taken place according to custom as
it is observed everywhere, then the monks lead the bishop with hymns from
the church to the Anastasis. As the bishop begins to draw near with hymns,
all the doors of the Anastasis basilica are opened, and all the people enter,
the faithful that is, not the catechumens. When the people are inside, the
bishop enters, and straightway goes behind the railings of the cave shrine.
First thanks are given to God (*aguntur gratiae Deo*), and thus a prayer for all.
Afterwards the deacon calls out that all, wherever they stand, are to bow
their heads, and then the bishop, standing behind the inner railings, blesses
them and afterwards goes out. As the bishop leaves, all approach to kiss his
hand. And thus it is that the dismissal is delayed until almost the fifth or
sixth hour.

252   *Itinerarium Egeriae* xxv, 4–5; *CCL* CLXXV, 70–1

> The Sunday order of services concludes with vespers while sext and none
> are omitted. Egeria closes this portion of her diary with the observation

that the psalms and antiphons are always appropriate, but unfortunately, as indicated above, she rarely specifies what they are.

And at the *lucernare* things are done the same as in the daily ritual. This order is thus observed on every day throughout the year, except on solemn feast days, and we will describe below how it is done on these. Now it is this which stands out in all of this, that they see to it that the psalms and antiphons are always appropriate, including those sung at night, those toward morning, and those throughout the day – at the sixth hour, the ninth hour and at *lucernare*; thus they are always so suitable and so appropriate that they pertain to the very thing that is being done.

253   *Itinerarium Egeriae* xxvii, 7–8; *CCL* CLXXV, 74

> The Lenten Friday vigil is described. For those who wish the distinction between responsorial and antiphonal psalmody to be clear cut, the passage must be disturbing. Most translators, in fact, reassemble the terms in various orders other than Egeria's in aid of the distinction.

But on Friday the vigil is celebrated in the Anastasis from that hour in which they came from Sion with hymns until morning, that is from the time of the *lucernare* until the approach of morning on the next day, that is Saturday. The Eucharist (*oblatio*) at the Anastasis is very early, so that the dismissal is given before sunrise. All night responsorial psalms are sung in turn (*uicibus*), antiphons in turn, and various readings in turn, all of which continue until morning.

254   *Itinerarium Egeriae* xliii, 5; *CCL* CLXXV, 85

> On the early afternoon of Pentecost a service is held at the Imbomom, the purported site of Christ's Ascension. The term *interponere* is of interest to the extent that it may bear on what German liturgical historians call *Zwischenpsalmodie* (see Stuiber, 1980), that is, the singing of an appropriate psalm after each reading within a series. The passage, incidentally, furnishes a rare instance of Egeria specifying readings.

As soon as they have climbed the Mount of Olives, that is the Eleona, they go first to the Imbomom, that is the place whence the Lord ascended into the heavens. And there the bishop sits, and the priests, and all the people too; readings are read there, interspersed (*interposite*) hymns are sung, and antiphons appropriate to the very day and place are sung; the prayers also, which are interspersed, always have such subject matter as befits the day and place. That passage of the Gospel is also read where it speaks of the Ascension of the Lord, and again that passage from the Acts of the Apostles is read where it speaks of the Ascension of the Lord into the heavens after his Resurrection.

Canons of Laodicea

A collection of sixty canons generally thought to date from the second half of the fourth century. Nothing is known for certain of the Council of Laodicea from which they purport to originate.

255   Canon 15; *Hefele-Leclercq* I, 2, 1007

> A document of central importance. Perhaps for the first time it: (1) specifies the cantor as a 'canonical' office; (2) mentions that he sings from the ambo; and (3) that he uses some sort of liturgical text.

No others are to sing (ψάλλειν) in church, besides the canonical cantors (κανονικῶν ψαλτῶν), who ascend the ambo and sing from a parchment (διφθέρας).

256   Canon 17; *Hefele-Leclercq* I, 2, 1009

> This regulation seems more likely to be meant for the office, say, the Sunday morning vigil, than the pre-eucharistic synaxis.

The psalms ought not to be sung one after the other in the assemblies (συνάζεσι), but a reading should be interpolated after each psalm.

257   Canon 23; *Hefele-Leclercq* I, 2, 1012

> The stole is reserved for the deacon, perhaps, rather than reader and cantor.

Neither the readers nor the cantors (ψάλτας) ought to wear the stole (ὡράριον) or thus to read and sing.

258   Canon 24; *Hefele-Leclercq* I, 2, 1012–13

> No clerics, including cantors, may frequent taverns.

The priestly orders from presbyters to deacons, and in turn those of the churchly order, to subdeacons, readers, cantors, exorcists, porters, and the order of ascetics, ought not to enter a tavern.

259   Canon 53; *Hefele-Leclercq* I, 2, 1023

> Christians must not dance at weddings.

Those Christians attending weddings ought not to leap and dance, but rather partake respectfully of the luncheon or dinner as befits Christians.

260 Canon 54; *Hefele-Leclercq* I, 2, 1023

> An even stricter standard of behavior is expected of clerics at such events.

Priests or clerics of whatever rank must not look upon the spectacles at weddings, or at banquets, but they must arise and depart from there before the entry of the musicians (θυμελιχούς).

261 Canon 59; *Hefele-Leclercq* I, 2, 1025

> A passage of some importance. The commentary of *Hefele-Leclercq* interprets it to mean that certain approved non-biblical hymns are allowed, but an outright ban seems more likely.

One must not recite privately composed psalms (ἰδιωτιχοὺς ψαλμούς) nor non-canonical books in the church, but only the canonical books of the Old and New Testament.

Canons of Basil

This collection of one hundred and six Alexandrian canons, originally in Greek, is published only in a German translation from an Arabic manuscript by Riedel. It is virtually impossible to assign a precise date to it since it appears to have been reworked over a number of centuries from the late fourth until the Arab conquest (*Riedel*, pp. 232–3). The collection is not to be confused with the genuine *Canonical Epistles* of St Basil.

262 Canon 36; *Riedel*, 256

> The virgin should sing psalms, presumably in private.

A virgin must not become involved in the cares and concerns of this world; she ought never to go to the place where a wedding or banquet is held. A virgin must employ her tongue frequently in singing psalms; she must be chaste, obedient and modest in speech.

263 Canon 37; *Riedel*, 257

> The profession of woman musician cited here is just one of a series forbidden to Christians. (See APOSTOLIC CONSTITUTIONS VIII, xxii, 9.)

A woman who dances in a tavern and who entices people through pretty singing and sweet sound, which is deceitful and full of seduction, shall, if she gives up this profession, wait forty days before she communicates; then she may receive the mysteries.

264   Canon 74; *Riedel,* 267

> The ecclesiastical reader may not play a musical instrument. Perhaps the
> circumstance that the reader is singled out here rather than the cantor
> indicates a comparatively early date for this particular canon. In the
> present translation the liberty is taken of substituting cithara for the
> obviously anachronistically guitar of *Riedel.*

When a reader learns to play the cithara, he shall be taught to confess it. If
he does not return to it, he will endure his punishment for seven weeks. If
he persists in it, he must be discharged and excluded from the church.

265   Canon 97; *Riedel,* 273

> Psalms are sung as faithful and catechumens gather for the pre-eucharistic
> synaxis. This is a unique reference, which unfortunately cannot be dated.
> Perhaps the omission of an Old Testament lesson and the usurpation of
> the psalmody by deacons indicates a comparatively late date.

When they begin to celebrate the mysteries, they should not do so in disorder, but should wait until the entire congregation has gathered; as long as
they are coming in they should read psalms. Then after the congregation is
assembled, there should be readings from the Apostles, then from the Acts
and from the Gospel. If the deacons read well, they should read the psalms;
and if the presbyters read well, they should read the Gospel. If they do not
read well, the oldest lectors should read the psalms, and the deacons the
Gospel. Only a deacon or a presbyter should read the Gospel in a catholic
church; none should overstep his rank.

266   Canon 97; *Riedel,* 274–5

> Canon 97 continues with its description of the Eucharist. Offertory
> psalmody is not mentioned, but communion psalmody is; the remarks
> quoted here appear in that context.

Those singing psalms at the altar shall not sing with pleasure, but with
understanding; they should sing nothing other than psalms . . . The congregation shall respond with vigor after every psalm. If anyone is physically
sick, so that he answers after the others, no blame resides in him; but if he is
healthy and keeps quiet, then one leaves him alone; he is not worthy of
blessing.

CHAPTER 10

Western authors of the fourth and early fifth centuries

Included here are the major western authors born in the fourth century with the exception of Augustine, who is reserved for the final chapter. They are five in number: Hilary of Poitiers, Ambrose, Niceta of Remesiana, Jerome and Cassian. Hilary, perhaps, makes the most modest contribution of the group with his psalm commentary, the first Latin example of the genre. Ambrose, of course, is well known as one of the most musically significant church fathers, while Niceta of Remesiana, comparably significant due to his remarkable sermon on psalmody, has been largely ignored until recent times. Jerome, the celebrated translator of the *Vulgate*, has left us numerous brief remarks on the place of music in the monastic and ascetic life, and finally Cassian is probably the most important contributor to our knowledge of psalmody in the monastic office prior to St Benedict.

Generally considered, these authors provide musical references very similar to those of their eastern contemporaries. They display the same position of antagonism toward pagan musical practice, the same cautious acceptance of academic music, and the same penchant for instrumental allegory; while in the area of liturgical music they describe the same phenomena of psalmody in the Eucharist, at vigils and in the daily round of monastic office hours. In this sense they merely corroborate what we already know, but there is one essential differentiating factor – that of chronology. Certain of the positive developments in liturgical song like the monastic cultivation of psalmody and the laity's enthusiasm for psalmodic vigils originate in the east and spread westwards. This circumstance grants us an historical perspective that might eventually be of immense help in understanding the period which is possibly the most important in the history of western ecclesiastical music prior to the time of the Carolingians.

Hilary of Poitiers (c.315–367)

Called the 'Athanasius of the West' because of his vigorous opposition to Arianism, Hilary was the first important Latin exegete and theologian. In 350, he was named bishop of Poitiers. His musical significance is twofold: he was the earliest composer of hymns in the west (see Mason, 1904), and wrote a psalm commentary in the typical allegorical style of Origen. Several passages from the latter are quoted below.

267 *Tractatus super psalmos, Instructio psalmorum* 1–2; *PL* IX, 232–3; *CSEL* XXII, 3–4

> Hilary's commentary opens with a preface (*Instructio psalmorum*) which places more emphasis than most of such prefaces on objective factors like the numbering of the psalms and the historical significance of the super-

scriptions. An attempt is made here to quote those passages which are of more interest to students of music history while at the same time giving a rounded view of the work's content. The first two capitula deal with broad issues like the proper title of the Psalter.

1 From the very writings they have left behind, however, we find that many hold opposing views of the Book of Psalms. For some of the Hebrews want the psalms to be divided into five books, such that the first would extend to the fortieth psalm, the second from the fortieth to the seventy-first, the third to the eighty-eighth, the fourth to the one hundred and fifth – so that each of these psalms would then end with 'Amen, Amen' – and the fifth, finally, would close with the one hundred and fiftieth psalm. Others, however, thought that the psalms should be inscribed 'Psalms of David', by which title they wanted it to be understood that they were all composed by David. But in accordance with apostolic authority we both say and write 'Book of Psalms', recalling that verse in the Acts of the Apostles: 'For it is written in the book of Psalms "Let his habitation become desolate and let another take his office"' (Acts 1.20). Hence they should not be called five books, as some of the Hebrews would have it, nor 'Psalms of David', after the naivete of others, but should instead be known as the 'Book of Psalms', in accordance with apostolic authority.

2 These psalms have several authors, however. David is given as the author in the inscription above some of the psalms, for some it is Solomon, for some Asaph, for some Idithum, for some the 'Sons of Chore', and for one it is Moses. So it is indeed ridiculous to call them 'Psalms of David' when their authors are given right there in the very titles.

268   *Instructio psalmorum* 5; *PL* ix, 235; *CSEL* xxii, 6–7

The psalms can only be understood as prophecies of Christ's life.

There should be no doubt that the things mentioned in the psalms must be understood in accordance with the teaching of the Gospel, such that regardless of the person in which the prophetic spirit has spoken, it should nonetheless be referred in its entirety to recognition of the coming of our Lord Jesus Christ, his incarnation, passion and kingdom, and to the glory and excellence of our own resurrection . . . For prophecy as a whole is woven together with allegories and types, through which are revealed all the mysteries of the only-begotten Son of God as he is born in the flesh, suffers, dies, rises again and, along with those glorified by him for their belief in him, reigns in eternity and judges all others. And because the scribes and Pharisees did not acknowledge that the Son of God was born in the flesh, and so denied everyone access to the prophetic understanding, they are condemned thus by the Lord: 'Woe to you who are learned in the Law, for you have taken away the key of knowledge: you have not entered in, and those entering in, you have hindered' (Lk 11.52).

> **269**   *Instructio psalmorum* 7; *PL* IX, 237; *CSEL* XXII, 8–9

> The very shape of the instrument on which David composed the psalms –
> the psaltery – testifies to their prophetic spirituality.

7 And though we know by the testimony of the Lord himself that everything
spoken by David came from the Holy Spirit, even the external form of this
prophecy teaches the very same thing, that knowledge of lofty and celestial
doctrine manifested itself in it. For the prophecy was delivered on that
musical instrument called psaltery in Greek and *nabla* in Hebrew, which is
unique in being the most upright of all musical instruments, having nothing
crooked or oblique about it, and whose musical harmony is not produced by
the motion of its lower parts. Instead, it is an instrument built in the shape
of the Lord's body and made without any inward or outward curve, an
instrument moved and struck from above and brought to life to sing of
supernal and heavenly teaching, not one that sounds with a base and
terrestrial spirit, as do the other earthly instruments. For the Lord did not
preach what is base and terrestrial while in the instrument of his own body,
as he himself declared: 'He who is of the earth belongs to the earth, and of
the earth he speaks; he who comes from heaven bears witness to what he has
seen and heard' (Jn 3.31–2).

270   *Instructio psalmorum* 8; *PL* IX, 238; *CSEL* XXII, 9–10

> The psalms were numbered not by the Hebrews, but by the authors of the
> Septuagint.

8 One should note that among the Hebrews there is no precise numbering
of the psalms; rather they are written with no indication of their order. They
are not designated as first, second, third, fiftieth or one hundredth, but are
run together with no distinction of order or number. For Esdras, as ancient
tradition maintains, collected and presented in one volume, what had been
disordered and scattered because of the diversity of authors and periods.
But when the seventy elders, who remained in the Synagogue to preserve
the Law's teaching in accordance with the tradition of Moses, were afterwards entrusted by King Ptolemy with the responsibility of translating the
entire Law from Hebrew into Greek, they grasped the excellence of the
psalms with a spiritual and heavenly knowledge and reduced them to
number and order.

271   *Instructio psalmorum* 17; *PL* IX, 243; *CSEL* XXII, 14–15

> There is a variety of superscriptions to the psalms: the names of authors,
> genre designations, etc. One must seek to understand these.

The titles of all the superscriptions are different, however. For in addition
to those which give the names of authors and indications of their circum-

stances of time period, there are others with titles such as 'unto the end' and others with simply 'psalm of a song' and 'song of a psalm'. Now it is necessary to grasp the various reasons underlying the different superscriptions ...

272   *Instructio psalmorum* 19; *PL* IX, 244; *CSEL* XXII, 15–16

> These four 'genre designations' have caused considerable confusion among musicologists. Much of this can be avoided simply by keeping in mind that they are exegetical in nature: they refer to Old Testament not contemporary Christian usage.

19 Now, the varieties of function and kind in the art of music are as follows. There is a 'psalm' when the voice rests and only the playing of the instrument is heard. There is a 'song' (*canticum*) when the chorus of singers, using its freedom, is not bound in musical deference to the instrument and enjoys a hymn with sonorous voice above. There is a 'song of a psalm' when after the instrument has played the singing chorus is heard, following it and vying with it, seeking to imitate the measures of the psaltery with the measures of the voice. There is a 'psalm of a song' when, after the chorus has sung, the art of the musical instrument is adapted to the hymn of human singing and the psaltery plays with equal sweetness to the measures of the singing voice. By these four types of the art of music, then, appropriate superscriptions are applied to each of the psalms individually, and the reason for each superscription is revealed in both the meaning of the psalms and the particulars of musical doctrine.

273   *Tractatus in psalmum lxv*, 3; *PL* IX, 425; *CSEL* XXII, 250

> The first example in this volume of a passage describing the *jubilus*. For literature on this much discussed phenomenon see AUGUSTINE, *In psalmum xxxii*, II, S. 1, 8. This example from Hilary is singular in two respects: it presents an interesting distinction between the Latin *jubilus* and the Greek ἀλαλαγμός ('shout'); and its definition of *jubilus* – in the second sentence here – is expressed in particularly obscure terms. That the translation has a degree of cogency is due to the efforts of Professor Dickson.

In Latin manuscripts we read: 'Rejoice (*iubilate*) in God, all ye earth'. Now, according to the conventions of our language, we give the name jubilus (*iubilum*) to the sound of a pastoral and rustic voice, when the sound of a voice prolonged and expressed forcefully is heard in the wilderness either answering or asking, in point of sense. In Greek books, however, which are closer to the Hebrew, it is not written with the same sense, for what they have is: 'Shout (ἀλαλάζατε) unto God, all ye earth'. Now, among the Greeks, the term shout (which is rendered in Latin as jubilus) means the cry of an army in battle, either when it routs the enemy or else proclaims a victorious outcome in a shout of joy. We gain a clearer understanding of this occurrence, that is, how translation weakens meaning, in another psalm, where we read: 'Clap your hands, all peoples, praise God in a shout of joy' (Ps 44.2). Now, a shout of joy (*vox exultationis*) does not mean the same thing as jubilus; but for the purpose of translation, since a proper term for 'shout of joy' is not available, 'shout of joy' is rendered by what is called jubilus.

Ambrose (c.339–397)

Born at Trier to a prominent governing family, Ambrose was himself a state official when in 374 he was offered the bishopric of Milan at the insistence of the people. Only a catechumen at the time, he accepted reluctantly, was immediately baptized and ordained, and subsequently devoted himself to the study of theology and the ascetic life. His tenure as bishop of Milan was distinguished by a vigorous defense of the Church against both Arianism and the authority of the Empire. He played an important part in the conversion of Augustine, who shared the contemporary admiration for his preaching.

The name of Ambrose has rich musical connotation since the Milanese chant bears it in roughly analogous fashion to that of Gregory and the Roman chant. Ambrose was also noted as a composer of Latin metrical hymns, and subsequent liturgical documents like the *Regula Benedicti* refer to office hymns as *ambrosiana*. As for his references to music, we owe a special debt to his many brief allusions to liturgical psalmody. These are widely scattered throughout his writings, but their study is greatly facilitated by the work of Leeb (1967).

The musical references presented here are given in the following order: those from works dealing with the psalms, from other exegetical works, from the letters, and from the remaining theological and ethical works.

274 *Explanatio psalmi i*, 6; *PL* xiv, 923; *CSEL* lxiv, 5–6

> Ambrose wrote extended expositions of selected Psalms, including an independent book-length exposition of Psalm 118. The exposition of Psalm 1 serves as a general introduction to the Psalter, more devotional in character than scientifically exegetical like that of Hilary. Capitulum 6, in the first of three excerpts given here, relates that the special office of sacred song is represented only sporadically throughout Scripture except in the Book of Psalms.

Yet it is David who was especially chosen by the Lord for this office, so that what in others seems to stand out only rarely in their works would in his shine forth continually and without ceasing. We read but one song (*canticum*) in the Book of Judges, while the rest runs its course in the manner of history, relating the deeds of the ancients. Isaiah wrote one song, in which he soothes the heart of his readers, whereas elsewhere he rages with the fearsome trumpet of rebuke. Not even those very enemies who persecuted him to the death because of the other things he said could reproach him for this song. Daniel and Habakkuk each wrote one. And Solomon, himself, David's son, although he is said to have sung countless songs, has left only one which the Church accepts, the Song of Songs; he did write

Proverbs however. Among others, then, one can encounter only isolated examples.

275   *Explanatio psalmi i*, 7; *PL* XIV, 923; *CSEL* LXIV, 6

> Capitulum 7 makes the point that the virtues of the various types of Scripture are combined in the psalms.

History teaches, the Law instructs, prophecy proclaims, reproach chastens and moralizing persuades; in the Book of Psalms there is the successful accomplishment of all this along with a kind of balm of human salvation. Whoever reads there, has a special remedy whereby he can cure the wounds of selfish passion. Whoever is willing to look closely, discovers a variety of contests prepared for him, as if in a communal gymnasium of souls or a stadium of virtue, from which he can select for himself the one for which he knows himself best suited, in which he can more easily win the crown. If one is eager to study the deeds of our forebears and wishes to imitate them, he finds contained within a single psalm the entire range of ancestral history so that he gains a treasury of memories as a stipend for his reading. Things explained with more brevity also seem easier.

276   *Explanatio psalmi i*, 9; *PL* XIV, 924–5; *CSEL* LXIV, 7–8

> Capitulum 9 is frequently cited for the occasional glimpse it affords of fourth-century psalmodic practice. Particularly interesting is the allusion to the faithful's inattention to the readings as opposed to the responsorial psalmody.

What is more pleasing than a psalm? David himself puts it nicely: 'Praise the Lord', he says, 'for a psalm is good' (Ps 146.1). And indeed! A psalm is the blessing of the people, the praise of God, the commendation of the multitude, the applause of all, the speech of every man, the voice of the Church, the sonorous profession of faith, devotion full of authority, the joy of liberty, the noise of good cheer, and the echo of gladness. It softens anger, it gives release from anxiety, it alleviates sorrow; it is protection at night, instruction by day, a shield in time of fear, a feast of holiness, the image of tranquility, a pledge of peace and harmony, which produces one song from various and sundry voices in the manner of a cithara. The day's dawning resounds with a psalm, with a psalm its passing echoes.

The Apostle admonishes women to be silent in church, yet they do well to join in a psalm; this is gratifying for all ages and fitting for both sexes. Old men ignore the stiffness of age to sing [a psalm], and melancholy veterans echo it in the joy of their hearts; young men sing one without the bane of lust, as do adolescents without threat from their insecure age or the temptation of sensual pleasure; even young women sing psalms with no loss of wifely decency, and girls sing a hymn to God with sweet and supple voice while maintaining decorum and suffering no lapse of modesty. Youth is eager to understand [a psalm], and the child who refuses to learn other things takes pleasure in contemplating it; it is a kind of play, productive of more learning than that which is dispensed with stern discipline. With what great effort is silence maintained in church during the readings (*cum lectiones leguntur*)! If just one person recites, the entire congregation makes noise; but when a psalm is read (*legitur*), it is itself the guarantor of silence because when all speak [in the response] no one makes noise. Kings put aside the arrogance of power and sing a psalm, as David himself was glad to be observed in this function; a psalm, then, is sung by emperors and rejoiced in by the people. Individuals vie in proclaiming what is of profit to all. A psalm is sung at home and repeated outdoors; it is learned without effort and retained with delight. A psalm joins those with differences, unites those at odds and reconciles those who have been offended, for who will not concede to him with whom one sings to God in one voice? It is after all a great bond of unity for the full number of people to join in one chorus. The strings of the cithara differ, but create one harmony (*symphonia*). The fingers of a musician (*artificis*) often go astray among the strings though they are very few in number, but among the people the Spirit musician knows not how to err.

277   *Explanatio psalmi xlv*, 15; *PL* xiv, 1140–1; *CSEL* lxiv, 340

A specific psalm verse is cited as psalm response.

Hence what was sung today as a response to the psalm (*psalmi responsorio decantatum est*), considerably corroborates our point: 'With expectation I have waited for the Lord, and he was attentive to me' (Ps 39.2).

278   *Expositio psalmi cxviii*, viii, 48; *PL* xv, 1314; *CSEL* lxii, 180

A reference to singing at midday Eucharist.

The fast is mandated: take care that you do not neglect it. If hunger urges you to a midday meal and lack of self-control disinclines you to fast, you are nonetheless better served by a heavenly banquet. Let not well prepared meals force you to miss the heavenly sacrament. Delay a little: the end of the day is not far removed. There are indeed many days of this sort when one ought to arrive in church right at midday, as hymns are to be sung and the sacrifice to be offered. Then indeed stand ready to receive this [spiritual] nourishment, to eat the body of the Lord Jesus, in which is the remission of sins and a pledge of divine reconciliation and eternal protection.

279   *Expositio psalmi cxviii*, xix, 22; *PL* xv, 1476; *CSEL* lxii, 433

> In commenting upon Psalm 118.148, Ambrose makes several brief refer-
> ences to psalmody, three of which are quoted here. (See also xx, 52.)

'My eyes have anticipated the morning that I might meditate upon thy
words' (Ps 118. 148). It says above: 'I anticipated ἐν ἀνωρίᾳ (Ps 118.147),
that is 'before the hour, before the time', while here it says 'morning',
indicating a different time for praying and singing psalms to the Lord.

280   *Expositio psalmi cxviii*, xix, 30; *PL* xv, 1478–9; *CSEL* lxii, 438

When the new day finds you meditating upon the word of God and when so
grateful a task as praying and singing psalms delights your mind, once
again you say to the Lord Jesus: 'You have made the passing of the morning
and the evening to be joyful' (Ps 64.9).

281   *Expositio psalmi cxviii*, xix, 32; *PL* xv, 1479; *CSEL* lxii, 438

At the least divide your time between God and the world. When the darkness of night prevents you from performing in public the deeds of this
world, then, as you have leisure time for God, give yourself to prayer, and,
lest you sleep, sing psalms, thus cheating your sleep by means of a benefi-
cent fraud. In the morning hasten to church and offer the first fruits of your
pious devotion, and afterwards, if worldly necessity calls, you are not
excluded from saying: 'My eyes have anticipated the morning that I might
meditate upon thy words' (Ps 118.148). You may now with peace of mind
proceed to your duties.

282   *Apologia prophetae Dauid* i, viii, 42; *PL* xiv, 867; *CSEL* xxxii–2, 325

> Ambrose mentions the singing of alleluia in the course of explaining how
> the number fifty is associated with pardon.

We receive into ourselves the coming grace of the Holy Spirit on the day of
Pentecost: fasting is at an end, God is praised and alleluia is sung.

283   *De Helia et ieiunio* xv, 55; *PL* xiv, 717; *CSEL* xxxii–2, 444–5

> In commenting upon Isaiah 5.11–12, Ambrose contrasts early morning
> carousing with prayer and psalmody at the same hour.

Therefore not without justification [does Isaiah say] woe unto them who
require the drink of intoxication in the morning, who ought to render praise
to God, to rise before dawn and meet in prayer the sun of justice, who visits
his own and rises before us, if we rise for Christ rather than for wine and
strong drink. Hymns are sung (*hymni dicuntur*), and you grasp the cithara?

Psalms are sung, and you take up the psaltery and tympanum? Woe indeed, because you disregard salvation and choose death.

284   *Expositio euangelii secundum Lucam* VII, 238; *PL* XV, 1763;
CSEL XXXII–4, 388

> In defining *symphonia* Ambrose mentions responsorial psalmody. On the omission of the comma between *psalmus* and *respondetur*, see Leeb (1967, p. 31).

For this is a symphony (*symphonia*), when there resounds in the church a united concord (*indiscreta concordia*) of differing ages and abilities as if of diverse strings; the psalm is responded to (*psalmus respondetur*), the amen is said.

285   *De uirginitate* XII, 69; *PL* XVI, 283; Cazzaniga, 32

> The dedicated virgin must rise early.

[Christ] seems to come late when you sleep too long; he seems to come late when you miss your prayers; he seems to come late when you fail to raise your voice in psalms.

286   *De interpellatione Job et Dauid* IV, vi, 23–4; *PL* XIV, 821.
CSEL XXXII–2, 284

> A rare, perhaps unique, usage by Ambrose of *psaltes*, the Greek term for cantor.

[Christ] upon the cross, when he gave up his spirit, said to the Father: 'Into thy hands I commend my spirit' (Lk 23.46). Therefore others ought not to add, as do the cantors (*psaltae*), 'Lord', which I have not found in my Latin codex, nor in the Greek, nor in the Gospel.

287   *De Jacob et uita beata* I, viii, 39; *PL* XIV, 614; *CSEL* XXXII–2, 30–1

> A man's body is compared to a broken musical instrument and his heart to the human voice. Could there be a connection with Raphael's famous painting of Saint Cecilia?

Just as he who ordinarily plays the cithara (*cithara canere*), if he saw that it was badly damaged, indeed unusable, its strings limp and its body broken, would set it aside and not feeling the need of its rhythms (*numeros*) would regale himself with his own voice; so would this man allow his corporeal cithara to lie at rest and find delight in his heart.

288   *De Jacob et uita beata* II, xii, 56; *PL* XIV, 637–8; *CSEL* XXXII–2, 68–9

> The martyrdom by Antiochus of the seven Maccabees and their mother
> produces figurative music.

What cithara could give forth sweeter song than her dying sons in their final
agony? For a spontaneous groaning burst from their lips, despite their
unwillingness. You might look upon their mangled bodies arranged in a row
as the strings of an instrument (*fila chordarum*), and you might hear in their
victorious sighs the sounding of the seven string psaltery. Not so were those
enticing songs of the fabled Sirens able to attract a listener; for they led one
to shipwreck while these led one to the triumphant sacrifice. Not so could
the song of the swan calm the ears and the spirit; for swans die by lot of
nature while these died out of love and devotion. Nor does the soft cooing
of doves in the solitary grove echo so sweetly as the last words of these as
they died. Nor does the moon shine forth so among the stars as this mother
among her sons, both when she led them to martyrdom as one lighting their
way, and when she lay among them embracing them as victors.

289   *Hexaemeron* III, v, 23; *PL* XIV, 165; *CSEL* XXXII–1, 74–5

> The islands of the sea provide an actual monastic refuge, while the waves
> of the sea provide a multifaceted image of psalmody.

Why should I mention the islands, ringed by the sea as by a necklace, where
those who have renounced the attractions of earthly indulgence and
resolved firmly to be chaste, choose to hide from the world and avoid the
dubious affairs of this life? The sea, then, is a sanctuary for temperance, a
training ground for continence, a retreat for austerity, a secure harbor,
peace on earth, and sobriety in this world. It is moreover an inducement to
devotion for these faithful and pious men, that as their psalmody (*cantus
psallentium*) vies with the sound of softly lapping waves, the islands applaud
with a gentle chorus of blessed undulations, and resound with the hymns of
the saints. How could I grasp the beauty of the sea in its entirety as viewed
by its Creator? Why say more? What is that harmony of the waves other than
the harmony of the people? Hence the Church is frequently and appropriately compared to the sea, first, because all its entrances are flooded by the
incoming tide of people, and then because it hums with the prayer of the
entire people like the washing of waves, and resounds with the singing of
psalm responses (*responsoriis psalmorum cantus*) like the crashing of breakers.

290   *Hexaemeron* IV, viii, 33; *PL* XIV, 204–5; *CSEL* XXXII–1, 139

> A play on the words *canticum* and *incantator*.

Many provoke the Church, but the charms (*carmina*) of the soothsayer's art
are not able to harm her. Those who enchant (*incantatores*) avail not where

the chant (*canticum*) of Christ is sung (*decantatur*) daily. The Church has her own enchanter (*incantatorem*), the Lord Jesus, by whom she has voided the spells of the magical charmers (*magorum incantantium carmina*) and the venom of serpents.

291   Epistle xx, 20; *PL* xvi, 1000

> Psalm 78 is read at a morning service; its first verse is employed as the response.

At the morning office (*matutinis horis*), as you will recall, brethren, there was read (*lectum*) what we sing in response (*respondemus*) with great sorrow of spirit: 'O God, the heathen have come into thy inheritance' (Ps 78.1).

292   Epistle xx, 24; *PL* xvi, 1001

> The events of 386, described in the famous passage of AUGUSTINE, *Confessions* ix, 7, are alluded to more briefly here.

I was not able to return home, because soldiers surrounded the basilica, keeping it under guard; we recited psalms with the brethren in the lesser basilica of the church.

293   Epistle xxix, 1; *PL* xvi, 1054

> Psalm 44.3 and Isaiah 52.7 are employed as verses at an evening vigil.

During the reading, when I had rested my mind somewhat (having abandoned my nocturnal study), I began to reflect upon that verse which we had used in the evening at the vigil (*uesperi in uigiliis*): 'You are the fairest of the sons of men' (Ps 44.3), and 'How beautiful are the feet of those who announce him' (Isa 52.7).

294   Epistle L, 16; *PL* xvi, 1107

> Ambrose complains to the emperor Theodosius about an order that monks be punished for burning a Valentinian shrine. The incident reveals the monks singing psalms in an outdoor procession.

And shall the pagan shrine of the Valentinians that was burned be avenged? For what is it other than a pagan shrine in which heathens gather? If the heathen call upon twelve gods, the Valentinians honor thirty-two Aeons which they refer to as gods. Now in this regard there has come to my attention an order that the shrine be avenged upon those monks who – angered by the effrontery of the Valentinians who had denied them access to that roadway along which by time honored custom and usage they went singing psalms in celebration of the martyred Maccabees – set fire to a shrine of theirs which had been hastily thrown up in some rural village or another.

295   Epistle LXIII, 82; *PL* XVI, 1211

> The disciples of Eusebius of Vercelli (c.371) live in a monastic community, perhaps the earliest of the sort in the west.

But enough has been said of the master, I should think; let us now pursue the life of his disciples, who have taken up that praise which day and night they proclaim in hymns (*hymnis personant*). This is indeed the service of angels, to be engaged always in the praise of God, and to reconcile and beseech the Lord with incessant prayer. They are diligent in their reading or keep their minds occupied with continual work; while separated from the company of women, they provide a safeguard for one another.

296   *De officiis* I, xli, 202; *PL* XVI, 84

> The cries of the martyred Maccabees are as music to their mother (see also *De Jacob et uita beata* II, xi, 56, quoted above).

What shall I say of the mother, who joyously looked upon the corpses of her sons as so many trophies, who delighted in their dying cries as in the singing of psalms, and saw in her offspring the fairest cithara of her womb and the harmony of devotion, surpassing the rhythm of any lyre (*omni lyrae numero*) in sweetness?

297   *De officiis* XLIV, 215; *PL* XVI, 87

> In specifying the skills of minor clerical officials Ambrose indicates a distinction between lector and cantor.

One is considered better qualified to enunciate a reading, another more pleasing with a psalm, another more solicitous to exorcize those burdened by an evil spirit, and another more suited to have charge of the sacred things.

298   *Sermo contra Auxentium de basilicis tradendis* XXXIV; *PL* XVI, 1017–18

> An apparent reference to the congregational singing of Ambrose's hymns (see also AUGUSTINE, *Liber retractationum* I, 20).

They also say that the people are led astray by the charms of my hymns (*hymnorum carminibus*). Certainly; I do not deny it. This is a mighty charm (*carmen*), more powerful than any other. For what avails more than the confession of the Trinity, which is proclaimed daily in the mouth of all the people? All vie eagerly among themselves to profess the faith; they know how to praise the Father, Son and Holy Spirit in verse (*in uersibus*). All then are rendered masters, who had scarcely managed to be disciples.

299   *De uirginibus ad Marcellinam sororem* I, iii, 12; *PL* XVI, 192;
Flor Patr XXXI, 23

> Ambrose addressed a treatise on virginity to his sister Marcellina. In this passage Miriam with tympanum stands as a figure of the singing church.

Miriam took up the tympanum and led the choral dance with virginal modesty (Ex 15.20). Now consider whose image she represented then. Was it not that of the Church, which as a virgin of unstained spirit has brought together the devout throng of people to sing sacred songs?

300   *De virginibus ad Marcellinam sororem* I, x, 60; *PL* XVI, 205;
Flor Patr XXXI, 43

> The nuns of Bononia sing 'spiritual songs'.

What shall I say of the virgins of Bononia . . . at one time they resound in spiritual song (*canticis spiritualibus personant*), and at another they provide their sustenance by their labors and seek similarly to provide the material of their charity with the work of their hands.

301   *De uirginibus ad Marcellinam sororem* III, iv, 19; *PL* XVI, 225;
Flor Patr XXXI, 71

> Evening psalmody is recommended to the devout virgin and contrasted with aulos playing prescribed by Pythagoras.

But I wish also that even in your bedchamber you weave together psalms with the Lord's prayer in frequent interchange, both as you stand vigil and before drowsiness suffuses your body; so that at the very beginning of rest sleep finds you free from anxiety over secular affairs and meditating upon those of heaven. And indeed he who first coined the name of philosophy itself, bade the tibia player, each day before going to bed, to play soothing tunes (*molliora canere*), in order to still his heart, disturbed by worldly cares. Yet he, like one who washes bricks, sought in vain to banish secular matters with secular means.

302   *De uirginibus ad Marcellinam sororem* III, v, 25; *PL* XVI, 227;
Flor Patr XXXI, 73–4

> A warning against the allurement of the dance.

There ought then to be a joy of the mind that knows what is right, not a joy aroused by disorderly banquets and nuptial concerts (*nuptialibus symphoniis*); for where the companion of luxury is unrestrained dancing (*extrema saltatio*), modesty is imperiled and temptation must be expected. From that sort of thing I wish the virgins of God to maintain their distance. As a certain secular teacher has said: 'No one dances when sober, unless he is insane!' (Cicero, *Pro Murena* vi). Now if according to the wisdom of the world it is drunkenness or madness that begets the dance, what sort of warning do we expect to be given in the exempla of Sacred Scripture, where John, prophet of Christ, was beheaded at the whim of a dancer? Is not this a case in which the attraction of the dance was deadlier than the madness of sacrilegious fury?

Niceta of Remesiana (d. after 414)

Born somewhere in Dacia in the second quarter of the century, Niceta was named bishop of Remesiana (present-day Bela Palanka, Yugoslavia) in about 370. Although well known in his time – Paulinus of Nola and Jerome speak highly of him – he was all but forgotten in subsequent centuries, and his works were attributed to various other authors. These were restored to him in the edition of Burn (1905). Among them are two sermons of great importance to liturgy and music: *De uigiliis seruorum Dei* and *De utilitate hymnorum*. Previous to Burn's edition they were known only in a grossly defective version attributed to the sixth-century Nicetius of Trier. They both appear thus in *PL* (vol. 68, cols. 365–76), while the second of the two appears in *Gerbert* (vol. 1, pp. 9–14). They appear, finally, in an edition of *Turner*, which offers improvements upon that of Burn. The sermon on vigils, not quoted here, indicates the prominent part played by psalmody in those services and closes with a promise to devote an entire sermon to the subject. This, quoted here in all its essential points, is one of the central patristic documents on ecclesiastical music. Both sermons are available in a rather free English translation in *FC* VII.

Morin (1894) and Burn (1926) ascribe the composition of the *Te Deum* to Niceta, although this is not universally accepted.

303   *De utilitate hymnorum* 2; *Turner*, 233–4

> After opening the sermon by reminding the faithful that he is fulfilling his promise to preach about singing, Niceta makes his first substantial point. Displaying a common sense remarkable for its time, he refutes the notion that 'singing in the heart' precludes actual sound.

I know that there are some, not only in our area but in the regions of the east, who consider the singing of psalms and hymns to be superfluous and little appropriate to divine religion. They think it enough if a psalm is spoken in the heart and frivolous if it is produced with the sound of one's lips, and they appropriate to this opinion of theirs the verse of the Apostle which he wrote to the Ephesians: 'Be filled with the Spirit, seeking in psalms, hymns and spiritual songs, singing and making melody to the Lord in your hearts.' Look, they say, the Apostle specifies that one must make melody in the heart, and not babble in the theatrical manner with sung melody (*uocis modulatione*), for it is sufficient to God 'who searches hearts' (Rom 8.27) that one sings in the secrecy of his heart. None the less, if the truth be told, just as I do not blame those who 'make melody in their heart' (for it is always beneficial to meditate in one's heart upon the things of God), so too do I praise those who glorify God with the sound of their voice.

Now before I offer testimony drawn from numerous Scriptural passages, by way of a preliminary objection I will refute their foolish talk by appealing to that very verse of the Apostle that many use against the singers. Certainly the Apostle says, 'be filled with the Spirit as you speak', but I believe also that he frees our mouths, loosens our tongues and opens our lips, for it is impossible for men 'to speak' without these organs; and just as heat differs from cold so does silence differ from speech. And since he adds 'speaking in psalms and hymns and songs', he would not have mentioned 'songs' if he had wished those 'making melody' to be altogether silent, for no one can sing by being absolutely quiet. When he says, then, 'in your hearts', he admonishes one not to sing with the voice alone and without the attention of the heart; as he says in another place, 'I will sing with the spirit, I will sing also with the understanding' (1 Cor 14.15), that is with both voice and thought.

304   *De utilitate hymnorum* 3–4; *Turner*, 234–5

> He then lists Old Testament figures, beginning with Moses and culminat-
> ing with David, who established precedents for the benefit of sacred song.

If we ask who among men was first to introduce this sort of singing, we will find none other than Moses . . .

4 After this you will find many, not only men but also women, who, filled with the divine Spirit, sung the mysteries of God, even before David, who was especially trained by the Lord in this office from childhood and was found worthy to be a prince among singers and a treasury of song. While still a lad, singing sweetly yet strongly to the cithara, he subdued the evil spirit which worked in Saul – not because such was the power of his cithara, but because a figure of the cross of Christ was mystically projected by the wood and the stretching of strings, so that it was the Passion itself that was sung and that subdued the spirit of the demon.

305   *De utilitate hymnorum* 5; *Turner*, 235

> Niceta catalogues the spiritual riches of the Psalter, a topos found in the
> writings of other patristic authors including BASIL, *In psalmum i*, 2 and
> AMBROSE, *Explanatio psalmi i*, 9.

What do you fail to find in the psalms of David that works toward the benefit, edification and consolation of the human species of whatever class, sex or age? The infant has here what he can suckle, the boy what he can cheer, the adolescent that by which he can mend his ways, the young man what he can follow and the old man material for prayer. A woman learns modesty, orphans find a father, widows a judge, the poor a protector and strangers a guide. Kings and judges hear what they should fear. A psalm consoles the sad, restrains the joyful, tempers the angry, refreshes the poor and chides the rich man to know himself. To absolutely all who will take it, the psalm offers an appropriate medicine; nor does it despise the sinner, but presses upon him the wholesome remedy of penitential tears.

306   *De utilitate hymnorum* 5; *Turner*, 235–6

> Psalms are especially effective because they add the sweetness of melody to the soundness of their doctrine; this idea also is frequently encountered in fourth-century encomiums of the Psalter, for example, JOHN CHRYSOSTOM, *In psalmum xli*, 1.

For since human nature rejects and avoids what is difficult, even if beneficial, and accepts virtually nothing unless it seems to offer pleasure, through David the Lord prepares for men this potion which is sweet by reason of its melody (*cantionem*) and effective in the cure of disease by reason of its strength. For a psalm is sweet to the ear when sung, it penetrates the soul when it gives pleasure, it is easily remembered when sung often, and what the harshness of the Law cannot force from the minds of man it excludes by the suavity of song. For whatever the Law, the Prophets and even the Gospels teach is contained as a remedy in the sweetness of these songs.

306   *De utilitate hymnorum* 7; *Turner*, 236–7

> Psalmody, the sacrifice of praise, is a spiritual sacrifice, superior to bloody sacrifice.

Rightly does the same prophet urge everybody and everything to the praise of God who rules over all: 'Let every spirit praise the Lord' (Ps 150.5). And promising that he himself would be the one who praises he said: 'I will praise the name of God in song, I will magnify him in praise; and it will please God better than a young calf that brings forth horns and hoofs' (Ps 68.31–2). Behold what is superior, behold the spiritual sacrifice, greater than all the sacrifices of victims. And justly so; if there indeed the irrational blood of animals was poured out, here is offered the reasonable praise of the soul itself and a good conscience. Rightly did the Lord say: 'The sacrifice of praise shall glorify me, and there is the way by which I will show him the salvation of God' (Ps 49.23). Praise the Lord in your life, then; 'offer a sacrifice of praise' (Ps 49.14), and thus is shown in your soul the way by which you come to his salvation.

308 *De utilitate hymnorum* 9; *Turner,* 237–8

> The carnal usages of the Old Testament such as circumcision and musical instruments have been rejected, while the spiritual usages such as psalmody (*laudatio*) have been retained.

It would be tedious, beloved, were I to recount every single detail that the history of the psalms contains, especially now that it is time that we must also present something from the New Testament in confirmation of the Old, lest one think that the office of psalmody (*psalmizandi*) is to be curtailed, inasmuch as many of the Old Law usages are now abolished. For what is carnal has been rejected, for example, circumcision, the Sabbath, sacrifices, discrimination among foods, trumpets, citharas, cymbals and tympana, all of which are understood to reside now in the bodily members of man and there better to sound. Daily ablution, observance of the new moons, that fastidious inspection of leprosy, have altogether ceased and gone their way along with whatever else of the sort was necessary at the time because of their immaturity. The other things which are spiritual – faith, piety, prayer, fasting, patience, chastity, praise (*laudatio*) – have been increased, not diminished.

309 *De utilitate hymnorum* 9–10; *Turner,* 238

> Niceta now catalogues the precedents for sacred song to be found in the New Testament (see the first chapter of the present volume for chapter and verse references).

Therefore in the Gospel you will first find Zachary, father of the great John, who 'prophesied' in the form of a hymn after his long silence. Nor did Elizabeth, so long barren, fail to 'magnify' God from her soul when her promised son had been born. And when Christ was born on earth, the army of angels sounded a song of praise (*laudem*), saying: 'Glory to God on high', and proclaiming 'peace on earth to men of good will' . . . And not to prolong this discourse, the Lord himself, a teacher in words and master in deeds, went out to the Mount of Olives with the disciples after singing a hymn . . .

10 The Apostles also are known to have done likewise when even in prison they did not cease to sing. And Paul, in turn, admonishes the prophets of the Church: 'When you come together,' he says, 'each one of you has a hymn, a teaching, a revelation; let all things be done for edification'. And again in another place: 'I will sing with the spirit', he says, 'I will sing with the mind also'. And James puts it thus in his epistle: 'Is anyone among you sad? Let him pray. Is any cheerful? Let him sing.' And John reports in Revelations that, as the Spirit revealed to him, he saw and heard the voice of the heavenly army 'like the sound of many waters and the sound of mighty thunderpeals, crying, Alleluia!'

310   *De utilitate hymnorum* 12; *Turner*, 239

> The language here shows a clear distinction between psalms and 'interspersed' readings.

What more appropriate than this sort of benefit? What more congenial than this form of pleasure? For we are delighted by the psalms, bedewed by the prayers and fed by the interspersed readings. And indeed, as the cheerful guests at a banquet take pleasure in the variety of courses, so our souls feast on the multiplicity of readings and the display of hymns.

311   *De utilitate hymnorum* 13; *Turner*, 239–40

> A unique passage. It is difficult to determine the meaning of the musically descriptive terms but the general sense is clear – Niceta advocates a carefully coordinated congregational singing.

Thus, beloved, let us sing with alert senses and a wakeful mind, as the psalmist (*hymnidicus*) exhorts: 'Because God is king of all the earth', he says, 'sing ye wisely' (Ps 46.8), so that a psalm is sung not only with the spirit, that is, the sound of the voice, but with the mind also (1 Cor 14.15), and so that we think of what we sing rather than allow our mind, seized by extraneous thoughts as is often the case, to lose the fruit of our labor. One must sing with a manner (*sonus*) and melody befitting holy religion; it must not proclaim theatrical distress but rather exhibit Christian simplicity in its very musical movement (*ipsa modulatione*); it must not remind one of anything theatrical, but rather create compunction in the listeners.

Further, our voice ought not to be dissonant (*dissona*) but consonant (*consona*). One ought not to drag out the singing (*protrahat*) while another cuts it short (*contrahat*), and one ought not to sing too low (*humiliet*) while another raises his voice (*extollat*). Rather each should strive to integrate his voice within the sound of the harmonious (*concinentis*) chorus and not project it outwardly in the manner of a cithara as if to make an immodest display . . . And for him who is not able to blend (*aequare*) and fit himself in with the others, it is better to sing in a subdued (*lenta*) voice than to make a great noise, for thus he performs both his liturgical function and avoids disturbing the singing brotherhood.

Jerome (341–420)

Born in Dalmatia to wealthy Christian parents, he studied the classics in Rome under Donatus. Subsequently he sojourned in Gall and at Aquileia, where he cultivated the ascetic life among friends of similar inclination. In about 372 he set out for Jerusalem, but was sidetracked by illness in Antioch where he perfected his schoolboy Greek. Next he lived for about three years in the desert of Chalcis and there learned Hebrew. In 397 he was ordained a priest at Antioch and then went to Constantinople where he developed an enthusiasm for Origenist exegesis under the influence of Gregory of Nazianzus. From 382 to 385 he was secretary to Pope Damasus at Rome and began his work of biblical translation which would cluminate eventually in the *Vulgate*. At Rome he also became the center of an ascetic circle of aristocratic women to whom he later directed rather severe advice in his much quoted letters. Finally in 385 he retired to the Holy Land and there spent the rest of his long life in literary activity, in directing his monastery and convents at Bethlehem, and in heated controversy. As for musical reference he makes an ordinary contribution to instrumental allegory in his works on the psalms, but a rather special one in his strictures to highborn ladies against secular musical enticements and in his liturgical advice to the monks and nuns under his tutelage. The material is quoted in the following order: references from works devoted to the psalms, from the letters and from other works.

312   *Tractatus de psalmo vii; CCL* LXXVIII, 19

Jerome's homilies on the psalms, *Tractatus siue homiliae in psalmos*, of which seventy-four are extant, were composed for his monastic community at Bethlehem. A number of them, including that quoted here, indicate that they were preached during a Sunday liturgical service at which the respective psalm had been heard. The reference to Alleluia in this example is initially puzzling, but explained by the custom of prefixing or appending Alleluia to psalms lacking it in the Hebrew Bible (see Jerome, *Commentarioli in psalmos* ciiii, 1). Typical passages of instrumental allegory, not quoted here, appear in connection with the appropriate psalms.

With regard to the seventh, that was itself sung under Alleluia (*sub alleluia*), because last Sunday the sixth psalm was read and we due to illness were not able to interpret it – now however the seventh psalm is read.

313   *Tractatus de psalmo ix, CCL* LXXVIII, 28

Again the relationship of homily to psalm is indicated.

The ninth psalm, which was sung by you to the Lord, is grand in its poetry and grand in its mysteries. But since we are not able to discuss it in its entirety, it will suffice for now to speak of its title.

314   *Tractatus de psalmo xiv; CCL* LXXVIII, 30

A third example; it gives the impression that the psalms were performed each Sunday in numerical sequence (see also *Tractatus de psalmo vii*, quoted above, on this second point).

Appropriately, the fourteenth psalm was read; and it occurs thus in sequence (*secundum ordinem*) and so seems read almost by design. The psalm is read in sequence – I believe this happens by a dispensation of God, that what might be of benefit to you was recited today in the normal order of exposition.

315   *Tractatus de psalmo cxliii; CCL* LXXVIII, 313

> The reference to the Gospel suggests that the Sunday service at which
> these homilies were read was the Eucharist.

Because of those who do not know the Latin language – allowing that we
have said much about the Gospel, we ought none the less to say something
about the Psalter, so that while some have been filled others will not go
away empty. But since the psalm is long, and if we wished to linger over
every verse, it would take all day, we ought briefly to reflect upon certain
facets of the sense rather than explain every word.

316   Pseudo-Jerome, *Brevarium in psalmos* xxxii; *PL* XXVI, 917

> In addition to his *Tractatus siue homiliae in psalmos* Jerome composed a
> *Commentarioli in psalmos*, brief notes on the psalms excerpted from various
> works of Origen. The standard passages of musical allegory are absent
> from this work, while they appear in a spurious work, *Breviarium in psalmos*.
> From the latter we quote only this brief reference to the *jubilus*.

It is called jubilus, because neither by words, nor syllables, nor letters, nor
voice, can it be expressed or comprehended how much man ought to praise
God.

317   Epistle XIV, *Ad Heliodorum monachum*, 10; *PL* XXII, 353; *CSEL* LIV, 59

> The letters of Jerome are rich in musical allusion. Here he uses the term
> *celeuma*, a boatman's cry, which some, rightly or wrongly, have associated
> with the notion of *jubilus* and the Alleluia (see AUGUSTINE, *De cantico nouo* 2).
> On the *celeuma* in general see Sheerin (1982).

But since my discourse has sailed free of reefs, and my frail skiff has proceeded from amid hollow crags and foaming breakers into deep water, the
sails must be spread to the wind; and now that the rocks of controversy are
behind us, the *celeuma* of the epilogue must be sung in the manner of sailors.
O desert of Christ blooming with flowers! O solitude . . .

318   Epistle XLVI, *Paulae et Eustochiae ad Marcellam* 12; *PL* XXII, 491;
CSEL LIV, 342–3

> In the Holy Land farmers sing Alleluia and the psalms of David in the
> fields. *Villa* OR *uillula* is Jerome's term for Bethlehem; see Kelly (1965,
> p. 129).

As we said above, in the village (*uillula*) of Christ all is simple, and aside
from psalms there is silence. Wherever you turn, the farm hand grasping the
plough handle sings Alleluia, the sweating reaper cheers himself with
psalms, and the vine dresser sings something of David as he prunes the vine

with his curved knife. These are the lays of this province, these, to put it in common parlance, its love songs . . .

319   Epistle LII, *Ad Nepotianum presbyterum* 5; *PL* XXII, 532; *CSEL* LIV, 423–4

> The cantor, along with other minor clerical officials, is placed in a curious light.

If you must visit a widow or a virgin because of your clerical office, never enter the house alone and take such companions so that association with them will not disgrace you. If a reader, an acolyte, or a cantor (*psaltes*) follows you, let them not be adorned with garments but with morals; nor let their hair be waved with a curling-iron, but let them declare modesty in their mien.

320   Epistle LIV, *Ad Furiam de uiduitate seruanda* 13; *PL* XXII, 556; *CSEL* LIV, 479–81

> The widow Furia must avoid, among others, musicians. Rather, she should imitate her kinswoman, a nun in Bethlehem (Eustochium?), who teaches a spiritual kind of music.

Avoid the company of young men. Let long-haired fellows, ornamented and wanton, not be seen under your roof. Let the male singer (*cantor*) be repelled as a bane, banish from your house female citharists (*fidicinas*) and harpists (*psaltrias*) and that devil's choir whose songs lead to death like those of the sirens . . . Oh if you could see your sister and if it were possible to hear in person the eloquence of her holy lips, you would perceive the mighty spirit within her tiny body and hear the entire content of the Old and New Testaments bubbling up from her heart! Fasting is her sport and prayer her recreation. She takes up the tympanum in imitation of Miriam and after Pharaoh is crowned sings before the choir of virgins: 'Let us sing to the Lord, for he has triumphed gloriously; the horse and the rider he has thrown into the sea' (Ex 15.1). These she instructs as harpists for Christ, these she teaches to be citharists for the Savior. Thus she passes the day and the night, awaiting the coming of the bridegroom with oil ready for the lamps. You, too, then – imitate your kinswoman . . .

321   Epistle LXXVII, *Ad Oceanum de morte Fabiola* 11; *PL* XXII, 697; *CSEL* LV, 48

> Psalms and cries of Alleluia are heard at Fabiola's funeral.

Hardly had she breathed forth her spirit, hardly had she returned the soul she owed to Christ, 'and now rumor flying, the herald of such grief' (Virgil, *Aen* XI.139), gathered together the population of the entire city for her obsequies. Psalms resounded and Alleluia echoed on high and shook the gilded ceilings of the temples.

322   Epistle cvii, *Ad Laetam de institutione filiae* 4; *PL* xxii, 871; *CSEL* iv, 293–4

> In a letter which Jerome wrote to Laeta on the rearing of her daughter Paula as a virgin, there are several references to music, five brief examples of which are given here. Jerome appears to advocate a monastic way of life for the child.

Thus must be educated the soul, whose future is to be a temple of the Lord. It must learn to hear nothing, to say nothing, which has no bearing on the fear of God. It must not comprehend foul words, nor have knowledge of worldly songs, and while still tender its tongue must be imbued with sweet psalms.

323   Epistle cvii, 4; *PL* xxii, 872; *CSEL* lv, 295

When she sees her grandfather, let her leap upon his chest, and hanging from his neck let her sing Alleluia to the reluctant old man.

324   Epistle cvii, 8; *PL* xxii, 875; *CSEL* lv, 299

> Most translations of this passage render *organa* as 'organ', while both syntax and contemporary usage call for the generic 'musical instruments'.

Let her be deaf to musical instruments (*organa*); let her not know why the tibia, lyre and cithara are made.

325   Epistle cvii, 9; *PL* xxii, 875; *CSEL* lv, 300

> The standard six monastic office hours are recommended (see also Epistle xxii, 37).

Let an elderly virgin of good faith, morals and modesty be placed in charge of her, who will instruct her and familiarize her by example to rise at night for prayer and psalms, to sing hymns at dawn, to stand in the ranks as a warrior for Christ at the third, sixth and ninth hours, and to proffer an evening (*uespertinum*) sacrifice at the lighting of the lamp (*lucernula*).

326   Epistle cvii, 12; *PL* xxii, 876; *CSEL* lv, 302

> In the final reference from this letter Jerome advocates the monastic practice of learning the Psalter (by heart, presumably; see Epistle cxxviii, 4, quoted below).

Let her first learn the Psalter, let her entertain herself with these songs and then be taught life's lessons in the Proverbs of Solomon.

327 Epistle cviii, *Epitaphium sanctae Paulae* 20; *PL* xxii, 896; *CSEL* lv, 335

> The elder Paula's nuns gathered for prayer and psalmody each day at the six appointed times. The church they attended on Sundays was probably Constantine's basilica of the Nativity.

She divided them into three groups and monasteries in such a way that, while separate for work and meals, they were brought together for psalmody and prayers. After the Alleluia was sung – the signal by which they were summoned to the collect (*collectam*) – no one was permitted to remain behind ... At dawn, at the third hour, the sixth, the ninth, evening, and the middle of the night they sang the Psalter in sequence (*per ordinem*); nor was it permitted that any of the sisters not know the psalms nor fail to learn a portion of the Holy Scriptures every day. On the Lord's day only they proceeded to the church next to where they lived, with each group following its own mother superior.

328 Epistle cxxv, *Ad Rusticum monachum* 15; *PL* xxii, 1081; *CSEL* lvi, 134

> Jerome recommends the common life of the monastery to Rusticus. In describing it he mentions singing. Note how he downplays 'sweetness of voice', reminding one of the similar caution in his *Commentarium in epistulam ad Ephesios* quoted below, and note also that an ordinary monk recites a psalm in his turn. I am indebted to Joseph Dyer for this reference.

And before sleep is fully satisfied you will be forced to rise; when your turn comes (*in ordine tuo*) you will recite (*dicas*) a psalm, in which sweetness of voice (*dulcedo uocis*) is not required but a proper mental disposition (*mentis affectus*). As the Apostle writes, 'I will sing with the spirit, I will sing with the mind also' (1 Cor 14.15), and 'singing in your hearts' (Eph 5.19); for he had read the precept, 'Sing with understanding' (Ps 46.8).

329 Epistle cviii, 29; *PL* xxii, 904–5; *CSEL* lv, 348

> At Paula's funeral rites psalms were sung in various languages.

There followed no weeping nor lamentations, as is the custom among people of the world, but crowds of monks struck up psalms in various languages ... Psalms resounded in the Greek, Latin and Syrian tongues in turn, not only for the three-day period that she was buried beneath the church, close by the cave of the Lord, but for the entire week ...

330 Epistle cxxviii, *Ad Pacatulam* 4; *PL* xxii, 1098; *CSEL* lvi, 160

> Jerome gives Gaudentius advice concerning his infant daughter Pacatula similar to that given Laeta concerning Paula (Epistle cvii, quoted above). It is curious that Jerome sees the church as a place of temptation (see also Epistle cxxx, 19).

Let her learn the Psalter by heart, and let her make the books of Solomon, the Gospels, the Epistles and the Prophets the treasure of her heart until the years of puberty. She ought not to go into public too frequently nor always seek out the crowded churches. Let her have all her pleasures in her own chamber. Let her never look upon young men, never those with curled hair who with sweetness of voice wound the spirit through the ears.

331   *In Isaiam* II, v, 20; *PL* XXIV, 86; *CCL* LXXIII, 77

> Jerome appears to refer to Ps 33.9 as a congregational response to the communion psalm. For references to the communion psalm not cited in this volume, see Jungmann (1951, I, pp. 392–4).

Each day, filled with the heavenly bread, we say, 'Taste and see how sweet is the Lord' (Ps 33.9).

332   Epistle CXXX, *Ad Demetriadem* 15; *PL* XXI, 1119; *CSEL* LVI, 195

> Again the monastic order of prayer and psalmody is recommended to a Roman lady, in this case the patrician virgin Demetrias.

In addition to the order of prayer and psalmody – which you must always observe at the third, sixth and ninth hours, at evening, in the middle of the night and at dawn – determine how many hours you ought to study Holy Scripture, how much time to read for the delight and composure of your spirit rather than its fatigue.

333   *Commentarium in epistulam ad Ephesios* III, v, 19; *PL* XXVI, 528–9

> In his commentary on the famous passage from the Epistle to the Ephesians (3.5), Jerome first gives exegetical definitions of the three psalm types, and then goes on to emphasize the importance of a singer's interior disposition as opposed to musical display. The office of cantor is implicit in the text.

'Addressing one another in psalms and hymns and spiritual songs (*canticis*), singing and making melody (*psallentes*) to the Lord with all your heart.' He who has abstained from the drunkenness of wine, in which is luxury, and in place of this has been filled with the Spirit, this one is able to take all things spiritually – psalms, hymns and songs. How psalms, hymns and songs differ among themselves we learn most thoroughly in the Psalter. But it must be said here briefly that hymns are those that proclaim the strength and majesty of God and ever express wonder over his favors and deeds – something all psalms do, to which Alleluia has been superscribed or appended. Psalms, however, apply properly to the ethical seat, so that by this organ of the body we might know what is to be done and what avoided. But he who treats of higher things, the subtle investigator who explains the harmony of the world and the order and concord existing among all creatures, this one sings a spiritual song. For certainly (to speak more plainly than we wish for the sake of the simple), the psalm pertains to the body and the song to the mind.

And we ought therefore to sing, to make melody and to praise the Lord more with spirit than the voice. This in fact is what is said: 'singing and making melody in your hearts to the Lord'. Let youth hear this, let them hear it whose duty it is to sing in the church, that God is to be sung to, not with the voice but with the heart – not in daubing the mouth and throat with some sweet medicine after the manner of tragedians, so that theatrical melodies and songs are heard in the church, but in fear, in work and in knowledge of the Scriptures. Although one might be, as they are wont to say, *kakophonos*, if he has performed good works, he is a sweet singer before God. Thus let the servant of Christ sing, so that not the voice of the singer but the words that are read give pleasure; in order that the evil spirit which was in Saul be cast out from those similarly possessed by it, and not introduced into those who have made of God's house a popular theatre.

334 *Dialogus contra pelagianos* I, 25; *PL* XXIII, 519

> Jerome expresses his view that women ought not to sing psalms in church through the person of the Augustinian Atticus, who argues against the contrary position of the Pelagian Critobulus. On the issue in general, see Quasten (1930, pp. 75–87).

Indeed your liberality is so great, that to win favor among your Amazons you write in another place, 'Women ought also to have knowledge of the law'; while the Apostle teaches that women must be silent in the church, and if there is something they do not know, they ought to ask their husbands at home (1 Cor 14.34–5). Nor is it enough for you to have given knowledge of the Scriptures to your army, but you must be regaled with their voices and songs, for you add in a title, 'That women ought also to sing psalms to the Lord'. But who does not know that women are to sing psalms in their chambers, away from the company of men and the crowded assembly? But you in truth grant what is not permitted, so that, with the support of their master, they flaunt what they ought to do modestly and without any witness.

335 *Contra Vigilantium* I, I; *PL* XXIII, 339

> Among the false notions of Vigilantius is confining the singing of the alleluia to Easter – actually Eastertide in all probability.

He says vigils are to be condemned, the Alleluia must never be sung except at Easter (*in Pascha*), continence is a heresy, and modesty a nursery of lust.

John Cassian (c.360–435)

Believed to have been born in Scythia – modern Rumania – he is first observed as a young monk at Bethlehem. In about 385 he left to spend several years studying monasticism in Egypt. Eventually he came west and established both a monastery and convent near Marseilles in about 415. There he wrote his two important works on monasticism, the *De institutis*, quoted here, and the *Collationes patrum*, a series of partially fictitious conversations with the desert fathers of Egypt. Books II and III of *De institutis* give detailed directions for the order of psalmody to be followed in the monastic office. Cassian proposes the Egyptian system with certain modifications to suit western circumstances. His recommendations had considerable influence upon subsequent monastic rules including that of Benedict. All the essential descriptive material is given here, while the entire work is available in *NPNF*, 2, 11. The standard study on Cassian is that of Chadwick (1968).

336   *De institutis coenobiorum* II, 2; *PL* XLIX, 77–9; *CSEL* XVII, 18

> There is widespread confusion over the number of psalms to be sung at the evening and nocturnal offices, which John proposes to allay by invoking the Egyptian precedent. Note the interesting, if obscure, use of the term antiphon. *Modulatio* is translated 'rhythm' here for want of a better alternative; see Augustine, *De musica* I, 2–3.

For we have found that many throughout different lands, according to the caprice of their mind – having, indeed, as the Apostle says, 'zeal for God, but not according to knowledge' (Rom 10.2) – have established for themselves various arrangements and regulations in this matter. For some have decided that twenty or thirty psalms ought to be recited each night, and that these ought to be prolonged by the melodies of antiphons and the addition of certain rhythms (*modulationum*). Others have sought even to exceed this number, while some have used eighteen. And in this way we have observed different rules established in different places, and the arrangements and regulations we have seen adopted are almost equal in number to the monasteries and cells we inspected. There are some also to whom it seemed right that in the daytime prayer offices themselves, that is, terce, sext and none, the number of psalms and prayers should correspond to the number of the hours in which these services are rendered to God; while it pleased some to assign the number six to each of the daytime meetings. Therefore I deem it necessary to propose the most ancient rule of the fathers, which is preserved now throughout all Egypt by the servants of God, so that the unformed infancy in Christ of your new monastery can be instructed by the venerable institutions of the earliest fathers.

337   *De institutis* II, 4; *PL* XLIX, 83–4; *CSEL* XVII, 20

> Twelve is the proper number, followed by a reading from the Old Testament and one from the New. The number was revealed by an angel.

Thus, as we have said, the number of twelve psalms is preserved throughout all of Egypt and the Thebaid both at the evening and the night offices, in such a way that afterwards two readings follow, one each from the Old and New Testaments. And this arrangement, established long ago, has endured intact at all the monasteries of those regions through so many ages up to the present day, because it is said by the elders not to have been established by human invention but to have been brought down to the fathers from heaven by the agency of an angel.

338 *De institutis* II, 5–6; *PL* XLIX, 86–9; *CSEL* XVII, 21–2

> Here the legend of the angel singer is told.

At that time, therefore, when the perfection of the primitive church remained inviolate, still fresh in the memory of its successors, and the burning faith of the few had not yet grown tepid in its dispersion among the many, the venerable fathers, alert to the needs of posterity, met to decide what plan of daily worship there ought to be for the whole body of the brotherhood . . . There was among them such a holy variety in their pious dispute over the rule of worship that the time of the most holy evening office arrived during their discussion, and as they wished to celebrate the daily rites of prayer one arose in their midst to sing psalms to the Lord. And while all sat, as is still the custom in the land of Egypt, concentrated upon the words of the singer with all their heart, after he had sung – with successive verses evenly pronounced (*contiguis uersibus parili pronuntiatione*) – eleven psalms separated by the interpolation of prayers, as he was finishing the twelfth, during the Alleluia response (*sub alleluiae responsiones*), he suddenly withdrew from the sight of all and thus brought an end to both the discussion and the ceremony.

6 Thereupon the venerable assembly of fathers, realizing that a general rule established for meetings of the brethren by the direction of an angel, was not done without the guidance of the Lord, determined that this number would be preserved at both the evening and nocturnal offices.

339 *De institutis* II, 6; *PL* XLIX, 89–90; *CSEL* XVII, 22–3

> Both lessons on Saturday, Sunday and during Eastertide are from the New Testament.

When they joined a pair of lessons to these psalms, one from the Old Testament and one from the New, they added them as something from their own tradition and as something extra for only those who wished it and who were eager to achieve the remembrance of the divine Scriptures by constant meditation. But on the Sabbath and the Lord's Day they recite both from the New Testament, one from the Apostle or the Acts of the Apostles and

one from the Gospels. And they do this also for the entire fifty days of the
Paschal season (*Quinquagensimae*) . . .

340   *De institutis* II, 8; *PL* XLIX, 94–5; *CSEL* XVII, 24

> In Cassian's province the doxology is sung after each psalm but in the east
> only after the antiphon. Perhaps this passage offers some hint as to the
> meaning of this persistently difficult term.

And what we have seen in this province, that after one sings to the end of the
psalm all stand and sing aloud 'Glory be to the Father and to the Son and
to the Holy Spirit', we have never heard throughout the entire east. Instead,
when the psalm is finished, there follows a prayer by the one who sings, all
the others remaining silent, and only the antiphon is ordinarily terminated
with this glorification of the Trinity.

341   *De institutis* II, 10; *PL* XLIX, 97–8; *CSEL* XVII, 25

> The psalmody is solo, not choral.

When, therefore, they come together to conduct the aforementioned services, which they call *synaxes*, all maintain such silence that even though so
great a number of brethren assemble, one would believe no man to be
present except he who rises in their midst to sing the psalm . . .

342   *De institutis* II, 11; *PL* XLIX, 99–101; *CSEL* XVII, 26–7

> A series of important particulars about the conduct of the psalmody. The
> breaking down of a psalm into segments helps to account for the great
> length of a service of only twelve psalms, while the tempo of the chanting
> must also have been very slow.

And therefore they do not even try to complete the very psalms which they
sing at their assembly in an unbroken recitation, but they work through
them section by section (*distinctim particulatimque*), according to the number
of verses, in two or three segments with prayers in between . . . This also is
observed among them with great care, that no psalm is sung with the
response Alleluia unless Alleluia appears inscribed in its title. They divide
the aforementioned number of twelve psalms in this manner: if there are
two brothers, each sings six; if three, four; and if four, three. They never sing
less than this number when assembled, so that however large a group has
come together, never more than four brothers sing in the synaxis.

343   *De institutis* II, 12; *PL* XLIX, 102; *CSEL* XVII, 27

> A sort of rest is provided by sitting during the psalmody.

They render this aforementioned canonical number of twelve psalms easier by a kind of bodily rest: all, except he who has stood up in their midst to sing the psalms, sit upon low benches while observing these rites of assembly according to custom and follow the voice of the singer with the utmost attention. For they are so wearied by the fasts and work of the entire day and night that, unless aided by this sort of rest, they could not get through this number while standing.

344   *De institutis* III, 1; *PL* XLIX, 111–12; *CSEL* XVII, 33

> Book II dealt with the evening and night offices after the Egyptian model. Book III will treat the three day offices of Terce, Sext and None as practised in Palestine and Syria. So states Cassian here, but actually he will also deal eventually with the controversial 'new' morning office.

I believe that with God's help and in so far as our meager talent was able, we have completed an exposition of the manner of nocturnal prayer and psalmody which prevails throughout Egypt. Now we must discuss the offices of terce, sext and none according to the rule of the Palestinian and Mesopotamian monasteries, which by their practices, as we said above in the prologue, temper the perfection of the Egyptians and the inimitable reign of their discipline.

345   *De institutis* III, 2; *PL* XLIX, 112–15; *CSEL* XVII, 34

> The Egyptians, rather than meeting at set times during the day, remain alone the entire day in one continuous office.

Now among the Egyptians these offices, which we fulfill for the Lord at separate hours and intervals of time when brought together by the call of the convener, are celebrated throughout the entire span of the day together with the work of their own free will. For they perform manual labor constantly while alone in their cells in such a way that meditation upon the psalms and other Scripture is never altogether omitted; and while mixing prayers and vows with this at every moment, they spend the entire day in these offices which we celebrate at set times. Therefore, apart from the evening and nocturnal assemblies, there is no public service celebrated by them in the course of the day except on the Sabbath and the Lord's Day, when they come together at the third hour for the purpose of Holy Communion.

346   *De institutis* III, 3; *PL* XLIX, 116–26; *CSEL* XVII, 34–8

> Cassian first specifies that three psalms are to be sung at each of the three day offices. There follows a long passage, omitted here, citing scriptural precedents for the choice of these hours, and finally a list of five offices

including his first mention of a morning office and his first description of the evening office as *lucernarium*.

And in the monasteries of Palestine, Mesopotamia and all of the east, the offices at the hours mentioned above are concluded each day with three psalms, so that continual prayer is offered to God at set times . . . But concerning the morning office, we are taught also by what it is customary to sing each day: 'O God, my God, to thee do I watch at break of day' (Ps 62.2); and, 'I will meditate on thee in the morning' (Ps 62.7); and, 'I anticipated the dawn and cried out' (Ps 118.147); and again, 'My eyes have anticipated the break of day, that I might meditate upon thy words' (Ps 118.148). At these hours also that head of the house in the Gospel hired workers for his vineyard. For he is described as hiring first at dawn, the time to which our morning office is assigned, then at the third hour, then the sixth, after this the ninth, and finally the eleventh, the hour at which the lighting of lamps (*lucernaris*) is observed.

347   *De institutis* III, 4; *PL* XLIX, 126–31; *CSEL* XVII, 38–9

> One of the most problematic passages in the literature of early monasticism. The traditional view is that it introduces a second morning office, that of prime, while the more recent view is that it refers simply to the one morning office of lauds. Interpreted either way, the passage has unresolved contradictions. Against the former view, for example, is the fact that Cassian calls two supposedly different offices by precisely the same term; against the latter is his statement that there is a total of seven offices. As a way out of the dilemma, Chadwick (1968, pp. 73–7) notes that Book III, 4–6 is irreconcilable as a whole with the rest of Cassian's work and suggests that it might be an interpolation. For more recent literature and discussion see Bradshaw (1982, pp. 107–10) and especially Taft (1984).

But you should know that this morning office (*hanc matutinam*) which is observed especially in the western regions, was originally established as a canonical function in our time and in our monastery, where our Lord Jesus Christ was born . . . For up to that time we find that when this morning office (*matutina hac sollemnitate*) – which is customarily celebrated in the monasteries of Gall a short period of time after the nocturnal psalms and prayers are ended – was completed at the same time as the morning vigils, the remaining hours were assigned by our elders to bodily refreshment. Indeed when the more lax abused this privilege and prolonged the period of sleep excessively, since there was no assembly which required them to rise from their beds and leave their cells until the third hour . . . a complaint was brought to the elders by some of the brothers who were more fervent in spirit and to whom this sort of negligence was hardly pleasing, and it was determined by them after long discussion and careful consideration that up until sunrise, when they could prepare their reading without blame or undertake their manual labor, rest might be allowed their tired bodies, and after this all would be summoned to rise from their beds at the same time for the observance of this office, and by reciting three psalms and prayers, according to the custom established long ago at the offices of terce and sext as a manifestation of devotion to the Trinity, they would accomplish in this uniform arrangement both an end to sleep and the beginning of work. This arrangement, granted that it seems to have come about by accident and that it appears to have been established only recently for the reason given above, provides us nevertheless with that number specified by blessed David, clearly and according to the letter (although it also has a spiritual meaning): 'Seven times a day I have given praise to thee, for the judgments of thy justice' (Ps 118.164).

348 *De institutis* III, 6; *PL* XLIX, 135–6; *CSEL* XVII, 40–1

> The ambiguity of the previously quoted passage continues; does he speak of one morning office or two?

We ought to know this, that nothing concerning the ancient custom of psalmody (*psalmorum*) was changed by our elders who decided that they ought to add this morning office, but it was carried out (*missam*) in the same order as it had always been celebrated previously in the night offices. For the hymns which they have adopted in this region at the morning office, at the close of the nightly vigils, which customarily end before daybreak after cockcrow, they sing today also: that is the one hundred and forty-eighth psalm, which begins, 'Praise the Lord from the heavens', and the rest which follow. The fiftieth psalm, however, and the sixty-second and the eighty-ninth have been assigned to this new service. Finally, the fiftieth psalm is sung today after the completion of the morning hymns in every church throughout Italy, a practice I do not doubt derived from no other source but here.

349 *De institutis* III, 8; *PL* XLIX, 140–4; *CSEL* XVII, 42–3

> In this description of the Sabbath vigil, at least some of the obscurity surrounding the term antiphon is lifted. If nothing else, it is dissociated from responsorial psalmody.

During the winter, therefore, when the nights are longer, our elders shortened the vigils which are celebrated once weekly on the eve of the dawning Sabbath to end at the fourth cockcrow, so that after a watch of the entire night their bodies, rested for the nearly two hours that remain, would by no means languish all day dull with drowsiness . . . Therefore, should vigils be protracted until dawn by a thoughtless and unreasonable excess, it is necessary that they be compensated with greater interest. Hence they divide them into threefold offices, so that the effort thus broken up with variety might relieve the exhaustion of the body with a sort of pleasure. For when they have sung three antiphons while standing, after this while sitting on the floor or on low benches they respond to three psalms sung by one of their number, each of them performed by a single brother succeeding another in turn, and to these they add three readings while still sitting in silence.

350   *De institutis* III, 11; *PL* XLIX, 149; *CSEL* XVII, 44

> On Sundays, when the Eucharist is celebrated, all the morning and midday offices are combined.

But one ought also to know that on the Lord's Day only one office is conducted before mealtime. Out of respect for this meeting itself as well as the Lord's communion they employ at it a more solemn and extended form of psalmody, prayers and readings, and they consider that terce and sext are included within it.

CHAPTER 11

Augustine and minor western authors

Augustine, the most renowned of all church fathers, east and west, makes an appropriately significant contribution to our subject, matched only by Ambrose, John Chrysostom and perhaps Basil. An appreciable number of his contemporaries, on the other hand, provide but a single passage for this volume. They are characterized here as minor authors because of their modest musical involvement, not necessarily because of their stature more generally considered. Among their isolated references are some of crucial importance. Gennadius for example, has left us the earliest expression of the notion that psalms ought to be thematically related to the readings they accompany, and Paulinus has complicated our understanding of Ambrose's famous musical vigil at Milan by using the term antiphon when describing it.

Augustine (354–430)

Perhaps the most important figure in the history of Christian thought, Augustine is rivalled only by Thomas Aquinas and perhaps Origen. We are well informed about his life due to the autobiographical *Confessions* (397–401) and *Retractationes* (427). He was born at Thagaste in North Africa to a pagan father and Christian mother, the sainted Monica. In 371 he was sent to Carthage to study rhetoric; here he lost what Christian faith he possessed and began the relationship with a mistress to whom he remained faithful until his conversion. In 373 his reading of Cicero's *Hortensius* inspired him to pursue the philosophical life which he experienced first as a devotee of Manicheism. He became disillusioned with this persuasion toward the end of his tenure as professor of liberal arts at his native Thagaste, c.375–83. He moved to Rome in 383 and then to Milan in 384 as professor of rhetoric. Here he came under the influence of figures like the Christian Neoplatonist Simplicianus and especially St Ambrose. He was led gradually through Neoplatonism to Christianity and, after a period of retreat at Cassiacum, was baptized on Easter Eve of 387. He returned to Thagaste in 388 where he formed a sort of monastery with a group of friends. While visiting Hippo in 391 he was acclaimed by the people and reluctantly submitted to ordination at the hands of the venerable bishop Valerius. He was made his coadjutor bishop in 395 and succeeded him at his death the following year. The next three and a half decades were spent in administering the diocese, preaching, writing and combating heresy. He died on 28 August 430 as the city of Hippo was under siege by the Vandals.

With the exception of Niceta's *De utilitate hymnorum*, Augustine has left us the only patristic work devoted entirely to music, his *De musica*, a treatise on music as a liberal art. Of even greater significance to our subject are the numerous brief references to liturgical psalmody scattered throughout his voluminous works. The material appears here in the following sequence: two well-known passages from the

Confessions, references from the *Ennarrationes in psalmos*, the sermons, the letters, and finally the remaining works in alphabetical order.

351   *Confessiones* IX, vi, 14–vii, 15; *PL* XXXII, 769–70; *CCL* XXVII, 141–2

> There has been much confusion over the part played by the so-called antiphonal psalmody in this passage; see Leeb (1967, pp. 90–110).

How much I wept at your hymns and canticles, deeply moved by the voices of your sweetly singing church. Those voices flowed into my ears, and the truth was poured out in my heart, whence a feeling of piety surged up and my tears ran down. And these things were good for me.

vii, 15 Not long since had the church of Milan begun this mode of consolation and exhortation, with the brethren singing zealously together with voice and heart. It was just a year, or not much more, since Justina, mother of the boy-emperor Valentinian, persecuted your servant Ambrose on behalf of her heresy, into which she had been seduced by the Arians. There my mother, your handmaid, bearing a principal part of the anxiety and sleeplessness, lived in prayer; while we, still cool to the heat of your spirit, were stirred nevertheless by the stunned and shaken city. At that time the custom began that hymns and psalms be sung after the manner of the eastern regions lest the people be worn out with the tedium of sorrow. The practice has been retained from that time until today and imitated by many, indeed, by almost all your congregations throughout the rest of the world.

352   *Confessiones* X, xxxiii, 49–50; *PL* XXXII, 799–800; *CCL* XXVII, 181–2

> In a passage unique among the church fathers for its aesthetic introspection, Augustine scruples over the pleasure he takes in melodious psalmody. Note the distinction he makes between 'speaking' and 'singing' in connection with Athanasius. For a passage in which Augustine describes his feelings during the private reading of the Psalter, see IX, iv, 8.

The delight of the ear drew me and held me more firmly, but you unbound and liberated me. Now I confess that I repose just a little in those sounds to which your words give life, when they are sung by a sweet and skilled voice; not such that I cling to them, but that I can rise out of them when I wish. But it is with the words by which they have life that they gain entry into me, and seek in my heart a place of some honor, even if I scarcely provide them a fitting one. Sometimes I seem to myself to grant them more respect than is fitting, when I sense that our souls are more piously and earnestly moved to the ardor of devotion by these sacred words when they are thus sung than when not thus sung, and that all the affections of our soul, by their own diversity, have their proper measures (*modos*) in voice and song, which are stimulated by I know not what secret correspondence. But the gratification of my flesh – to which I ought not to surrender my mind to be enervated –

frequently leads me astray, as the senses do not accompany reason in such a way as patiently to follow; but having gained admission only because of it, seek even to run ahead and lead it. I sin thus in these things unknowingly, but afterwards I know.

50 Sometimes, however, in avoiding this deception too vigorously, I err by excessive severity, and sometimes so much so that I wish every melody of the sweet songs to which the Davidic Psalter is usually set, to be banished from my ears and from the church itself. And safer to me seems what I remember was often told me concerning Athanasius, bishop of Alexandria, who required the reader of the psalm to perform it with so little inflection (*flexu*) of voice that it was closer to speaking (*pronuntianti*) than to singing (*canenti*).

However, when I recall the tears which I shed at the song of the Church in the first days of my recovered faith, and even now as I am moved not by the song but by the things which are sung, when sung with fluent voice and music that is most appropriate (*conuenientissima modulatione*), I acknowledge again the great benefit of this practice. Thus I vacillate between the peril of pleasure and the value of the experience, and I am led more – while advocating no irrevocable position – to endorse the custom of singing in church so that by the pleasure of hearing the weaker soul might be elevated to an attitude of devotion. Yet when it happens to me that the song moves me more than the thing which is sung, I confess that I have sinned blamefully and then prefer not to hear the singer. Look at my condition! Weep with me and weep for me, you who so control your inner feelings that only good comes forth. And you who do not behave thus, these things move you not. You however, O Lord my God, give ear, look and see, have pity and heal me, in whose sight I have become an enigma unto myself; and this itself is my weakness.

353 *In psalmum xxi*, ii, 24; *PL* xxxvi, 177; *CCL* xxxviii, 128

> Augustine's vast *Ennarrationes in psalmos* originated partly as sermons and partly as dictated writings (*partim sermocinando in populis, partim dictando exposui; In psalmum cxviii, Prooemium*). In addition to instrumental allegory at the expected places, there are numerous other references to music. Of particular interest are those which specify that the psalm in question had been sung earlier in the service. The standard work on liturgical references in Augustine's writings is Roetzer (1930).
>
> This passage suggests that the late fourth-century Alleluia is an acclamation like the Amen.

'You that fear the Lord, praise him' (Ps 21.24). Wherever God is feared and praised, there is the church of Christ. Observe, my brothers, whether in these days Amen and Alleluia are said throughout the entire world without cause. Is God not feared there? Is God not praised there?

354   *In psalmum xxix*, II, 1; *PL* XXXVI, 216; *CCL* XXXVIII, 173–4

> An example of the sort of passage referred to in the previous head note; the reference to the Gospel might indicate that the service in question is the Eucharist.

This indeed have we sung: 'I will extol thee, O Lord, for thou hast drawn me up, and hast not let my foes rejoice over me' (Ps 29.1). If we have learned from the Holy Scriptures who are our enemies, we know the truth of this canticle . . . For what we just now heard when the Gospel was being read . . .

355   *In psalmum xxxii*, II, S. 1, 5; *PL* XXXVI, 279–80; *CCL* XXXVIII, 250

> The institution of vigils in a particular location has brought about the banishment of instruments previously heard there. The location might have been the burial site of St Cyprian (*Sermo* CCCXI, 5). The passage continues with a lengthy exposition of the allegorical distinction between cithara and psaltery.

Did not the establishment of these vigils in the name of Christ bring it about that citharas be banished from this place? But here they are ordered to sound: 'Praise the Lord', he says, 'on the cithara, sing to him on the psaltery of ten strings' (Ps 32.2). Let none turn his heart to theatrical instruments. What one is commanded here, he has within himself, as it says in another place: 'In me, O God, are vows of praise which I will pay thee' (Ps 55.12). They remember, those who were here some time ago, when I, to the best of my ability, specified in my discourse what difference exists between cithara and psaltery . . . And now, not inappropriately, I will repeat it . . .

356   *In psalmum xxxii*, II, S. 1, 8; *PL* XXXVI, 283; *CCL* xxxviii, 254

> After discoursing upon the New Song, mentioned in verse three, Augustine turns to the term *iubilatio*, used later in the same verse. Musicologists have persistently associated such patristic descriptions of the *jubilus* with the Alleluia of the Mass although there is nothing in the texts to justify this. For a perceptive reader of patristic texts who long since noted this discrepancy, see Gélineau (1962, p. 172); for further Augustinian references to the *jubilus*, see Gérold (1831, pp. 121–2); and for a comparative musicological study of the phenomenon, see Wiora (1962). On the Alleluia of the Mass as such, see Froger (1948), Bailey (1983) and especially Martimort (1970).

Sing 'in jubilation' (Ps 32.3). For this is to sing well to God, to sing in jubilation. What is it to sing in jubilation? To be unable to understand, to express in words, what is sung in the heart. For they who sing, either in the harvest, in the vineyard, or in some other arduous occupation, after beginning to manifest their gladness in the words of songs, are filled with such joy that they cannot express it in words, and turn from the syllables of words and proceed to the sound of jubilation. The jubilus is something which signifies that the heart labors with what it cannot utter. And whom does jubilation befit but the ineffable God? For he is ineffable whom you cannot speak. And if you cannot speak him, yet ought not to be silent, what remains but that you jubilate; so that the heart rejoices without words, and the great expanse of joy has not the limits of syllables? 'Sing well unto him in jubilation' (Ps 32.3).

357   *In psalmum xl*, 1; *PL* xxxvi, 453; *CCL* xxxviii, 447

> The psalm response is taken from the middle verse rather than the first.

First, what we have sung in response to the reader (*legenti*), although it is from the middle of the psalm, we will take the beginning of our discourse from it: 'My enemies have spoken evil against me: when shall he die and his name perish?' (Ps 40.6).

358   *In psalmum lvi*, 16; *PL* xxxvi, 671; *CCL* xxxix, 705

> Before embarking upon an allegorical exposition of the distinction between psaltery and cithara, Augustine throws some light on the etymology of the term *organum*. (See also *In psalmum cl*, 7, quoted below.)

'Arise, psaltery and cithara' (Ps 56.9). What does he call upon to arise? I see two instruments, and yet I see one body of Christ; one flesh as risen again, but two instruments have arisen. The one instrument is the psaltery, the other is the cithara. All musicians' implements (*instrumenta*) are called instruments (*organa*). Not only is that called an instrument, which is large and blown into by bellows, but whatever is adapted to song (*cantilenam*), and is corporeal, and utilized as an implement by he who plays (*cantat*), is called an instrument. Now these two instruments differ from each other; and I wish, so far as the Lord grants, to point out to you how they differ and why they differ . . .

359   *In psalmum lxvii*, 1; *PL* xxxvi, 812–13; *CCL* xxxix, 868–9

> Augustine, generally studious in pursuing allegorical exegetical distinctions, here draws the line. He accepts the typical explanation of the psalm title *in finem*, and the distinction between *psalmus* and *canticum*, but will not enter into the distinction between *psalmus cantici* and *canticum psalmi*. (On *psalmus* versus *canticum* see also *In psalmum iv*, 1.)

The title of this psalm seems not to require laborious discussion, but appears to be simple and easy. For it stands thus: 'In the end, for David himself, a psalm of a song (*psalmus cantici*)'. In many psalms already, we have advised you what 'in the end' means, since 'Christ is the end of the Law, that everyone who has faith may be justified' (Rom 10.4); he is the end who perfects, not who consumes or destroys. However, should anyone attempt to investigate what 'psalm of song' means, and why not either 'psalm' or 'song', but both together, and what is the difference between 'psalm of a song' and 'song of a psalm', since certain psalms are inscribed with such titles; he will discover, perhaps, something which we leave to those who are keener and have more free time than we do. Some before us have distinguished between 'song' and 'psalm', that since a song is pronounced with the mouth, but a psalm is sung together with a visible instrument, that is the psaltery, it appears that by a song the mind's understanding is signified and by a psalm the body's activities.

360   *In psalmum lxxii*, 1; *PL* xxxvi, 914; *CCL* xxxix, 986

> A frequently quoted definition of hymn. Augustine refers, however, to a category of psalm not a non-biblical hymn.

Hymns are praises of God with song; hymns are songs containing the praise of God. If there be praise, and it is not of God, it is not a hymn; if there be praise, and praise of God, and it is not sung, it is not a hymn. If it is to be a hymn, therefore, it must have three things: praise, and that of God, and song.

361   *In psalmum xcix*, 4; *PL* xxxvii, 1272; *CCL* xxxix, 1394

> Another description of the *jubilus* (see *In psalmum xxxii*, II, S. 1, 8, quoted above).

One who jubilates (*iubilat*) does not speak words, but it is rather a sort of sound of joy without words, since it is the voice of a soul poured out in joy and expressing, as best it can, the feeling, though not grasping the sense. A man delighting in his joy, from some words which cannot be spoken or understood, bursts forth in a certain voice of exultation without words, so that it seems he does indeed rejoice with his own voice, but as if, because filled with too much joy, he cannot explain in words what it is in which he delights. You observe this even in those who sing improperly. Now our jubilation will not be such as theirs, for we ought to jubilate in justification, while they jubilate in iniquity; we, then, in confession, they in confusion. Yet that you might understand what I say, call to mind what you well know, that it is especially those who perform some task in the fields who jubilate. Mowers and vintagers and those who gather other products, happy in the abundance of harvest and gladdened by the very richness and fecundity of the earth, sing in joy. And between the songs which they express in words, they insert certain sounds without words in the elevation of an exultant spirit, and this is called jubilation.

362 *In psalmum cvi*, 1; *PL* XXXVII, 1419; *CCL* XL, 1570

> Alleluia is sung audibly at specified times, but always in the 'mouth of the heart'. Note that Alleluia appearing as a psalm title occasions the remark.

Its title need not be discussed now, for it is Alleluia, indeed Alleluia twice. It is our custom to sing it at a specified time during the year (*sollemniter*), according to the ancient tradition of the Church, for we do not sing it on certain days without the sacrament. Indeed we sing Alleluia on specified days, but we think it every day. For if by this word is meant the praise of God, then, even if not in the mouth of the flesh, certainly in the mouth of the heart, 'His praise is always in my mouth' (Ps 33.3).

363 *In psalmum cx*, 1; *PL* XXXII, 1463; *CCL* XL, 1620–1

> Alleluia is sung during the fifty days of the Paschal season after the forty days of Lent.

The days have come for us to sing Alleluia . . . Be present in spirit, good singers, sons of the praise and eternal glory of the true and incorruptible God. Stand attentive, you who know how to sing and make melody (*psallere*) in your hearts to the Lord, giving thanks always in all things (Ep 5.20); and praise God, for this is Alleluia. Now indeed these days come only to pass away, and pass away to come again . . . For as these days, with grateful gladness, regularly follow the preceding days of Quadragesima each year, by which is signified the sorrow of this life before the resurrection of the Lord's body . . . and signified by the number forty . . . But signified by the number fifty after the resurrection of the Lord, when we sing Alleluia, is not the end and passing of a certain season, but that blessed eternity; because the denarius added to forty pays the wage of the faithful who toil in this life . . .

364 *In psalmum cxix*, 1; *PL* XXXVII, 1596; *CCL* XL, 1776

> Responsorial psalmody in a liturgical service.

The psalm which we have just now heard sung and responded to in singing, is short and highly beneficial.

365 *In psalmum cxxxii*, 1–2; *PL* XXXVII, 1729; *CCL* XL, 1926–7

> The sound of Psalm 132.1 inspires the monastic life.

This is a short psalm, but one well known and often quoted. 'Behold how good and sweet it is when brothers dwell in unity' (Ps 132.1). That sound is so sweet that even those who do not know the Psalter quote this verse. It is so sweet, as sweet as is the charity which makes brothers dwell in unity . . .
2 For these words of the Psalter, this sweet sound, this lovely melody (*suauis*

melodia) – as much in the song as in the understanding – has even begotten monasteries. By this sound were the brethren stirred who wished to live in common; this verse was their trumpet.

366   *In psalmum cxxxviii*, 1; *PL* xxxvii, 1784; *CCL* xl, 1990

The reader – not the cantor, one notes – sings the wrong psalm. For two additional passages in the *Ennarrationes* where Augustine cites the singing of a specific psalm, see cxxiii, 1–2 and cxxxvi, 1.

We had prepared for ourselves a short psalm, which we had ordered to be sung by the reader (*lectore*); but as it seems, when the time came he was confused and read a different one rather than the other. We have chosen to follow the will of God in the error of the reader, rather than our own will in our previous intention.

367   *In psalmum cl*, 7; *PL* xxxvii, 1964; *CCL* xl, 2195

A fuller etymological note on the term *organum* than that of *In psalmum lvi*, 16. It serves as a corrective to modern authors who take the term, as it appears in commentaries on Psalm 150, to refer to the organ.

'Praise him on strings and the instrument (*in chordis et organo*)' (Ps 150.4). Both the psaltery and the cithara, which were mentioned above, have strings. *Organum*, however, is a general term for all instruments (*uasorum*) of music, although the usage has now been established, that by *organa* is meant specifically those which are inflated by bellows (a type of instrument I do not believe is meant here). For, since *organum* is a Greek word, referring generally, as I have said, to all musical instruments; that to which bellows are fitted they call by another Greek name, while its being called *organum* is more a Latin and even colloquial usage. Therefore when he said 'on strings and the instrument', it seems to me that he wished to indicate some instrument which has strings.

368   *In psalmum cl*, 8; *PL* xxxvii, 1965; *CCL* xl, 2196

Augustine turns to *ars musica* for a threefold classification of sound (see also *De doctrina christiana* ii, xvii, 27, quoted below).

Nor do I think that what the musicians say should be ignored ... that there are three kinds of sound, by voice, by breath, and by striking (*uoce, flatu, pulsu*): by voice, that is by the throat and wind pipe of a singing man without any sort of instrument; by breath, as with the tibia or anything of that kind; by striking, as with the cithara or anything of that sort. Thus no type is omitted here [in Psalm 150]: for there is voice in the chorus, breath in the trumpet and striking in the cithara; just like mind, spirit and body, but through similarity, not actual properties.

369   *Sermo* xiv, *de uerso 14, psalmi ix,* 1; *PL* xxxviii, 111; *CCL* xli, 185

There is a vast quantity of extant sermons by Augustine, many of which are classified among the treatises and exegetical works, most notably the *Ennarrationes in psalmos*. However, the number of those appearing under the simple rubric of *sermo* is itself so large that it is being brought entirely under scholarly control only in recent years (Verbraken, 1976). The Maurist Benedictines first published the collected sermons in 1683, numbering those they deemed authentic 1–363 and those inauthentic 364–94. Their work is reproduced substantially unchanged in *PL*. Many additional sermons have come to light throughout the centuries and Dom Morin published these – some one hundred and thirty-eight at the time – in 1930. Finally in 1961 Dom Cyrille Lambot began a critical edition within the *CCL* series that integrates the two collections, but by 1985 only one volume had appeared. The new edition will retain the organization and numbering of the Maurist edition with the necessary insertions.

    The Maurist edition opens with sermons based on the Old Testament, and in the section dealing with the psalms there are several examples based on a single verse which indicate that it had been sung previously, presumably as a psalm response. One of these is quoted here (see also *Sermo* xvii, 1; 1; xxi, 1; and xxiv, 1). For an example where the responsorial function is made explicit, see *Sermo* ccclii, 1, quoted below.

We sang to the Lord and said, 'To thee is the poor man left; thou will be a helper to the orphan' (Ps 9B.14).

370   *Sermo* xxix A, *de uerso 1, psalmi cxvii,* 1; *CCL* xli, 378

Alleluia is sung as the response to Psalm 117, the Easter gradual psalm. This is not surprising since Alleluia is the biblically indicated response for the psalm, but note that JOHN CHRYSOSTOM, *In psalmum cxvii,* 1, gives verse 24 – *Haec dies,* the proper medieval gradual response – as that sung by his congregation. (I am indebted to Peter Jeffery for the Augustinian reference as well as for a related one: *In psalmum cxvii,* 2.)

'Give praise to the Lord, for he is good: for his mercy endureth forever' (Ps 117.1). What the Holy Spirit has advised us in the words (*uoce*) of the psalm, to which we responded with one mouth and one heart Alleluia – which means praise the Lord in Latin – this the same Holy Spirit advises you through my words (*uoce*): 'Give praise to the Lord . . .'

371   *Sermo* clxv, *de uerbis Apostoli, Eph.* iii, 13–18, 1; *PL* xxxviii, 902

The psalm, at the Eucharist apparently, is referred to as a reading. For a similar passage, see *Sermo* clxxvi, 1; see also *Vita S. Martini* ix.

We heard the Apostle, we heard the Psalm, we heard the Gospel; all the divine readings (*diuinae lectiones*) sound together so that we place hope not in ourselves but in the Lord.

372   *Sermo* CXCVIII, *de calendis Januariis* II, 1–2; *PL* XXXVIII, 1024

> The faithful have just sung Psalm 105.47 at a New Year's Day service, presumably as a refrain. Does this indicate a 'proper' gradual?

For you were singing this: 'Save us, O Lord our God, and gather us from among the heathen, that we may give thanks to thy holy name' (Ps 105.47). Now, if this festival of the heathen which takes place today with worldly and carnal rejoicing, with the noise of the vain and most immoral songs, with banqueting and shameful dancing in celebration of this false feast day – if these things which the heathen do do not please you, then you will be gathered from among the heathen.

2 You have indeed sung it, and the sound of this divine song echoes still in your ears: 'Save us, O Lord our God, and gather us from among the heathen'.

373   *Sermo* CCLII, *in diebus paschalibus* XXIII, 9; *PL* XXXVIII, 1176

> In several sermons from the Paschal season Augustine mentions that Alleluia is sung during these fifty days (see also CCX, 6; CCLIV, 5; CCLV, 1; CCLVI, 1–3). Here he indicated its singing at two services, perhaps the Sunday morning vigil and Eucharist. Note the interchangeability of the verbs *dicere* and *cantare*.

Is it by chance that these days which we now celebrate number fifty? Indeed it is not without reason, my brothers, that the Church maintains the usage of ancient tradition that the Alleluia be sung (*dicatur*) throughout these fifty days. For Alleluia means the praise of God, and therefore it signifies to us who toil what occupies our time of rest. For when after this period of toil we come to that time of rest, our only business will be the praise of God, our activity there will be Alleluia. What is Alleluia? Praise God. Who can praise God without ceasing but the angels? They hunger not, nor thirst nor grow sick, nor die. Now we also have sung (*diximus*) Alleluia; it was sung (*cantatum est*) early in the morning, and since we were already present, we sang (*diximus*) Alleluia a short time before.

374   *Sermo* CCCLII, *de utilitate agendae poenitentiae* II, 1; *PL* XXXIX, 1548–50

> A particularly clear indication of a psalm verse used as response to the solo psalm singer (see also *Sermo* CCCVI, 1).

The voice of the penitent is recognized in the words with which we respond to the singer (*psallenti*): 'Hide thy face from my song, and blot out all my iniquities' (Ps 50.11).

375 Epistle XXIX, 10–11; *PL* XXXIII, 119–20; *CSEL* XXXIV, 121–2

> The 'evil custom' to which Augustine refers is a tradition of unrestrained eating and drinking in church on the feast of St Leontius, sometime bishop of Hippo. Note the distinction between Scripture reading and psalmody. Note also the musical role of the 'brethren', presumably monks.

When, after these things were accomplished, I saw that all were of one mind to proceed in good will, despising that evil custom, I exhorted them to spend the noon hour in divine readings and psalm singing (*diuinis lectionibus et psalmis*) . . . 11 In the afternoon, however, there was a larger crowd than in the morning, and until the time we came out with the bishop, reading alternated with psalmody (*legebatur alternatim et psallebatur*); and as we approached two psalms were read. Then the old man ordered me, though unwilling and wishing this perilous day to be at an end, to say something to them . . . And when, in accord with the time, something of the sort had been said along with what the Lord had deigned to inspire in me, vespers (*uespertina*) were celebrated, as is the daily custom. And as we departed with the bishop the brethren (*fratres*) sang hymns (*hymnos dixerunt*) in the same place, while a considerable crowd of both sexes remained until dark and sang (*psallente*).

376 Epistle LV, 32; *PL* XXXIII, 220; *CSEL* XXXIV, 207

> Alleluia is sung everywhere during the fifty days of Paschaltide, but in some locations is also sung at other times. One notes, incidentally, in the many patristic references to the Alleluia, nothing to indicate that they refer specifically to the Alleluia of the Mass, as many musicologists assume they do.

Yet it is not observed universally that Alleluia is sung in the church throughout these fifty days only; for it is sung variously on other days at one place or the other – on these same days, however, everywhere.

377 Epistle LV, 34–5; *PL* XXXIII, 221; *CSEL* XXXIV, 208–9

> Augustine defends the custom of singing in church.

But if the objection is so slight that greater benefits are to be expected for those who are earnest than damage to be feared from slanderers, then the practice ought without hesitation to be maintained, especially when it can be defended from the Scriptures, as can the singing of hymns and psalms, since we have the example and precepts of the Lord himself and of the Apostles. There are various ways of realizing this practice, which is so effective in stirring the soul with piety and in kindling the sentiment of divine love, and many members of the church in Africa are rather sluggish about it, so that the Donatists reproach us because in church we sing the divine songs of the prophets in a sober manner, while they inflame their revelry as if by trumpet calls for the singing of psalms composed by human ingenuity. When, then, is it not the proper time for the brethren gathered in church to sing what is holy – unless there is reading or discourse or prayer in the clear voice of bishops or common prayer led by the voice of the deacon?

35 And at other times I simply do not see what could be done by Christian congregations that is better, what more beneficial, what more holy.

378   Epistle CLVIII, 2; *PL* XXXIII, 694; *CSEL* XLIV, III, 490

> Singing and celebration of the Eucharist at the obsequies of Augustine's young secretary.

We celebrate his obsequies with fitting honor, worthy of such a soul; for we praised the Lord in hymns for three days around his tomb, and on the third day we offered the sacrament of redemption.

379   Epistle CCXI, 7; *PL* XXXIII, 960; *CSEL* LVII, 361

> This letter is one of the many documents, authentic and inauthentic, involved in the complex question of St Augustine's 'rule'; see Bonner (1963, pp. 396–7) and Verheijen (1967). For another example, clearly inauthentic, see *Regula secunda* ii, quoted below.

Be instant in prayer at the appointed hours and times. Let no one do anything in the oratorio (*oratorio*) other than that for which it was made and from which it derives its name, so that if nuns who have the free time wish to pray even outside the regular hours, others who wish to do something else there will not prove an obstacle to them. When you pray to God in psalms and hymns, let what is pronounced by the voice be meditated upon in the heart; and do not sing something unless you read that it is to be sung, for what is not thus noted to be sung, ought not to be sung.

380   *De cantico nouo* 2; *PL* XL, 680

> In an extended metaphor, the life of a Christian is pictured as a journey to heaven by ship. In one sentence the boatman's cry, the *celeuma*, is identified with the Alleluia.

May our protection, the grace of Christ, be present; let us sing our sweet *celeuma*, Alleluia, so that joyful and secure we might enter the eternal and most blessed homeland.

381   *De doctrina christiana* II, xvi, 26; *PL* XXXIV, 48–9; *CCL* XXXII, 51–2

> *De doctrina christiana* purports to explain how classical learning is to be used in the exposition of Scripture. The process is obviously allegorical. Here number and music are singled out.

Indeed, an ignorance of certain musical questions shuts off and conceals much. For on the basis of a distinction between psaltery and cithara a certain writer has aptly explained some figures of things, and among the learned it is fittingly queried whether the psaltery of ten strings obeys some law of music which required that number of strings, or whether, if this is not the case, that number should be considered to result from something more sacred, either from the Ten Commandments (a number which, if examined, can be referred to nothing but creature and Creator), or from the explanation of the number ten given above [II, xvi, 25]. And that number of the building of the Temple mentioned in the Gospel, namely forty-six years, sounds with I know not what musical significance; and when referred to the structure of the Lord's body – the reason why mention is made of the Temple – it forces not a few heretics to acknowledge that the Son of God was clothed not in a false but in a true human body. And we find both number and music honorably placed in many passages of the sacred Scriptures.

382   *De doctrina christiana* II, xvii, 27; *PL* XXXIV, 49; *CCL* XXXII, 52–3

> Augustine continued with Varro's rationalistic explanation of the origin of the nine Muses; it involves the three ways of producing sound (see *In psalmum cl*, 8, quoted above).

Jupiter, then, did not beget the nine Muses, but three artists created three each. And that city did not decide upon the number three because it had seen the Muses in a dream or because they had presented themselves in such a number to anyone's eyes, but because it is easily observed that all sound which furnishes the material of music (*cantilenarum*) is threefold in nature. For it is produced either by voice (*uoce*), as with those who sing with their throats and without an instrument, or by breath (*flatu*), as with trumpets and tibias, or by striking (*pulsu*), as with citharas and tympana and whatever other instruments sound when beaten.

383   *De doctrina christiana* II, xviii, 28; *PL* XXXIV, 49; *CCL* XXXII, 53

> Augustine closes the section on music by arguing that one, while avoiding real musical instruments, should use the knowledge of them in interpreting Scripture.

But whether the fact of the matter is as Varro has related, or is not so, we must nevertheless not shun music because of the superstition of the heathen, if we are able to snatch from it anything useful for the understanding of the Holy Scriptures. Nor should we be involved with their theatrical frivoloties, if we consider some point concerning citharas and other instruments which might be of aid in comprehending spiritual things.

384   *Liber retractationum* I, 20; *PL* XXXII, 618; *CSEL* XXXVI, 97–8

> An Ambrosian hymn is confirmed as authentic, and its widespread usage is suggested.

In one passage of this book I said about the Apostle Peter that 'on him as upon a rock the Church was built'. The same idea is sung from the mouth of many in the verses of the most blessed Ambrose, where he says of the crowing of the cock: 'This man himself, rock of the Church at the cockcrow washed away his guilt'.

385   *Liber retractationum* II, 37; *PL* XXXII, 634; *CSEL* XXXVI, 144

> A passage of great significance: it indicates that the communion psalm and another psalm, apparently the gradual, had been introduced at Carthage only in Augustine's time – but see Dyer (1981).

Meanwhile a certain Hilary, a lay catholic of tribune rank, angered I know not why against the ministers of God, as often happens, attacked the custom which had begun then in Carthage – in abusive, censorious terms, whenever possible, asserting it ought not to be – of singing (*dicerentur*) at the altar hymns from the Book of Psalms both before the oblation and while what had been offered was distributed to the people. I responded to him at the urging of the brethren, and the book was called *Against Hilary*.

386   *De musica* I, iv, 5–7; *PL* XXXII, 1085–7

> *De musica*, only one work in an ambitiously conceived series on the liberal arts, is itself incomplete in that it deals with metrics and rhythmics while leaving harmonics to a similarly projected but not realized volume. However, as a substantial work on *musica* it occupies an important place in the pre-history of medieval music theory. At the same time it can be said to occupy an equally important place in the history of aesthetic philosophy. Much has been written about it from the perspective of various disciplines; as a starting point the reader is directed to O'Connell (1978, pp. 178–88) on the central question of the relationship of the first five books to the sixth. Quoted here is only the beginning and end of a long passage comparing practical musicians to birds, which would seem to play a part in the medieval topos of *musicus et cantor*; see Gurlitt (1950) and also *In psalmum xviii*, II, 1. The entire treatise is translated in *FC* IV.

Tell me then, I ask, whether all these who guided by a certain sense sing well seem to you to be like that nightingale, that is, they do it sweetly and harmoniously (*numerose*), although if asked about these numbers, or about the intervals of high and low notes, could not reply . . . If all tibia players and string players and others of this sort have science, then I think there is nothing more tawdry and base than this discipline.

387 *De opere monachorum* xvii, 20; *PL* XL, 564–5; *CSEL* XLI, 564–5

Monks must not neglect manual labor entirely in order to devote themselves to prayer, reading and psalmody; actually they can sing psalms from
memory during work. For another appearance of the word *celeuma*, see *De
cantico nouo* 2, quoted above.

I would like to know what they who do not wish to work manually are
supposed to do – for what activity they are to be free. For prayers, they reply,
and psalms and reading and the word of God . . . In fact those working with
their hands are easily able to sing the divine songs also and to lighten the
labor itself with a kind of divine *celeuma*. Or are we unaware of what vanities
and often even scandals of theatrical tales to which all workmen lend their
hearts and tongues while their hands do not withdraw from their task?
Therefore what prevents the servant of God while working with his hands
from meditating on the Law of the Lord and singing (*psallere*) to the name of
the Lord most high – provided of course that he has time set aside to learn
that which he will recall from memory?

388 *De trinitate* IV, 2, 4; *PL* XLII, 889; *CCL* L, 164–5

The theological context of this musical reference is too complex for easy
summarization. Suffice it to say that a 'co-adaptation' or congruency
between sinful man and righteous God is established when the Divine
Word takes on the burdens of the flesh. While Augustine is explaining this,
it occurs to him that a good analogy exists in what the Greeks call
'harmony'.

For I mean by this co-adaptation – as occurs to me just now – what the
Greeks call ἁρμονία. But this is not the place to demonstrate the power of
the consonance of single to double that is found in us especially and is
naturally so implanted within us – and by whom except by him who created
us? – that not even the unskilled can fail to notice it whether singing themselves or listening to others. Through it, indeed, high and low notes are so
in concord that whoever departs from it offends grievously not just the
discipline, in which most are inexpert, but our very sense of hearing. But a
long discourse is required to demonstrate this, while one who knows how,
can make it clear to the ears themselves on a well-regulated monochord.

389 Pseudo-Augustine, *Sermo* CCCLXXII, *De natiuitate Domini* IV, 3.
PL XXXIX, 1663

A reference to the liturgical singing of an Ambrosian hymn. Among the
reasons the Maurists give for denying authenticity to this sermon is
Augustine's opposition to non-biblical hymnody (*PL* XXXIX, 1661, note b).
But see above, *liber retractationum* I, 20.

Thus it is written: 'And he rejoices as a giant in running his course' (Ps 18.6). For he descended and he ran, he ascended and he sat. You know that you are accustomed to proclaim this: 'After he had arisen, he ascended into heaven and sitteth at the right hand of the Father'. Blessed Ambrose has sung very concisely and most beautifully of this journey of our giant in the hymn which you sang a short while ago. In speaking of the Lord Christ he said: 'His going out from the Father, his re-entrance to the Father; his excursion to the very depths, his return to the seat of God'.

390   Pseudo-Augustine, *Regula secunda* ii; *PL* xxxII, 1449–50;
          De Bruyne, 318–19

> Of the various documents relating to the Augustinian 'rule', this makes the weakest claim for authenticity; see Bonner (1963, pp. 396–7). *De Bruyne* attributes it to Benedict no less, while Verheijen (1967, vol. 2, pp. 125–74) attributes it to Alypius, Augustine's associate at Thagaste. Perhaps the musical terminology suggests a somewhat later date.

Now we describe how we ought to pray and sing psalms. At lauds (*matutinis*) three psalms are recited (*dicantur*): the sixty-second, the fifth and the eighty-ninth; at terce the first psalm is recited responsorially (*ad respondendum*), then there are two antiphons (*antiphonae*), a reading and a 'closing' (*completorium*); it is the same at sext and none; while at lamp-lighting (*lucernarium*) there is one responsorial psalm (*psalmus responsorius*), four antiphons, another responsorial psalm, a reading and a 'closing'. And at a suitable interval after vespers there are readings while all are seated and then the customary psalms preceding sleep. For the night offices (*nocturnae orationes*), during the months of November, December, January and February, there are twelve antiphons, six psalms and three readings; during March, April, September and October, ten antiphons, five psalms and three readings; during May, June, July and August, eight antiphons, four psalms and two readings.

Minor western authors

391   Julius Firmicus Maternus (d. after 360) *De errore profanarum religionum* iv, 2) *PL* xII, 990; *Ziegler*, 11

> Priests of the air goddess adorn themselves as women and prophesy to the accompaniment of tibia music. For similar examples of musically inspired cult practices, see Quasten (1930, pp. 35–40).

Then when they had thus made themselves estranged from men, filled with the music (*cantu*) of tibias they call upon their goddess so that infected by a wicked spirit they might ostensibly predict the future to foolish people.

392 GAUDENTIUS OF BRESCIA (d. after 406) *Sermo* VIII; *PL* xx, 890;
CSEL, LXVIII, 64–5

> Gaudentius contrasts the immoral pagan domestic banquet with its ideal
> Christian counterpart.

You will at last be able to preserve this [your faith] if you avoid drunkenness
and shameful banquets, where the serpentine movements of lewd women
stir one to illicit desire, where the lyre and tibia sound, and where, finally,
every sort of musician (*musicorum*) makes noise amid the cymbals of the
dancers. Those are wretched homes which differ in nothing from theatres.
I beg you, let all this be taken from your midst. Let the house of the
Christian and the baptized man be free of the devil's choir; let it simply be
human, let it be hospitable; let it be sanctified with continuous prayer; let
it be filled with psalms, hymns and spiritual songs . . .

393 PAULINUS (d. after 422) *Vita sancti Ambrosii* 13; *PL* XIV, 31;
Pellegrino, 68

> Paulinus, former secretary of Ambrose who wrote his biography in 422 on
> the advice of Augustine, used the term antiphon in his reference to the
> famous events described by AUGUSTINE, *Confessiones*, IX, 6. See Leeb (1967,
> pp. 98–103).

At this time antiphons, hymns and vigils first began to be celebrated in the
church of Milan. And dedication to this practice endures to the present day,
not only in the same church but throughout virtually every province of the
west.

394 PAULINUS OF NOLA (d. 431) *Carmen* XVII, 109–10; *PL* LXI, 485;
CSEL XXX, 86

> Paulinus, bishop of Nola, was among the foremost Christian poets of
> antiquity. He makes reference here to the boatman's *celeuma*. See Wille
> (1967, pp. 373–403) for several additional passages from Paulinus.

The cheerful sailors will sing the accustomed *celeuma* in the rhythmical
verses of hymns (*uersis modulis in hymnos*).

395 POPE CELESTINE I (d. 432) sermon fragment quoted by Arnobius
Junior, *Conflictus Arnobii catholici cum Serapione aegyptio de Deo trino et
uno* XIII. *PL* LIII, 289

> In the mid-fifth century Arnobius quotes Pope Celestine's reference to the
> singing of an Ambrosian hymn; see Jeffery (1984, p. 162).

I recall that on the day of the birth of our Lord Jesus Christ Ambrose of blessed memory had all the people sing with one voice, *Veni redemptor gentium* . . .

396   *Vita Melaniae Junioris* 47; *Rampolla*, 26 [Latin], 67 [Greek]

> The life of Melania the Younger (d. 438), existing in roughly contemporary Latin and Greek versions, presents an example of monastic psalmodic terminology.

He set down this rule for nighttime: that without interruption three responsories (responsoria – ὑποψάλματα) be completed; and three readings (*lectiones* – ἀναγνώσεις), and at the time of the morning office, fifteen antiphons (*antiphonae* – ἀντίφωνα).

397   ARNOBIUS JUNIOR, *In psalmum cxlviii*; *PL* LIII, 566

> Arnobius, writing in the mid-fifth century, implies that Psalm 148 is sung at the morning office in the universal church.

To us, I say, who everyday by the trumpet of this psalm, throughout the whole world, as soon as the light of dawn begins to introduce the start of day, urge everything in heaven and on earth to the praise and blessing of God.

398   GENNADIUS, *De uiris illustribus* 80; *PL* LVIII, 1103–4; *TU* XIV, 1a, 88

> Writing in about 480 Gennadius gives us what might be the earliest extant reference to the concept that psalms relate thematically to readings. The passage goes somewhat beyond the chronological limit of this volume, but is included because of its special relevance to the numerous earlier passages which spoke of psalms as independent Scripture readings rather than sung items subordinate to readings. *Psalmorum capitula*, incidentally, is translated simply as 'psalms' on the ground that individual psalms were originally viewed as chapters of the Book of Psalms.

Musaeus, priest of the church of Marseilles, a man learned in the Divine Scripture and refined by the most subtle exercise of its interpretation, schooled also in the language, selected, at the urging of the holy bishop Venerius, readings from the Holy Writings appropriate to the feast days of the entire year and responsorial psalms (*responsoria psalmorum capitula*) appropriate to the season and to the readings. This most necessary task is ratified by the lectors in church . . .

Epilogue

If the volume ends here abruptly, it does so along with the peak period of patristic production. By the middle of the fifth century all the great church fathers had passed from the scene and with them the flow of commentary on liturgical chant and contemporary musical life. This is true of the west especially, where there is a gap in the sources corresponding roughly to the period of the so-called Dark Ages. Monastic rules such as St Benedict's great exemplar constitute something of an exception; they provide us with an outline of the monastic office, but we must await the beginning of the eighth century and the *Ordines Romani* for similar information on the Roman Mass. This interim period – broadly considered that extending from the patristic period to the Carolingians – is one of special challenge to the music historian, but it can be attacked more effectively once the gains of the fourth and early fifth century are consolidated.

Bibliography

Texts and abbreviations

ACW   *Ancient Christian writers*, J. Quasten and others, eds., Westminster, Md. and London, 1946 ff.

AF I   *Die apostolischen Väter*, F. X. Funk, ed., Tübingen, 1906.

AF II   *Patres apostolici*, vol. 2, F. Diekamp, ed., Tübingen, 1913.

ANF   *The ante-Nicene fathers*, A. Roberts and J. Donaldson, eds., American revision of the Edinburgh edition, 10 vols., Buffalo, 1885–96, various reprints.

Bonnet   *Acta apostolorum apocrypha*, M. Bonnet, ed., Leipzig, 1898, reprint Hildesheim, 1959.

Boon   *Pachomiana latina*, A. Boon, ed., Bibliothèque de la Revue d'histoire ecclésiastique 7, Louvain, 1932.

Botte   *La tradition apostolique de Saint-Hippolyte*, B. Botte, ed., Liturgiewissenschaftliche Quellen und Forschungen 39, Münster in Westphalia, 1963.

Butler   *The Lausiac History of Palladius*, C. Butler, ed., Cambridge, 1898, reprint Hildesheim, 1967.

Cazzaniga *S. Ambrosii Mediolanensis episcopi de virginitate liber unus*, I. Cazzaniga, ed., Turin, 1954.

CCG   *Corpus christianorum, series graeca*. E. Dekkers and others, eds., Turnholt, 1977 ff.

CCL   *Corpus christianorum, series latina*, E. Dekkers and others, eds., Turnholt, 1953 ff.

Charlesworth *The Odes of Solomon*, translated and edited by J. Charlesworth, 2nd edn, Missoula, Montana, 1977.

CSCO   *Corpus scriptorum christianorum orientalium*, Paris and other locations, 1903 ff.

CSEL   *Corpus scriptorum ecclesiasticorum latinorum*, Vienna, 1866 ff.

De Bruyne D. De Bruyne, 'La première règle de Saint-Benoît', *Revue Bénédictine*, 42 (1930), pp. 316–42.

Devreesse *Le Commentaire de Theodore de Mopsueste sur les psaumes*, R. Devreesse, ed., Studi e Testi 93, Vatican, 1939.

FC   *Fathers of the Church*, R. Deferrari and others, eds., New York, 1947 ff.

Flor Patr *Florilegium patristicum*, J. Zellinger and B. Geyer, eds., Bonn, 1904 ff.

Frankenberg *Evagrius Ponticus*, W. Frankenberg, ed., Abhandlungen der königlichen Gesellschaft der Wissenschaften zu Göttingen, Philologisch-historische Klasse, neue Folge, XIII–2, Berlin, 1912.

Funk   *Didascalia et Constitutiones Apostolorum*, F. X. Funk, ed., 2 vols., Paderborn, 1905.

GCS   *Die griechischen christlichen Schriftsteller der ersten drei Jahrhunderte*, Leipzig, 1897–1941, Berlin and Leipzig, 1953, Berlin, 1954 ff.

(Volume numbers assigned in the present work are those of individual authors rather than of the series as a whole.)

Geffcken   *Die Oracula Sibyllina*, J. Geffcken, ed., *GCS*, Leipzig, 1902.

Gerbert   *Scriptores ecclesiastici de musica sacra potissimum*, M. Gerbert, ed., 3 vols., St Blaise Abbey, 1784, reprint Hildesheim, 1963.

Gingras   *Egeria: Diary of a Pilgrimage*, translated and annotated by G. Gingras, *ACW* 38, New York, 1970.

Halkin   *Sancti Pachomii vitae graecae*, F. Halkin, ed., *Subsidia Hagiographica* 19, Brussels, 1932.

Hefele-Leclercq   C. J. Hefele *Histoire de conciles*, translated and annotated by H. Leclercq, 11 vols., Paris, 1907–52.

LCL   *Loeb classical library*, London and Cambridge, Mass., 1912 ff.

Morin   *Sancti Augustini sermones post Maurinos reperti*, G. Morin, ed., Miscellanea Augustiniana 1, Rome, 1930.

Nau   F. Nau 'Histoires des solitaires Égyptiens', *Revue de l'orient chrétien*, 13–18 (1908–13).

NPNF   *The Nicene and post-Nicene fathers*, P. Schaff and N. Wace, eds., American revision of the Edinburgh edition, 1st series, 10 vols., New York, 1890–1900, 2nd series, 10 vols., New York, 1902–7, various reprints.

Otto   *Justini philosophi et martyris opera quae feruntur omnia*, K. Otto, 3rd edn, 5 vols., Jena, 1876–81, reprint Jena, 1966–71.

Pellegrino   *Paolino di Milano, Vita di S. Ambrogio*, M. Pellegrino, ed., Rome, 1961.

PG   *Patrologiae cursus completus, series graeca*, J. P. Migne, ed., 162 vols., Paris, 1857–66.

PL   *Patrologiae cursus completus, series latina*, J. P. Migne, ed., 221 vols., Paris 1844–64. (The columnarization given in the present work is that of the original edition. The plates for several volumes were destroyed in the disastrous fire of 1868 at Migne's printshop, necessitating a second edition with different (slightly higher) columnarization. The volumes involved here are I, IV, XIV, XV, XVI and XXVI.)

Rampolla   *Santa Melania Giuniore senatrice romana*, M. Rampolla, ed., Rome, 1905.

Riedel   *Die Kirchenrechtsquellen des Patriarchats Alexandrien*, translated and and annotated by W. Riedel, Leipzig, 1900.

SC   *Sources chrétiennes*, Paris, 1940 FF.

Strunk   *Source readings in music history*, O. Strunk, ed., New York, 1950.

Terzaghi   *Synesii Cyrensis hymni*, N. Terzaghi, ed., Rome, 1944.

Thomson   *Athanasius Contra gentes* and *De incarnatione*, translated and edited by R. Thomson, Oxford, 1971.

TU   *Texte und Untersuchungen zur Geschichte der altchristlichen Literatur*, founded by O. Gebhardt and A. Harnack, Leipzig, 1882 ff.

Turner   Turner, C. 'Niceta of Remesiana II. Introduction and text of *De psalmodiae bono*', *Journal of Theological Studies*, 24 (1922–3), pp. 225–50.

Veilleux   *Pachomian koinonia*, 3 vols., translated and annotated by A. Veilleux, *Cistercian Studies* 45–7, Kalamazoo, 1980.

Wilkinson   *Egeria's travels*, translated and annotated by J. Wilkinson, London, 1971.

Wilson   Edgar Hennecke: *New Testament Apocrypha*, W. Schneemelcher, ed., translations edited by R. Wilson, 2 vols., London, 1963–5.

Ziegler   *Iuli Firmici Materni V C De errore profanarum religionum*, K. Ziegler, ed., Leipzig, 1907.

Studies cited

Abert, H. *Die Musikanschauung des Mittelalters und ihre Grundlagen*, Halle, 1905, reprint Tutzig, 1964.

Adam, A. *Die Psalmen des Thomas und das Perlenlied als Zeugnisse vorchristlichen Gnosis*, Beihefte zur Zeitschrift für die neutestamentliche Wissenschaft 24, Berlin, 1959.

Altaner, B. *Patrologie*, revised by A. Stuiber, Freiburg, 1966, translation of earlier edition by H. Graef, *Patrology*, New York, 1960.

Andresen, C. 'Die Kritik der alten Kirche am Tanz der Spätantike', in *Der Tanz in der modernen Gesellschaft*, F. Heyer, ed., Hamburg, 1958, pp. 139–68.

Bailey, T. *The Ambrosian Alleluias*, Englefield Green, 1983.

Barnes, T. *Tertullian, a historical and literary study*, Oxford, 1971.

Beck, E. and others. 'Éphrem le Syrien', *Dictionnaire de Spiritualité*, Paris, 1960, vol. 4, cols. 788–822.

Bonner, G. *St Augustine of Hippo, Life and Controversies*, Philadelphia, 1963.

Bousset, W. *Apophthegmata, Studien zur Geschichte des ältesten Mönchtums*, Tübingen, 1923.

Bradshaw, P. *Daily prayer in the early church*, London, 1981.

Burn, A. *Niceta of Remesiana, his life and works*, Cambridge, 1905.
The hymn 'Te deum' and its author, London, 1926.

Chadwick, H. 'Some reflections on the character and theology of the *Odes of Solomon*', *Kyriakon: Festschrift Johannes Quasten*, P. Granfield and J. Jungmann, eds., 2 vols. Münster in Westphalia, 1970, pp. 266–70.

Chadwick, O. *John Cassian, a study in primitive monasticism*, 2nd edn, Cambridge, 1968.

Chitty, D. *The desert a city*, Oxford, 1966.

Cross, F., ed. *The Oxford dictionary of the Christian Church*, 2nd edn, with E. Livingstone, London, 1974.

Dekkers, E. 'Were the early monks liturgical?', *Collectanae Ordinis Cisterciensium Reformatorum*, 22 (1960), pp. 120–37.

Dix, Gregory, ed. *The treatise on the Apostolic Tradition of St Hippolytus of Rome*, reissued by H. Chadwick, London, 1968.
The shape of the liturgy, London, 1945.

Dodds, E. R. *Pagan and Christian in an age of anxiety*, Cambridge, 1965.

Dyer, J. 'Augustine and the "Hymni ante oblatium", the earliest offertory chants?', *Revue des études Augustiniennes*, 27 (1981), pp. 85–99.

Fedwick, P., ed. *Basil of Caesarea, Christian, humanist, ascetic*, 2 vols., Toronto, 1981.

Finesinger, S. 'Hebrew instruments in OT', *Hebrew Union College Annual*, 3 (1926), pp. 21–75.

Foley, E. 'The cantor in historical perspective', *Worship*, 56 (1982), pp. 194–213.

Foster, J. 'The harp at Ephesus', *The Expository Times*, 74 (1962–3), p. 156.

Froger, J. 'L'alleluia dans l'usage romain et la réforme de Saint-Grégoire', *Ephemerides liturgicae*, 42 (1948), pp. 6–48.

Geffcken, J. *Komposition und Entstehungszeit der Oracula Sibyllina*, *TU* 8, Leipzig, 1902, reprint Leipzig, 1967.

Gélineau, J. *Chant et musique dans le culte chrétien*, Paris, 1962, cited here from *Voices and instruments in Christian worship*, translated by C. Howell, Collegeville, Minnesota, 1964.
'Les psaumes a l'époque patristique', *La Maison-Dieu*, 135 (1978), pp. 99–116.

Gérold, T. *Les pères de l'église et la musique*, Strasbourg, 1931, reprint Geneva, 1973.

Gurlitt, W. 'Zur Bedeutungsgeschichte von musicus und cantor bei Isidor von Sevilla', *Abhandlungen der Mainzer Akademie der Wissenschaften, geistes- und sozialwissenschaftliche Klasse* No. 7, Wiesbaden, 1950, pp. 539–58.

Guy, J. *Recherches sur la tradition grecque des Apophthegmata Patrum, Subsidia hagiographica* 36, Brussels, 1962.

Hammerstein, R. *Die Musik der Engel*, Bern, 1962.

Hannick, C. 'Christian Church, music of the early', *New Grove dictionary of music and musicians*, S. Sadie, ed., London, 1980, vol. 4, pp. 363–71.

Hatch, E. *The influence of Greek ideas on Christianity*, London, 1898, reprint New York, 1957.

Holleman, A. 'The Oxyrhynchus papyrus 1786 and the relationship between ancient Greek and early Christian music', *Vigiliae christianae*, 26 (1972), pp. 1–17.

Hucke, H. 'Die Entwicklung des christlichen Kultgesangs zum gregorianischen Gesang', *Römische Quartalschrift für christliche Altertumskunde und Kirchengeschichte*, 48 (1953), pp. 147–94.

Husmann, H. 'Syrian church music', *New Grove dictionary of music and musicians*, S. Sadie, ed., London, 1980, vol. 18, pp. 472–81.

Jeffery, P. 'The introduction of psalmody into the Roman Mass by Pope Celestine I (422–32)', *Archiv für Liturgiewissenschaft* 26 (1984), pp. 147–65.

Jones, C., Wainright, G., and Yarnold, E. *The study of liturgy*, London, 1978.

Jungmann, J. *Missarum sollemnia: eine genetische Erklärung der romanischen Messe*, 4th edn, Vienna, 1958, translation of earlier edition by F. Brunner, *The Mass of the Roman rite: its origins and development*, New York, 1951.

Kaczynski, R. *Das Wort Gottes in Liturgie und Alltag der Gemeinden des Johannes Chrysostomus*, Freiburger Theologische Studien 94, Freiburg, Basel and Vienna, 1974.

Kelley, J. *Jerome, his life, writings and controversies*, New York, 1975.

Kraeling, C. and Mowry, L. 'Music in the Bible', *The New Oxford history of music*, vol. 1, E. Wellesz, ed., London, 1957, pp. 283–312.

Kraemer, C. 'Pliny and the early church service', *Classical Philology*, 29 (1934), pp. 293–300.

Kroll, J. *Die christliche Hymnodik bis zu Klemens von Alexandreia*, Darmstadt, 1921, reprint Darmstadt, 1968.

Kümmel, W. *Einleitung in das Neue Testament*, 14th edn of Feine and Behm's handbook, Heidelberg, 1965, translated by A. Martill, *Introduction to the New Testament*, Nashville, 1966.

Lampe, G. *A patristic Greek lexicon*, Oxford, 1961.

Leeb, H. *Die psalmodie bei Ambrosius*, Wiener Beiträge zur Theologie 18, Vienna, 1967.

Lippman, E. *Musical thought in ancient Greece*, New York, 1964.

Lorenz, R. 'Die Anfänge des abendländischen Mönchtums im 4. Jahrhundert', *Zeitschrift für Kirchengeschichte*, 77 (1966), pp. 1–61.

McKinnon, J. 'The meaning of the patristic polemic against musical instruments', *Current musicology*, 1 (1965), pp. 69–82.

'Musical instruments in medieval psalm commentaries and psalters', *Journal of the American Musicological Society*, 21 (1968), pp. 3–20.

'Jubal vel Pythagoras, quis sit inventor musicae: thoughts on musical historiography from Boethius to Burney', *The Musical Quarterly*, 64 (1978), pp. 1–28.

'The exclusion of musical instruments from the ancient Synagogue', *Proceedings of the Royal Musical Association*, 106 (1979–80), pp. 77–87.

'*Canticum novum* in the Isabella Book', *Mediaevalia*, 2 (1976), pp. 107–22.

Martimort, A. 'Origine et signification de l'alleluia de la messe romaine', *Kyriakon*:

Festschrift Johannes Quasten, P. Granfield and J. Jungmann, eds., 2 vols., Münster in Westphalia, 1970, pp. 811–34.

Martin, R. 'Aspects of worship in the New Testament Church', *Vox evangelica* II, R. Martin, ed., London, 1963, pp. 6–32.

Worship in the early Church, London, 1964, reprint Grand Rapids, 1975.

Mason, A. 'The first Latin Christian poet', *Journal of Theological Studies*, 5 (1904), pp. 413–32.

Mateos, J. 'L'office monastique à la fin du ive siècle: Antioche, Palestine, Cappadoce', *Oriens christianus*, 47 (1963), pp. 53–88.

'La psalmodie dans le rite byzantine', *Proche-Orient chrétien*, 15 (1965), pp. 107–26.

'The origine of the divine office', *Worship*, 41 (1967), pp. 477–85.

Mathews, T. *The early churches of Constantinople: architecture and laiturgy*, University Park, Pa., 1971.

Meeks, W. *The first urban Christians*, New Haven and London, 1983.

Morin, G. 'Nouvelles recherches sur l'auteur de Te deum', *Revue Bénédictine*, 11 (1894), pp. 49–77; 337–45.

Mowry, L. 'Revelation 4–5 and early Christian liturgical usage', *Journal of Biblical Literature*, 71 (1952), pp. 75–84.

O'Connell, R. *Art and the Christian intelligence in St Augustine*, Cambridge, Mass., 1978.

Pagels, E. *The Gnostic Gospels*, New York, 1979.

Paverd, E. *Zur Geschichte der Messliturgie in Antiocheia und Konstantinopel gegen Ende des vierten Jahrhunderts*, Orientalia christiana analecta 187, Rome 1970.

Quasten, J. *Musik und Gesang in den Kulten der heidnischen Antike und christlichen Frühzeit*, Münster in Westphalia, 1930, cited here from *Music and worship in pagan and Christian antiquity*, translated from 2nd edn of 1973 by B. Ramsey, Washington, D.C., 1983.

Patrology, 3 vols., Utrecht and Westminster, Md., 1950–60.

'Carmen', *Real Lexikon für Antike und Christentum*, vol. 2, 1954, cols. 901–10.

Renoux, A. 'Un manuscrit du lectionnaire Arménien de Jérusalem', *Muséon*, 74 (1961), pp. 361–85; 'Addenda et corrigenda', 75 (1962), pp. 385–98.

Roetzer, T. *Des heiligen Augustinus Schriften als liturgiegeschichtliche Quelle*, Munich, 1930.

Schmitz, J. *Gottesdienst im altchristlichen Mailand*, Theophaneia 25, Cologne, 1975.

Sheerin, D. '*Celeuma* in Christian Latin: lexical and literary notes', *Traditio*, 38 (1982), pp. 45–74.

Skeris, R. *Chrōma Theou*, Altotting, 1976.

Smith, J. 'The ancient Synagogue, the early Church and singing', *Music and Letters*, 65 (1984), pp. 1–16.

Smith, W. *Musical aspects of the New Testament*, Amsterdam, 1962.

Souter, A. *A Glossary of later Latin to 600 A.D.*, Oxford, 1949.

Steger, A. 'Psalmenlesung oder Zwischengesang?', *Pietas: Festschrift für Bernhard Kötting*, E. Dassmann and K. Frank, eds., Munster in Westphalia, 1980.

Taft, R. 'Praise in the desert: the Coptic monastic office yesterday and today', *Worship*, 56 (1982), pp. 513–36.

'Quaestiones disputatae in the history of the liturgy of the hours: the origins of nocturnes, matins, prime', *Worship*, 58 (1984), pp. 130–58.

Veilleux, A. *La liturgie dans le cénobitisme Pachômien au quatrième siècle*, Studia Anselmiana 57, Rome, 1968.

Verbraken, P. *Études critiques sur les sermons authentiques de Saint Augustin*, Instrumenta patristica 12, The Hague, 1976.

Verheijen, L. *La Règle de saint Augustin*, 2 vols., Paris, 1967.

Wagner, D. *The seven liberal arts in the middle ages*, Bloomington, Ind., 1983.

Wagner, P. *Einführung in die Gregorianischen Melodien*, 3 vols., Leipzig, 1911–12, translation of vol. 1 from an earlier edition by A. Orne and E. Wyatt, *Introduction to the Gregorian melodies*, London, 1907.

Ward, B. *Apophthegmata Patrum*, New York, 1980.

Werner, E. *The Sacred Bridge*, London and New York, 1959.

' "If I speak in the tongues of men . . . " St Paul's attitude to music', *Journal of the American Musicological Society*, 13 (1960), pp. 18–23.

Wessely, O. 'Die Musikanschauung des Abtes Pambo', *Anzeiger der Österreichischen Akademie der Wissenschaften: philosophischhistorische Klasse*, 89 (1952), pp. 46–62.

Wilken, R. *John Chrysostom and the Jews*, Berkeley, Los Angeles and London, 1983.

Wille, G. *Musica romana: die Bedeutung der Musik im Leben der Römer*, Amsterdam, 1967.

Winkler, G. 'Über die Kathedralvesper in den verschiedenen Riten des Ostens und Westens', *Archiv für Liturgiewissenschaft*, 16 (1974), pp. 53–102.

Wiora, W. *Die vier Weltalter der Musik*, Stuttgart, 1961, cited here from *The four ages of music*, translated by M. D. Herter Norton, New York, 1965.

'Jubilare sine verbis', *In memoriam Jacques Handschin*, H. Anglès and others, eds., Strasbourg, 1962.

Index of musical and liturgical terms and concepts

Numbers in the index refer to items in the volume, not pages. Only the primary source material, along with its head-notes, is indexed; the Preface, Introduction and introductory portions of individual chapters are not. The juxtaposition of terms and concepts does not necessarily imply the author's view on a controversial subject. For example, the heading 'cithara, Christian usage' means only that the passages indicated might suggest to some the Christian usage of the instrument.